W9-BHV-743

The Writing Process

Quentin L. Gehle

Duncan J. Rollo

The Writing Process

St. Martin's Press   New York

ACKNOWLEDGMENTS

Reprinted by permission of Charles Scribner's Sons from
The Year of the Whale by Victor B. Scheffer. Copyright ©
1969 by Victor B. Scheffer.

"Bird Droppings," reprinted by permission from *Time,*
The Weekly Newsmagazine. Copyright Time Inc. 1973.

"Rod McKuen: Boring, Banal Bathos," by Tom Shales, reprinted by permission of the *Washington Post.* © The
Washington Post.

Excerpt from "Can't Anyone Here Speak English?" reprinted by permission from *Time,* The Weekly Newsmagazine. Copyright Time Inc. 1975

Preface

The purpose of this text is to help students become confident and effective writers. This aim, we believe, is best accomplished by a clear focus on the *process* of writing—an orderly yet flexible sequence of interrelated tasks that leads from topic selection through revision to the finished composition. Since the writing process involves a series of choices the writer must make, we offer clear and detailed analysis of what the important choices consist of, and we provide guidance and recommendations to help the writer reach the necessary rhetorical decisions.

The organization of this text should help take much of the mystery out of writing for many students. We take little for granted. We begin with an overview of the essay, discuss and illustrate the four types of nonfiction prose, and explain the elements essential to any discourse. We then turn our attention to the writing process. The chapters on prewriting deal at length with planning: how to select a topic, how to create a thesis statement that will guide the rest of the paper, how to plan and organize the paper, and how to find a style suitable to a particular audience. The chapters on developing an essay acquaint the student with the means for carrying out his or her intention as set forth in the thesis statement. Here, we discuss paragraphs, topic sentences, introductions, conclusions, and titles. The chapters on methods of development provide, we believe, an unusually thorough explanation of the ways of building and ordering content in both paragraphs and complete essays. Because revising a paper is an integral part of the writing process, we do not relegate revision to handbook status. Rather, we guide the student through revision and show him or her how to improve diction, avoid illogic, make sentences more effective, and check for correct grammar and punctuation. A list of revision symbols keyed to the text pages is provided at the back of the book for easy reference. Finally, the appendices reinforce the entire writing process: Appendix A illustrates the evolution of a paper through three drafts; Appendix B applies the writing process to research papers and provides a sample paper; Appendix C serves as a reference for grammar terms.

The principles that we discuss throughout this text are constantly and immediately reinforced by exercises that invite the student to apply what he or she has just read. These exercises are not arbitrarily grouped at the ends of chapters or sections but placed within the text at the points where they will do the most good. In addition, we avoid the abstract by providing abundant examples that range from individual sentences to paragraphs and complete essays—more than half of them written by students. We believe that the frequent use of student examples will enable the students who use this book to see that effective writing is not only for the professional. Finally, boxed summaries throughout the chapters reinforce specific writing principles and processes and also make the text easy to use and review.

For many useful suggestions and criticisms we wish to thank Duane C. Nichols, Wilson C. Snipes, Thomas F. Marshall, Donald C. Stewart, Patrick W. Shaw, Sharon Drake, and Kendall C. Patterson.

We also wish to express our gratitude to Patricia Klossner of St. Martin's Press for her steady encouragement and guidance, and to Nancy Perry, also of St. Martin's, for her advice and careful attention to the manuscript. Among the students to whom we are indebted for allowing us to reprint their paragraphs and essays are Kathy Lautermilch, William Good, Alan Stadler, Jr., and Mildred Andrews.

Finally, we owe a special thanks to our wives, Linda Gehle and Paula Rollo, for their kindly tolerance as well as for their critical suggestions.

Quentin L. Gehle
VIRGINIA POLYTECHNIC INSTITUTE
AND STATE UNIVERSITY

Duncan J. Rollo
BRIARCLIFF COLLEGE

Contents

PART TWO   The Development Process

13   Improving Your Sentences   157

14 Checking Mechanics 183

APPENDICES

Appendix A   A Paper Undergoing Revision   203

Appendix B   Writing the Research Paper   209

Appendix C   Grammar Terms   **241**

The Writing Process

A Preview of   1
the Writing Process

This is a textbook designed to give you practice in the central tasks associated with what we call the writing process. It is useful to think of writing as a *process*, because the idea of process suggests not just one but a series of ongoing activities. These activities are in some ways separate and·orderly, in other ways interconnected and interchanging. By stopping to look closely at some of the basic activities involved in the writing process, the text aims to help you gain greater control over your written communication.

In our study, we shall see the writing process as a series of tasks, each of which can be explored in turn. Approaching each task separately allows us to maintain a reassuring amount of order in our work. At the same time, by gaining a hold on one aspect of the process at a time, we grow to appreciate how the various tasks are interconnected and interchanging. For example, you may be hurriedly checking a paper for typing errors when you realize that you want to rework your introduction. That too is part of the writing process, a process that is orderly but that is also ongoing and fundamentally creative. Every paper you will ever write will develop in a different way for you. This text focuses on certain basics of the writing process which, once you begin to understand them, offer you more conscious control in writing.

The book is organized so as to parallel the writing process in important ways. There are three main sections. The first, "The Prewriting Process," discusses getting off to a good start, one of the tasks at which inexperienced writers are often least skilled. The second section, "The Development Process," gives guidance in building, supporting, and closing a paper. Finally, "The Revision Process" suggests a broad range of approaches for strengthening the composition. (A listing of terms of grammatical interest is also available toward the back of the book, as are an appendix on writing research papers and an appendix tracing one student paper as it undergoes revisions.)

Many of the models used for analysis throughout the text are themes written by students in introductory courses in college composition. These papers vary widely and are not included as separate approaches to a single implied standard of correctness but as interesting approaches to the particular writing task under discussion. Some papers have been thoroughly revised, others have not.

THE IMPORTANCE OF FORM

The matter of form, or shape or structure, is basic to all writing. When we write, we give formal expression to ideas and information. When we do so, of course, the writing process merges with our thought processes. Let us begin our study of the writing process by looking for a moment at the human mind itself.

The human mind is surprisingly chaotic much of the time. It tends toward unstructured, free association as it skips from place to place, from time to time. The following example suggests some of the things that may go through an individual's mind as he thinks through a problem—in this case, the problem of getting a summer job to help pay school expenses:

> Need money——summer job——wish I were rich——what kind of job——remember being a caddie——age fourteen——remember the guy who broke par——big tip——hope I'll get a good job after graduation——wish my grades were better——high school was easier——honor roll——same year I waited on tables——lousy money——couldn't even afford a car——like to get a Porsche someday——really like to drive——need money for that——how much——car, tuition, living——want to feel free——be my own boss——sense of freedom——wish I were rich——get a dune buggy——great that summer at Malibu——

At this point, the person's thoughts are only loose associations. One fragmented notion dissolves into another, which triggers still another, in a long train of free association.

Suppose you wished to find an idea for an essay in the above example of loosely structured thought. You would need to know that effective writing develops from *directed* thinking. You would consciously look for meaning in your thoughts. One useful way of doing so is to ask yourself a series of leading questions which can help you discard irrelevancies and concentrate on the problem at hand. The following example illustrates the questions that the individual thinking about summer employment might ask himself in a conscious effort to find meaning in his thoughts:

I need a summer job .... WHY?
To allow me to return to school ..... HOW MUCH MONEY IS NEEDED?
Fifteen hundred dollars .... WHAT KIND OF JOB?
Want a sense of freedom .... WHAT DO I ENJOY DOING?
Cars fascinate me .... IS THERE A RELATION BETWEEN CARS AND JOBS?
Sense of freedom..................... ANYTHING ELSE?
Potential for making money from driving cars

The person may now conclude that a driving job will give him the money he needs, allow him to return to school, and prove interesting and satisfying. In this instance, directed thinking has resulted in a specific decision.

Like thinking, writing must be deliberate and directed if it is to accomplish anything. If you simply begin putting words on paper without directing your thought to a particular point, issue, or problem, you may waste your time and your audience's also. If you hope that one sentence will magically lead to another, you will most likely end up with a chaotic paper, one which lacks *unity* (recognizable order between the elements in the sentences) and *coherence* (logical connection between sentences).

SEEING THE WHOLE ESSAY

One of the pitfalls of writing is the failure to keep the whole composition in mind at all times, even when wrestling with a tiny detail. If the writer forgets where he is going, the reader too will be lost. To emphasize the importance of seeing the whole essay, this text begins with some generalizations on and suggestions for composing a complete essay. Such an essay is one with an *introduction* that attracts the reader's attention and states the main point of the essay, a *body* that provides convincing support for the main point, and a *conclusion* that ends the essay by reinforcing the main point with a summary, prediction, question, or recommendations.

Subsequent chapters of the text present fuller explanations of writing terminology and detailed discussion of the process of locating a topic, developing a thesis to control that topic, filling out the body of the essay with appropriate explanation and support, devising a fitting introduction and conclusion, and revising the paper according to the conventions of standard English and proper logic. By practicing the writing of complete compositions, by working through the detailed steps of the writing process, by trial-and-error writing exercises, and, especially, by paying close attention to your instructor's comments on and reactions to your writing efforts, you can improve your writing effectiveness.

The Essential Elements

An essay has not only an introduction, body, and conclusion but also certain other essential elements.

1. The most important element in the introduction is the *thesis statement.* The thesis statement is a generalization which states precisely what your topic is, how you have limited your topic, and how you will organize your topic. The thesis statement may be presented in one sentence, or it may consist of several sentences, depending on the complexity of your topic.

2. Paragraphs in the body of the paper usually contain *topic sentences.* A topic sentence alerts the reader as to which aspect of the thesis statement you are covering in that particular paragraph. Normally, the topic sentence is most effective when placed at the beginning of the paragraph, though it may also appear in the middle or at the end. Sometimes the topic sentence of the individual paragraph is merely implied, left unstated.

3. Each paragraph in the body of the paper normally provides *specific support* for the thesis. Support usually consists of *details,* and the details may be presented in a variety of ways, such as narration, analogy, classification, and concession (all of which, and others, are discussed individually later in the text). Details form the evidence which persuades the reader to believe what you are saying. *Specific details* are items which can be mistaken for no others: for example, "dogs" is not specific; "Irish setters" is more specific; and "Mr. Johnson's pair of Irish setters" is specific. "A majority of children love ice-cream" is not specific; "Of the 400 children in Plantagenet County, 311 love ice-cream" is specific. Try to give enough support in the body to make the material convincing.

4. The conclusion of the paper reinforces the thesis statement. It may summarize or it may offer a recommendation, a question, or a prediction. It is usually brief and to the point.

Writing that follows this structure and contains these elements will be effective whether it is an English composition, a lab report, or a business or personal letter.

The following student essay contains each of the elements we expect in effective writing—a thesis statement, topic sentences, specific support, and a conclusion:

SADISM AND SELF-RIGHTEOUSNESS

Last spring I overheard a college professor remark to a minister, "I was shocked to hear a group of students urging that boy to jump from his perch on top of the univer- **INTRODUCTION** sity tower." *Although many persons commonly express loathing upon hearing of others reveling in sensational detail, these same persons often enjoy sensational events themselves.*

Thesis Statement

It may be that people like to feel superior to those who enjoyed a grisly event first-hand. This past June, I attended a small political meeting in an affluent Cleveland suburb. During his talk, the candidate for sheriff dwelled on a single subject: the murder of a young woman which took place only a block from the local jail. He condemned the immorality of the act. His face was red with anger, and he damned the perpetrator of the crime. He even attacked the newspaper which featured the story in great detail, **BODY-1** recording the one-inch radius of the bullet holes, the three square yards of carpet stained by the victim's blood, and the exact posture of the fallen victim's limbs. His eyes seemed to shine with superiority as he spoke of the evil of the paper's commercial motivation; the lurid account had apparently increased the journal's circulation that week by over 12,000 copies. The middle-aged, well-dressed gentleman seated next to me was apparently enjoying the speech. His face wore a look of smug self-righteousness.

Topic Sentence

Specific Support

It may be, too, that people just like to be cruel. *Television reporting practices suggest that a large segment of the audience has a strong, vicarious sense of sadism.* Night after night for several weeks, television network news reporters offered coverage of the return of prisoners-of-war from Vietnam. On nearly every occasion that a plane **BODY-2** brought home newly released prisoners, reporters appeared at the airport. Shoving the microphone into the face of a woman whose husband was to have been on the flight (but, for some reason or other, missed it), a reporter would ask, "How do you feel?" Frequently the woman would be unwilling to answer and would look at the reporter with disgust showing through her tears. There was no real "news" in the woman's emotions. But there was morbid, sadistic interest.

Topic Sentence

Specific Support

Perhaps the restoration of public executions would make everyone—except the victims—happier. The self-righteous **CONCLUSION** could feel much self-righteousness condemning the large and enthusiastic crowds which would gather for such spectacles. The general public would have advance notice about where and when the spectacle would take place—it would not have to concern itself with trying to drive past the university tower at just the right moment.

Some Helpful Hints

In addition to the four essential elements of an effective essay—thesis statement, topic sentences, specific support, and conclusion—the following five guidelines may prove helpful to you:

1. *Your writing should be logically sound* and *grammatically correct.* The topic itself should be treated without introducing irrelevant matters or appealing to the emotions of the reader. Every point should be clearly presented, with the elements arranged in a coherent and unified manner. Sentences should be well constructed and should consist of the fewest number of words necessary to convey your meaning. Grammar and mechanics should follow "standard" or "correct" usage.*

2. *Diction (word choice and arrangement) should be precise and, in the supporting material, highly specific.* Try to state your message so that the reader cannot misunderstand you; don't quit work when it is merely possible for him to understand.

3. *Consider your audience.* Use words that will be understandable to your audience, and maintain a respectful tone toward its members. Organize and develop your main point in a logical and emphatic manner.

4. *Consider revising your writing through at least three drafts.*

5. *Proofread carefully.* If the material is worth the audience's careful attention, it also deserves your own careful attention.

Types of Nonfiction Prose

There are four basic types of nonfiction prose—the kind you will be required to write in a standard composition course. They include *exposition, narration, description,* and *argumentation.*

Exposition: explains or clarifies. There are two kinds of expository writing: *process* and *analysis. Process* tells how to do something. *Analysis* either groups several ele-

---

* The Conference on College Composition and Communication recently issued a statement acknowledging that individual dialects have their own merit and importance. Standard English is the written usage practiced by the educated populace.

ments into categories *(classification)* or describes the
characteristics of a single element *(definition)*.

Narration: gives an account of an action or a series of actions.

Description: portrays a person, place, or object or a combination
of persons, places, or objects.

Argumentation: presents a course of reasoning.

These four basic types of nonfiction prose usually appear in combinations. An argument, for example, may make use of description as part
of the supporting evidence. A narration may have a strong element of
description in it also. A description may incorporate exposition.

In the following selection, Victor B. Scheffer combines various types
of nonfiction prose to advance an ecological argument against the
senseless exploitation of the whale:

**EXPOSITION/
DESCRIPTION**

The eastern limit of the sea pasture in which the Little
Calf and his family are feeding today is the coastal strip of
central California. This humid strip is the habitat or native haunt of a peculiar race of men who see in any new
event, in any change of circumstance, a potential source
of dollar revenue. They speak of the "fast buck," though
only to members of their own kind. To others they speak
of "opportunity," "advancement," "progress," or "improvement." Each member of the race has an angle. His
delight is to guess the other's angle while concealing his
own.

**Transitional
Paragraph**

All this sets the stage for a certain July event.

NARRATION

During the night, a dead sperm whale floats on a flood
tide to a beach north of the Golden Gate. It is a small
whale, only twenty-two feet long. It comes to rest in a fog.
No one knows it is there until a beachcomber, searching
for glass balls and odd bits of driftwood, sees the dark
thing in the surf at four in the morning. He rubs his eyes,
then runs to a seaside cafe that serves early breakfast to
the perch fishermen. He calls his friend McGill. McGill is
a member of the special race. He runs a tourist trap at
Sausalito. It sits beside the road, and its on-and-off red
light should be a warning to navigators of the road but
instead it lures them in. Here they buy souvenirs of the
West (made in Japan and Czechoslovakia). They buy deli-
cate carvings on genuine simulated ivory depicting an
Eskimo pressing his sledge dogs to the limit (made ten at
a time with a master template and a routing machine in a
Market Street basement).

NARRATION

McGill rouses from sleep and gets the message. At once alert, his eyes glisten and shift; a fleeting smile crosses his lips. "Be right over," he says as he jumps into his pants. "Get back and stake out a claim on that there whale!"

NARRATION/
DESCRIPTION

The beachcomber is paid off with a five-dollar bill and a share of stock in McGill Enterprises (worth perhaps a dollar and a half), and soon McGill himself has the whale on a truck, towing it to Santa Clarissima. Here he bargains with a mortician to embalm it. The mortician, too, is one of the fast-buck race. He telephones to a supplier; he orders more formalin-and-mercury than a respectable undertaker would use in a disaster.

After an all-night operation the whale is rigid. A blue-gray film settles over its eyes and its tongue pulls back in a queer triangle, though no one knows the difference. McGill hoses the body down and covers it with a tarpaulin, then heads for the nearest sign shop.

In just thirty-six hours after it stranded in the haunts of California man, the whale stares into the distance, resting on the truck, while above it a sign proclaims:

NARRATION/
DETAILS

BIGGEST LIVING THING ON EARTH   TOUCH IT
FEEL IT   A FULL-GROWN WHALE FROM THE
ABISMAL DEPTHS OF THE SEA   THE
LEVIATHAN OF HOLY WRIT   ONE
DAY ONLY   ONE DOLLAR

Each night the truck moves in darkness to a roadside stand at the edge of a small town and each morning the flow of visitors begins. The whale is a gold mine. July turns to August, and the thermometer climbs to one hundred and five. An ineffable vapor rises from the patient corpse. When McGill eats a hamburger it tastes like whale and when he eats an egg it tastes like whale. During the day he begins to hate this whale and in his dreams at night he is pursued by whales in great variety, all of which he hates.

DESCRIPTION

The exhibit is shopworn, too. Along its graying sides are carved initials, and the names of motorcycle gangs and schools and lovers and political candidates. The eyes have long since disappeared and a half-dozen teeth have been pried loose behind McGill's back.

NARRATION/
EXPOSITION

When the whiskey, too, begins to taste like whale, McGill is alarmed. He changes the sign to

FOR SALE, YOUR PRICE

but he has no offer. The town marshal suggests that per-

NARRATION/ EXPOSITION
> haps the whale has outstayed its welcome, though the marshal personally has nothing against a good, clean, educational-type exhibit. McGill has in mind a solution. It is typical of his kind to anticipate a way out, with several good alternatives.

NARRATION
> That night he drives a hundred miles to a lookout point on the Palisade Drive. He loosens the fastenings on the whale, backs the truck swiftly to the concrete guardrail and jumps on the brake as the rear tires hit. The truck rears like a frightened mustang and its burden slides into empty space. Ages later (it seems) a distant crash merges with the sound of the booming surf and the whale returns to its primordial home.

The Year of the Whale

THE WHOLE ESSAY: FOUR DEMONSTRATION MODELS

The following student essays illustrate four basic kinds of nonfiction prose; each provides the four elements necessary for an effective paper —thesis statement, topic sentences, specific support, and conclusion. You may wish to look back at these four essays from time to time as you work through the text and discover in detail what the process of effective writing involves.

Exposition Illustrated

This essay is primarily *exposition*. The writer also uses *description*.

MONSTER WATCH

Whether through fear or curiosity, people have long been fascinated by monsters. Each year, there are a number of accounts of sightings of the Yeti, Tibet's Abominable Snowman, and Big Foot, an ape-like creature that reportedly haunts the California redwood country. Yet the **INTRODUCTION** most famous creature is Scotland's Loch Ness Monster ("Nessie"), and the number of sightings each year (coupled with some rather convincing photographs) has resulted in serious scientific inquiry. When I visited Loch **Thesis Statement** Ness last year, I learned of two scientific theories that attempt to explain the existence of this creature.

Even in the bright summer sunlight, Loch Ness is a foreboding place. The loch itself stretches and winds for

Topic Sentence { miles, and its waters are cloudy, a result of the peat which permeates it. The cloudiness of the water is significant for the first theory: that prehistoric sea creatures were trapped in the loch by earth shifts which sealed their passageway to the ocean. Over the centuries, these crea-

BODY-1

tures adapted to fresh water, but were concealed from man's eyes by the peat in the water and by the loch's isolated geographic position. The trailers which house the Loch Ness Inquiry surround the loch, and I was shown a

Specific Support { number of pictures that testify to the existence of a large-bodied, long-necked, small-headed creature that looks very much like the prehistoric plesiosaur. The most interesting of these was taken at night in 1936, and although the picture is murky, a rather large creature is discernible.

Topic Sentence { The second theory is also credible, though not nearly so exotic as the first. Some scientists claim that the monster is really a giant squid, similar to those which inhabit the ocean depths. It, too, was trapped by earth shifts. The

BODY-2

Specific Support { squid, these scientists claim, is used to darkness and would have little trouble navigating in the loch's murky waters. Again, an assortment of pictures lends credibility to this theory.

Specific Support { Sightings of the monster go back to the ninth century, and, as it would be unrealistic to expect any creature to live such a length of time, proponents of both theories agree on one thing: there is more than one monster in the loch. Many scientists claim that nine individual creatures would be necessary to continue the species in an area the size of Loch Ness. This multiple monster idea helps ex-

BODY-3

Topic Sentence { plain why there have been simultaneous sightings at different ends of the lake.

Whether or not "Nessie" exists is still open to debate. And if it does, it is still uncertain which theory (if either) is correct. But after seeing the evidence, and realizing that like most people I am fascinated by the unknown, my visit to Loch Ness has made a believer of me.

CONCLUSION

Narration Illustrated

This essay is *narration*. Notice that the unifying concept expressed in the thesis statement is an impression the writer formed about the events. The progression is chronological, and the writer uses *description*.

THE RIGHT TO HUMAN DIGNITY

Thesis Statement

Visiting Mr. Kessler in the hospital gave me a sense that an ill person, as regarded by hospital personnel, is no more important than a piece of furniture. This attitude was conveyed to me by one of the nurses, whom I knew from another social context—my church; I found it as well in Mr. Kessler's doctor.

INTRODUCTION

Topic Sentence

Though a stroke had reduced Mr. Kessler to something approaching the state of an object of furniture—he could not see or speak, and he was paralyzed from the neck down—he was still worthy of the dignity which being human should confer, and he did not deserve the impersonal treatment he received from Mrs. Kraft, the nurse. A

Specific Support

man of fifty, Mr. Kessler had been a shy but always polite neighbor of mine. Late one evening last February he suffered a stroke. A week later, following his removal from the intensive care unit, I went to the hospital to visit him. Since he could not communicate, I decided to sit by his bed for a few minutes, first just to silently indicate my respect for him, and second to give me the opportunity to speak to his wife, who might also visit him. During the half-hour I was there, Mrs. Kraft, whom I had known from church as a normally kind and gracious person, appeared. She greeted me warmly; then, as if she were straightening the cushions on a sofa, she rearranged the pillow under the patient's head so that the tube in his mouth was better positioned. Raising his head with her left hand, she plumped up the pillow with her right. Then, instead of gently letting his head down again, she simply withdrew her hand and let his head drop.

BODY-1

(Implied Topic Sentence)

Specific Support

A few minutes later, Dr. Cox appeared. Without a word to me or to the comatose patient, he briskly placed his thumb on Mr. Kessler's eye and pushed up the eyelid. The doctor's demeanor was such that he might as well have been readjusting the position of a loose button on an upholstered cushion. Dr. Cox left as swiftly as he had entered. Neither he nor Mrs. Kraft had noticed the empty intravenous fluid bottle or the wilting flowers in need of water, standing in a vase on a shelf beside the bed.

BODY-2

I ended my silent vigil a few minutes later. Pausing at the nurse's desk on the way out, I mentioned the empty i.v. bottle to Mrs. Kraft, but I said nothing about the flowers, thinking that it would be foolish to request any nonessential service. Mrs. Kraft, however, was engrossed

CONCLUSION

in a Louis Lamour novel and, without looking up, muttered, "I'll see to it."

Description Illustrated

This essay is *description*. As in the preceding essay, the thesis statement announces the dominant impression, which gives unity to the selection of details in the essay.

HISTORY GLIMPSED THROUGH ART

Even though America has much to offer of historical interest, the tourist who earnestly seeks a fuller sense of history and tradition should greatly enjoy some of the cathedrals, castles, and museums of England: Canterbury, Ely, Stoke Poges, Chartwell, Winchester, and Glastonbury. One of the richest sources of British history is Windsor Castle, the traditional home of the royal family. Constructed in the Middle Ages, the castle offers the tourist **INTRODUCTION** 800 years of British elegance and glory. Of all the rooms accessible to the tourist, the one which best offers the **Thesis Statement** grace and dignity of English history is the King's Dressing Room. It will have particular appeal to the person who appreciates fine paintings.

(Implied Topic Sentence) As one enters the room, he can see in the center of the wall to his left the famous Van Dyke portrait of Charles I. The brilliant colors reveal a quiet, almost muted, intensity **Specific Support** of facial expression. The portrait is striking for its symmetry; the graceful lines capture the elegance of pre-Restoration England. Juxtaposed to the Van Dyke hang portraits by Dürer and Holbein, masters of the German and Dutch traditions. **BODY-1**

Topic Sentence To his right, the tourist finds two portraits by Rembrandt, the more engaging of the two being the portrait of the artist's mother. The somber background enhances the soft features of the gentle lady, the deeply penetrating **Specific Support** eyes contrast with the mild luster of her gown, and the feeling one gets is of gentle, not haughty, dignity. On the **BODY-2** same wall hangs Rembrandt's portrait of a young man, whose pensive gaze evokes a calmness in the beholder.

Topic Sentence It is, however, the center wall that is most striking. Andrea del Sarto's portrait of a Florentine lady brings to mind both the opulence and the decadence of the high **Specific Support** Renaissance in Italy. It is only just, however, that another painting by Rembrandt—his acclaimed self-portrait— **BODY-3**

Specific Support holds the most prominent position. The viewer is at once held only by the lifelike detail of the face of the master himself. The grace and the dignity of this exquisite collection of paintings is suitably revealed by the soft radiance of a frescoed nineteenth-century ceiling and by the shimmering elegance of an eighteenth-century chandelier.

Not only can the interested tourist find the sense of British history in the King's Dressing Room, for the various paintings were acquired during different reigns, but **CONCLUSION** he can also feel the grandeur of the best art Europe has offered. Nowhere are so many rich paintings set in such a scene of monarchical tradition.

Argumentation Illustrated

The following essay is essentially *argumentation*. Notice how the introduction identifies the basis for the writer's stand—the realm of information from which she has formed her conclusions.

ABORTION: AN APPEAL TO REASON

What I resent most about the current controversy on abortion is that many persons find it so easy to take single-minded stands, totally pro or totally con. I think it patently unfair for anyone to condemn or approve the practice as a whole, without taking into account the morality of the decision of the individual who chooses either **INTRODUCTION** to give birth to an unplanned, unwanted child or to have

Thesis Statement the birth aborted. My experience with two close friends— one who chose to have the abortion and one who chose to give birth to her child—has demonstrated for me the moral complexity of the abortion issue and shown the unfairness of judging the issue other than on the particulars of an individual case.

Topic Sentence My friend Sue chose to have an abortion when she was two months pregnant; to me her decision was morally justified. First, her father declared that, were she to embarrass him by producing an illegitimate child, she would have to find a home elsewhere, and that he would in no way finance her college education. Sue was seventeen, **Specific Support** she had a good academic record, and, with a college educa- **BODY-1** tion, she could pursue a challenging career. Second, she felt she was too young to get married, and she did not love the child's father. However, the most compelling reason for her decision to seek an abortion was that the

Specific Support

doctor told her, for reasons she did not disclose to me, that her physical health would be jeopardized if she had the child. In addition, her mental health was in danger: Sue had had a nervous breakdown two years before when her mother died in a car accident. For all the above reasons, I think Sue was justified in seeking an abortion.

Topic Sentence

When another friend, Janet, also seventeen, discovered that she was pregnant, she decided to have the baby; this decision I also found morally proper. First, her physical health was good, and, though the unexpected pregnancy put a strain on her, her mental health was sound and her outlook remained generally cheerful. Her parents supported her decision to have the baby and then put it up for adoption. Janet was interviewed by an understanding, intelligent caseworker at the County Welfare Office, who assured her that the child would be placed in a family that had adequate financial resources to care for and educate the child, and that strongly desired a child to love and raise. Having the baby, with such little risk to herself physically and emotionally, became a positive goal for Janet; for her, abortion would have been morally the wrong solution to her problem.

BODY-2

Specific Support

Prolifers might condemn Sue; ecologists worrying about the population increase might condemn Janet. Each woman, however, made the proper decision.

CONCLUSION

PART ONE

The Prewriting Process

This part of the text discusses *prewriting,* the beginning of the writing process. Prewriting can be thought of as deciding where you are going to go before you set out to get there. Many writing problems are actually problems that could have been avoided if prewriting tasks had been carried out.

As a means of getting underway, the prewriting process enables you to define a general subject area, select a topic, create a thesis statement, organize the material, and decide on a style of presentation. Prewriting, therefore, is planning; it means making rational, conscious choices about your paper *before* you begin writing it.

Part one discusses these aspects of the prewriting process:

> exploring your alternatives
> arriving at a subject and topic
> discovering your thesis
> organizing the composition
> finding a suitable style

Exploring   2
Your Alternatives

One of the tasks of prewriting is picking the most fruitful subject areas that you might write about. This part of the writing process offers rewards in proportion to the energy you devote to it. Here are four *strategy questions* that can spur your thinking about the alternative possibilities open to you as a writer.

What Am I Going to Write About?

Write about what you know. Don't assume that you know little that could possibly interest a reader; don't assume that you should leave writing to people who lead exciting lives.

The question of what to write about requires honesty and ego. Certainly, admit the limitations of your experience, but recognize also that no one else sees the world exactly as you do. Your experiences are probably shared by many persons, but because your perception of them is original, you can transform these experiences into interesting, worthwhile, and even exciting essays.

Finding material is an active process. Probe your mind to discover what and why you believe as you do. What is your experience? What are your interests, opinions, goals? Why did you vote for a particular candidate in the last election? What bothers you about certain fashions or customs or regulations? Finally, realize that no one wants to read the same thing over and over. Instead of writing generally about how some people are bored by spectator sports, describe your own feelings as you sat through an afternoon watching a football game in which the final score was 77–0.

Why Am I Writing About It?

Write about things that are important to you, and attempt to make them important to an audience. This does not mean that you should write essays about the nature of God, the design of the universe, or the development of civilization in the western world. It means, rather, that you should write about those things to which you assign value—a walk on a beach, the inflationary price of oil, or a humorous incident at a fraternity party.

You need also to recognize that writing can be both selfish and selfless: selfish because you gain insight from writing as you explore and discover what you think and why; selfless because, through your writing, you *do* something to or for an audience. Whether you narrate an experience, explain a process, describe a person, or argue for a point, you give an audience a perspective it did not have before. Writing should be a broadening experience for you, and reading what you have written should be a broadening experience for an audience.

How Am I Going to Say It?

Effective writing accomplishes what you intend it to accomplish. You must therefore find a tone that is suitable for your subject matter. For example, a paper on the horrors of a Nazi concentration camp would seem tasteless if it employed a light, frivolous tone; a love letter would seem ludicrous if it began with "Dear Madam." Also, be honest and fair. Avoid illogical leaps (such as "All Southerners are hospitable"). Avoid personal prejudices (such as "Don't trust anyone over thirty"). Provide evidence to back up generalizations. Be exact. Be precise.

Your presentation will reveal your attitude toward your subject, and you want to suggest a sense of commitment to that subject. Avoid generalities and words and expressions that have become almost meaningless (a "nice person," "a meaningful relationship"), and pay particular attention to logic, mechanics, and grammar. If your presentation is sloppy, your reader may conclude that you don't care about your essay, or worse, that you don't care about him.

Who Is My Audience, and How Do I
Appeal to That Audience?

You don't live in a vacuum, and you shouldn't write in one either. Your reader will assign to you a personality on the basis of his perception of you; you, in turn, must know who your reader is and direct your writing at that specific audience. A letter to Aunt Millie shouldn't sound like a chemistry report, but if you don't consciously analyze your audience, this may be the result. Remember that just as there is a person behind your words, there is a person who will read your words. For your presentation to be effective, it must be tailored to your reader.

Assume that any audience is intelligent, and treat it with the respect that you would desire were you part of that audience. You want to present your thought in a manner that you can take pride in, and you do this by appropriate prewriting, which helps to create an orderly, unified, and coherent essay. In addition, you can show respect for your audience by careful revision to make sure that there are no errors of fact, vague wording, or contradictions in what you have written and by thorough proofreading to correct for errors in grammar, punctuation, spelling, and the like. Careful revising will ensure that you place no barriers between your thoughts and your audience's reception of them. Finally, anticipate. A good writer anticipates possible audience reactions, reservations, and even counterarguments as he plans his writing strategy.

Naturally, answers to these four strategy questions are dependent on a number of variables (for example, specific topics will sometimes be assigned in college), but you will increase your writing effectiveness if you remain aware that the four strategy questions begin the prewriting process.

EXERCISE

The following essay is the work of a student writer who appears to have failed to consider writing strategy. Read the essay, keeping in mind the four strategy questions previously discussed. Then respond to the questions that follow the essay.

COLLEGE GRADES

Although I don't know a whole lot about the college grading system, having just arrived on campus, I do know that the average college student shouldn't have to put up with grades. After all, we would all like to think we have a scholarly streak and that we have come to college to gain the wisdom of a Sir Thomas More, the humor of a Mark Twane and the creative abilities of a Thomas Edison.

I had a friend once who went away to college. He was a really good guy. He worked for the church and was really popular in high school. He went away to college and was booted out by a bunch of guys with big degrees who said his grades weren't any good. This my friend told me was really unfair. The college wouldn't treat him like an individual.

I feel like a college should treat everyone like an individual, and how can they if they only see you in terms of As and Bs etc.

The real reason I'm against grades is that they put alot of pressure on you. If you don't get good grades, you really here about it from your nagging parents, they don't understand that theres alot more to college than grades: your social life, athletics, and alot of other things.

Students are suppose to come to school to study. That's where the word student comes from. But is that motivating young men and women fresh out of high school, toward enrollment on many college campuses across the nation. Most of my, friends don't think so anymore than they think grades are fair. They feel like the pressure grades put on an individual are just excuses for the college to make us conform to it's system. I've also heard that alot of colleges accept alot more students than they have room for just to get your money and then kick you out after one semester. Call that fair?

What most college students should do is rebel against the grading system. If an individual wants to get a college diploma and if he's spent alot of time and money on it the college should treat him like a individual and try to help him out instead of flunking him out.

So as I begin my career at State University, I've decided not to pay much attention to grades. After all, I've got alot going for me I don't want to give up. I'm alive and in my opinion (and to me my opinion is important) being alive and happy is better than worrying about little marks on tests and papers.

Questions

1. Does this writer understand his topic? How can you tell?
2. In which paragraph does the writer indicate specifically what his topic will be? What purpose(s) is served by the first three paragraphs?
3. Do the writer's paragraphs follow logically? Is it easy for you to follow his thinking?
4. Does the writer care about his topic? How do you know?
5. Has the writer been considerate of his audience?
6. What kind of person do you see behind the writer's words? Why?

"College Grades" is obviously a weak paper. Because the writer failed to direct his thought at the specific topic, because he failed to consider writing strategy, he simply transferred the chaos of his mind to paper. And the paper, unfortunately, is revealing. In it, the author implies the following: I don't care about my topic; I don't care how my audience sees me; my audience is not worth the time it would take to think, revise, and proofread.

Now examine the instructor's comments on the student's paper:

COLLEGE GRADES

Can you better convince the reader that you know your topic thoroughly?

diction

Although I don't know a whole lot about the college grading system, having just arrived on campus, I do know that the average college student shouldn't have to put up with grades. After all, we would all like to

How does this statement follow from the previous one?

think we have a scholarly streak and that we have come to college to gain the wisdom of a Sir Thomas More, the humor of a Mark Twane and the creative abilities of a Thomas Edison.

Avoid such awkward repetition.

Check rule on comma in a series.

diction

Exactly how is this example related to your thesis?

I had a friend once who went away to college. He was a really good guy. He worked for the church and was really popular in high school. He

diction

went away to college and was booted out by a bunch of guys with big degrees who said his grades weren't any good. This my friend told me was really unfair. The college wouldn't treat him like an individual.

Can you make your diction more precise?

"think" point of view shift. Doesn't this hurt your first three paragraphs?

I feel like a college should treat everyone like an individual, and how can they if they only see you in terms of As and Bs etc. [The real reason] I'm against grades is that they put alot of pressure

apostrophe

Avoid abbreviations.

Be precise.

Find a precise substitute for "a lot."

apostrophe

comma splice

on you. If you don't get good grades, you really here about it from your nagging parents, they don't understand that theres alot more to college than grades: your social life, athletics, and alot of other things.

Be more specific.

Use past participle.

Students are suppose to come to school to study. [That's where the word student comes from.] But is that motivating young men and women

necessary?

Unclear pronoun reference.

trite expressions

comma

fresh out of high school toward enrollment on many college campuses across the nation. Most of my friends don't think so anymore than they think grades are fair. They feel like the pressure grades put on an individual

imprecise diction

unclear pronoun reference

are just excuses for the college to make us conform to it's system. I've also heard that alot of colleges accept alot more students than they have room for just to get your money and then kick you out after one semester.

Check pronoun forms.

Unclear pronoun reference

fragment

Call that fair?

wordy

[What most] college students should [do is] rebel against the grading system. If an individual wants to get a college diploma and if he's spent

Check rule on comma with adverb clause.

alot of time and money on it, the college should treat him like a individual and try to help him out instead of flunking him out.

Be specific.

diction

Weak transition

So as I begin my career at State University, I've decided not to pay much attention to grades. After all, I've got alot going for me I don't

vague

want to give up. I'm alive and in my opinion [and to me my opinion is important] being alive and happy is better than worrying about little marks on tests and papers.

unnecessary

EXERCISE

Examine the following student paper in light of the four strategy questions previously discussed.

HO-HUM

My high school commencement speaker accomplished one thing: he persuaded me that high school commencement speakers should be abolished. His speech was too long and too dull, and he had distracting mannerisms.

The length of Mr. Beak's speech was exceeded only by its dullness. The speech began at 9:00 in the evening and rambled on for one hour and forty-five minutes, during which time the members of the audience could be observed yawning, coughing, and counting the bricks in the gymnasium wall. The worst thing about the talk, though, was its dullness. The topic was "The Need for Higher Education in a Changing World," a talk most us had heard in one form or another from assorted guidance counselors, progressive teachers, and parents. Naturally, the speech was peppered with countless trite expressions, such as "twenty years from now we shall all look back," "at this point in time," "the happiest days of your lives," "the challenge of the future," and "our responsibility as citizens." As Mr. Beak droned on, the person seated to my right (the class clown) pretended to fall into a coma, dropping his head on my shoulder. It was the most exciting moment of the evening.

Because Mr. Beak's chief "claim to fame" was his position as State Coordinator for Humanistic Advancement, it was assumed that he would be an effective speaker; however, Mr. Beak was obviously used to committee meetings and seminars rather than crowds of 500. Thus, he seemed a bit awe-struck to find himself at the podium addressing a sea of faces. Unfortunately, however, after a couple of feeble jokes, he erroneously assumed that the crowd had warmed to him; thus, in spite of a bad lisp, frequent stuttering, and wild gesturing with both hands and one eyebrow, Mr. Beak delivered what he obviously thought to be a timely message to an indifferent audience. We soon realized that indeed there was a need for higher education in a changing world.

If my commencement experience was typical, and many of my peers assure me that it was, perhaps our public institutions should begin to rethink having this yearly form of torture. Although some kind of commencement ceremony may well be necessary to formalize the high school education experience, it seems ridiculous to end one's secondary education on such a weak note.

Questions

1. In which paragraph does the writer indicate specifically what his topic will be?
2. Does the first paragraph indicate how the whole paper will be organized?
3. Does the writer fulfill his organizational plan?
4. Do the paragraphs follow one another logically?
5. Does the writer appear to care about his topic? How do you know?
6. Has the writer considered his audience? How do you know?
7. What kind of person do you sense behind this writer's words? Why?

"Ho-Hum" is a much stronger paper than "College Grades." When you examine the instructor's comments on "Ho-Hum," you will see that, while he suggests some revisions, he never is forced to wonder what the writer's topic is, nor is he ever unsure about the direction of the writer's thought. The writer has considered writing strategy before beginning to compose, so the instructor is able to devote most of his comments to possible ways in which the paper might be improved.

HO-HUM

Consider developing the introduction slightly. Perhaps you could open with a quotation or an anecdote.

My high school commencement speaker accomplished one thing: he persuaded me that high school commencement speakers should be abolished. His speech was too long and too dull, and he had distracting mannerisms.

Your thesis is effective — it clearly establishes your organization.

The length of Mr. Beak's speech was exceeded only by its dullness. The speech began at 9:00 in the evening and rambled on for one hour and forty-five minutes, during which time the members of the audience could be observed yawning, coughing, and counting the bricks in the gymnasium wall.

The descriptive detail reinforces your topic sentence well.

The worst <u>thing</u> about the talk, though, was its dullness. The topic was "The Need for Higher Education in a Changing World," a talk most us had heard in one form or another from assorted guidance counselors, progressive teachers, and parents. Naturally, the speech was peppered with countless trite expressions, such as "twenty years from now we shall all look back," "at this point in time," "the happiest days of your lives," "the challenge of the future," and "our responsibility as citizens." As Mr. Beak droned on, the person seated to my right (the class clown) pretended to fall into a coma, dropping his head on my shoulder. It was the most exciting moment of the evening.

Can you find a more precise word?

effective, specific examples

trite

Because Mr. Beak's chief ⑪claim to fame⑫ was his position as State Coordinator for Humanistic Advancement, it was assumed that he would be an effective speaker; however, Mr. Beak was obviously used to committee meetings and seminars rather than crowds of 500. Thus, he seemed a bit

Check quotation conventions.

The structure makes this sentence confusing. Did Mr. Beak think the audience was in-different ?

awe-struck to find himself at the podium addressing a sea of faces. Unfortunately, however, after a couple of feeble jokes, he erroneously assumed that the crowd had warmed to him; thus, in spite of a bad lisp, frequent stuttering, and wild gesturing with both hands and one eyebrow, Mr. Beak delivered what he obviously thought to be a timely message to an indifferent audience. We soon realized that indeed there was a need for higher education in a changing world.

The conclusion convincingly reemphasizes your thesis.

If my commencement experience was typical, and many of my peers assure me that it was, perhaps our public institutions should begin to rethink having this yearly form of torture. Although some kind of commencement ceremony may well be necessary to formalize the high school education experience, it seems ridiculous to end one's secondary education on such *trite* a weak note.

Arriving at a   3
Subject and Topic

The prewriting process is both expansive and narrowing. On the one hand, it invites the writer to consider broad possibilities in his search for something to write about. On the other hand, it involves a sharp narrowing of focus once suitable material comes into view. Selection is largely a matter of focus. Once promising ideas suggest themselves, you will want to place them under the microscope of thought to examine them clearly.

As the prewriting process proceeds, it is important to be clear about the distinction between the subject of your paper and its topic. For our purposes, a *subject* is a general field of knowledge or experience; a *topic* is the specific focus or limitation that a writer gives that subject. This example suggests the difference:

SUBJECT	TOPIC
tennis	the basic difference between wooden and metal tennis rackets

Note that a topic is more specific than a subject. In the example above, the topic imposes a limitation on the subject.

Determining topic requires that you identify what the limits of the essay will allow you to say about a general field of knowledge or experience. Common sense tells you that "tennis" is far too wide a field to examine in a short paper. Had you the time and knowledge, you could write a book on tennis. You could trace its history, catalog its rules, explain the fundamental tennis strokes, distinguish between types of tennis balls, examine the various tennis associations, and explore a hundred other components that together make up tennis. But if you tried to write an essay on "tennis" or "music" or "animals" or any subject, your paper would have little value; its content would be so general that it would do nothing to or for the reader. (Remember the second strategy question.)

Any subject can lead to a number of topics suitable for an essay. The following diagram illustrates some topics derived from the subject "tennis." It also suggests the basic essay type that each topic might generate:

SUBJECT	TOPIC	ESSAY TYPE
	how to select tennis shoes	exposition/description
	basic tennis equipment	exposition/description
tennis	my most memorable tennis match	narration
	how to hit the backhand	exposition/description
	advantages of indoor tennis	argumentation

EXERCISES

1. The following topics are all components of the subject "tennis." Indicate which topics would generate lengthy papers. Which topics would require further limitations? Indicate also the basic essay type each topic would generate.
   a. the most gripping tennis match I have watched
   b. basic tennis etiquette
   c. why mixed doubles should be banned
   d. the importance of concentration in tennis
   e. a history of the United States Lawn Tennis Association
   f. politics and the 1977 Davis Cup
   g. why we should suspend professional tennis players who violate standards of good sportsmanship
   h. how tennis clothing manufacturers are robbing the public
   i. fundamentals of tennis strategy
   j. perfecting the drop shot
2. Examine the following list of subjects for papers. Select three of these subjects and originate five topics for each.
   a. animals
   b. birds
   c. children
   d. dinosaurs
   e. ecology
   f. food
   g. golf
   n. novels
   o. October
   p. pizza
   q. queen
   r. racism
   s. sex
   t. theater

h. his and hers	u. utopia
i. Italy	v. vehicles
j. judo	w. war
k. kites	x. Xerox machines
l. love	y. youth
m. money	z. zoos

The topic selection process requires that you direct attention to one aspect of your total experience. Many inexperienced writers, however, claim that finding a topic within the subject areas of their lives is difficult—that beginning the paper is the greatest challenge.

The following discussion has two objectives: (1) to make you aware of subjects for writing and (2) to explain how these subjects may be translated into workable topics.

USING PRIMARY AND SECONDARY EXPERIENCE

In his essay "Self-Reliance," Ralph Waldo Emerson advises that "man should learn to detect and watch that gleam of light which flashes across his mind from within." Emerson, one of America's foremost essayists, is telling us to follow where our own experience leads. This is particularly good advice for the writer. You might think of your experience as including two types: *primary experience,* that which you have been directly exposed to by observing and interacting with other people and with your environment, and *secondary experience,* that which you have gained indirectly through hearing of the experience of someone else.

Each person's perception of experience is different from anyone else's. Were two six-year-old children of similar intelligence placed for an hour in identical bare rooms, their perceptions about that hour would differ because each would bring a different background to the experience. One child, for example, might upon emerging not only describe feelings of excitement and adventure but also tell of creating a fantasy of being aboard a spaceship. The second child might tell of feelings of loneliness and frustration and relate an elaborate fantasy of being trapped in an iceberg under the sea. The children's perceptions would differ because of differences in their past experience: one child had recently paid close attention to television accounts of a space flight; the other child had recently returned from a winter visit to a snowbound village on the Maine coast. These differing experiences—and many others—would color the way in which each perceived later events that were physically identical. Every individual's perceptions of both primary and secondary experiences are original. It is this originality that allows a writer to bring a fresh perspective to any material.

To derive the greatest benefit from your own unique perspective as a writer requires that you be conscious of your experience and that you be willing to analyze it. Becoming more aware of everyday experiences may yield an insight worth communicating, as it did for this writer:

> I always enjoyed talking with Bob. We both owned compact cars, and our conversation usually turned to comparison of gas mileage, where to get the best and least expensive repair work done, and how fast our cars could go in various gears. On reflection, however, I realize that the conversations were more than merely information exchanges. Each of us, I now see, had the underlying motive of saying to the other, "I'm better than you." This conclusion becomes obvious to me as I analyze the pattern in our conversations, which consisted almost entirely of comparisons: "I got 30 miles per gallon last week. How was your mileage?" "I got 28." I can remember the sense of satisfaction I felt on hearing that response. When I analyze our other conversations—on repair costs, speed achieved, and resale values—the same pattern emerges.

In the above paragraph, the writer's analysis of experience has led to a realization of the thoughts and feelings underlying his conversations with his friend. By giving written form to the experience, the writer has come to understand it. And the insight he gives the reader is worthwhile.

Following are four excerpts from writers who use personal experience in different ways and to different ends. The first, from *The Journal of John Woolman,* is by an eighteenth-century Quaker writer. Woolman uses personal experience to write a *descriptive* passage in which he re-creates a sense of disgust with himself resulting from a thoughtless boyhood prank:

> A thing remarkable in my childhood was, that once, going to a neighbour's house, I saw, on the way, a robin sitting on her nest, and as I came near she went off, but, having young ones, flew about, and with many cries expressed her concern for them; I stood and threw stones at her, till, one striking her, she fell down dead: at first I was pleased with the exploit, but after a few minutes was seized with horror, as having, in a sportive way, killed an innocent creature while she was careful for her young: I beheld her lying dead, and thought those young ones, for which she was so careful, must now perish for want of their dam to nourish them; and, after some painful considerations on the subject, I climbed up the tree,

took all the young birds, and killed them; supposing that better than to leave them to pine away and die miserably: and believed, in this case, that scripture-proverb was fulfilled, "The tender mercies of the wicked are cruel."

Because Woolman is primarily interested in capturing the painful boyhood memory, he presents a single incident in vivid detail, concrete and specific even in his recollection of the killing of the baby birds. For Woolman, personal experience is a way of reliving a painful lesson learned early in life: that man cannot reconcile cruelty with his conscience. Here, personal experience enables him to make an abstraction concrete.

Personal experience can also form the basis for *narration*. In *Life on the Mississippi*, Mark Twain uses his boyhood memories in a narrative passage about the arrival of a steamboat in a small town:

> Once a day a cheap, gaudy packet arrived upward from St. Louis, and another downward from Keokuk. Before these events, the day was glorious with expectancy; after them, the day was a dead and empty thing. Not only the boys, but the whole village, felt this. After all these years I can picture that old time to myself now, just as it was then: the white town drowsing in the sunshine of a summer's morning; the streets empty, or pretty nearly so; one or two clerks sitting in front of the Water Street stores, with their splint-bottomed chairs tilted back against the wall, chins on breasts, hats slouched over their faces, asleep—with shingle-shavings enough around to show what broke them down; a sow and a litter of pigs loafing along the sidewalk, doing a good business in watermelon rinds and seeds; two or three lonely little freight piles scattered about the "levee"; a pile of "skids" on the slope of the stone-paved wharf, and the fragrant town drunkard asleep in the shadow of them. . . . Drays, carts, men, boys, all go hurrying from many quarters to a common center, the wharf. Assembled there, the people fasten their eyes upon the coming boat as upon a wonder they are seeing for the first time. And the boat *is* rather a handsome sight, too. She is long and sharp and trim and pretty; she has two tall, fancy-topped chimneys, with a gilded device of some kind swung between them; a fanciful pilothouse, all glass and "gingerbread," perched on top of the "texas" deck behind them.

In recounting the incident, Twain also provides an analysis of what it means. He moves from present awareness as an adult to past awareness as a child—the "cheap, gaudy packet" becomes a "handsome sight . . . sharp and trim and pretty." Here, recounting a personal experience suggests the continuing growth and movement of the mind's perspective.

Stephen Crane, in an account of a near disaster at sea, uses *description* within a narrative structure. In the following excerpt from his story "The Open Boat," Crane's re-creation of his first-hand experience transmits emotions and attitudes forcefully:

A seat in this boat was not unlike a seat upon a bucking broncho, and by the same token, a broncho is not much smaller. The craft pranced and reared and plunged like an animal. As each wave came, and she rose for it, she seemed like a horse making at a fence outrageously high. The manner of her scramble over these walls of water is a mystic thing, and, moreover, at the top of them were ordinarily these problems in white water, the foam racing down from the summit of each wave requiring a new leap, and a leap from the air. Then, after scornfully bumping a crest, she would slide and race and splash down a long incline, and arrive bobbing and nodding in front of the next menace.

Crane concentrates exclusively on the physical sensations of the boat ride, avoiding direct commentary, because he knows that the power of description, based on personal experience, is enough to establish his major point: the menace of the sea.

In the following passage from *Walden*, Henry David Thoreau uses personal experience to explain how and why he built the cellar for his house at Walden Pond:

I dug my cellar in the side of a hill sloping to the south, where a woodchuck had formerly dug his burrow, down through sumach and blackberry roots, and the lowest stain of vegetation, six feet square by seven deep, to a fine sand where potatoes would not freeze in any winter. The sides were left shelving, and not stoned; but the sun having never shone on them, the sand still keeps its place. It was but two hours' work. I took particular pleasure in this breaking of ground, for in almost all latitudes men dig into the earth for an equable temperature. Under the most splendid house in the city is still to be found the cellar where they store their roots as of old, and long after the superstructure has disappeared posterity remark its dent in the earth. The house is still but a sort of porch at the entrance of a burrow.

This passage is basically *expository*—it explains. Thoreau not only recounts his cellar-digging experience but offers his reasons for digging the cellar "seven [feet] deep . . . where potatoes would not freeze in any winter." He uses personal experience and exposition to further one of his themes in *Walden:* that man, by simplifying his life, can improve the quality of it.

> **A personal experience can serve the writer in any of the following ways:**
>
> - as a means of making an abstraction concrete and forceful
> - as a means of contemplating, recounting, and providing perspective on an incident
> - as a means of making writing authentic and therefore credible
> - as a means of furthering an idea, concept, or theme

EXERCISE

Drawing upon your personal experience, select an event that resulted in your achieving a degree of insight and awareness. Describe the incident, examine how it altered your perspective, and explain what you gained from it. If you were to write an essay on this experience, what kind of essay would it be—narrative, descriptive, or expository?

Evaluating Personal Experience

Personal experience is also the basis for evaluation. Because in evaluating something you are essentially saying that it is good or bad—that it has value or lacks value—writing of this kind is more likely to arouse disagreement in your reader. For example, it is unlikely that a reader would dispute your contention that viewing sailboats on an April day is a tranquil and refreshing experience, but that same reader might react much more dramatically to your contention that *Gone With the Wind* is a bad movie. Before writing an evaluation, it is necessary to subject your personal experience to careful analysis.

To evaluate is to judge. When someone asks your opinion of a particular restaurant, he is really asking you to judge that restaurant according to specific *criteria*—standards that you believe a restaurant should meet. If, for example, you believe that a good restaurant is characterized by prompt, attentive service, a wide selection of American and Continental dishes, cleanliness, and moderate prices, you must impose each of these *criteria* on the restaurant in question. When you pronounce the restaurant "good," you are basing your judgment on the restaurant's ability to meet your standards. Naturally, you must be both fair and realistic about criteria: you would not judge a fast-food restaurant by the same standards you would use to judge an expensive, elegant restaurant; nor would you judge a comedy by criteria appropriate to a tragedy.

When you write an evaluation, you need to be able to assume that your judgment is correct and that your audience can be convinced that your judgment is correct. Realize that you are arguing a point. In order to convince your audience, you must first discover *why* you think as you do.

The following film review illustrates the process of making a judgment in writing.

BIRD DROPPINGS

If one must spend the better part of two hours following the adventures of a bird, far better that the hero be Daffy Duck than Jonathan Livingston Seagull. Jonathan, for the information of any recluse who might not have heard or misanthropes who just don't care, is an adventurous seagull who wants to "fly where no seagull has flown before," to "know what there is to know of this life." This angers his flock. An outraged Elder announces, "You are henceforth and forever outcast," and Jonathan takes it on the wing.

He seems to fly into a series of picture postcards of Yosemite, of Death Valley, of the frozen North. Eventually, settling down in the snow, he expires, his tail feathers quaking as he gives up the ghost. The ghost, however, will not be given up so easily and flies off to some spiritual never-never land. There, it—or he—is instructed in higher wisdom by a bird called Chiang, whose lessons in life and philosophy and heightened consciousness take a hint from Dale Carnegie, a leaf from Dr. Norman Vincent Peale and a volume from Kahlil Gibran. Thus enlightened, Jonathan is apparently reborn. He returns to his flock and spreads the good word in a sort of Sermon on the Garbage Mount: "Listen everybody! There's no limit to how high we can fly! We can dive for fish and never have to live on garbage again!"

Not that he actually talks, of course. Jonathan and the rest of his feathered friends are real birds—not mechanical, not animated—but their voices and interior monologues are rendered by actors. James Franciscus speaks for Jonathan, Juliet Mills for his love interest, Hal Holbrook for the Elder, Richard Crenna and Dorothy McGuire for Jonathan's parents. None of these actors has chosen to be included in the film's credits, a privilege only the least charitable would question.

Jonathan Livingston Seagull is the warmest, most goodhearted, most tuneful (score by Neil Diamond) piece of moral uplift since the musical version of *Lost Horizon*. Years hence, scholars may debate the significance of the fact that the wise elder in Shangri-La and the wise bird here are both called Chiang. Surely it is no mere coincidence. A homage, perhaps. Or maybe a moment of mystic communion, a stroke of magic enlightenment of the sort that Jonathan is always shoving his beak into.

Richard Bach, who wrote the original book, is much agitated over this film version, which has allegedly altered many of the "ideas" in the book and his original screenplay. The book has about as many ideas as *The Little Engine That Could*; in fact, buried under all the vomitous theosophy, it has the same idea. Ideology aside, the movie's casting could open up a whole new style of film making. Think of it: *Pigeons on Mean Streets*, about a bunch of tough young New York birds. Or what about a remake of *Four Feathers?*

Time, November 12, 1973

The judgment expressed in this review is based on four criteria:

JUDGMENT	CRITERIA
	The movie lacks *freshness.*
This is a *bad* movie.	The movie lacks *intellectual honesty.*
	The movie lacks *originality.*
	The movie lacks *ideas.*

Note that whenever the reviewer offers a particular criterion he provides a suitable example.

It is fair to say that another reviewer may find value in the same movie. He may, in fact, judge it to be a very good movie and give equally convincing reasons for his opinion:

JUDGMENT	CRITERIA
	The movie is *visually beautiful.*
This is a *good* movie.	The movie is *morally uplifting.*
	The movie praises *universal values.*

In the preceding examples, one judgment does not invalidate the other; they are simply based on different criteria.

Whenever you evaluate personal experience, you should not be influenced by anyone else's judgment. Your only task is to convince your reader that your judgment is valid. You must therefore explain with care the criteria upon which your judgment is based. Remember, your reader has no opportunity to question; you have only one opportunity to explain.

The magazines and books you read; the television programs and movies you see; the concerts, sports events, and talks you attend; the record albums you hear; even the people you meet and the situations you find yourself in—these (and many more) are all subjects for your judgment. And they are all potential topics for your writing.

> **Here is a review of the steps for evaluating personal experience:**
>
> - Reach a critical judgment.
>
> - Identify your criteria for that judgment.
>
> - Make sure that your judgment is based on suitable criteria (for example, the fact that a particular football player gives time to charities is unrelated to the quality of his playing).

EXERCISE

Following is a series of student and professional essays and reviews. In each, determine (1) the writer's judgment and (2) the specific criteria on which the writer bases that judgment.

Review of a Talk

AN ASSAULT ON RAPE

Overshadowed by the taboos of a past era, rape and rape prevention are two subjects which most people avoid but which, nevertheless, need to be dealt with directly. One of the few people who have taken the time to study and formulate the most effective means of rape prevention is Frederic Storaska. Author of the book *How to Say No to a Rapist and Survive,* Storaska is also a skillful lecturer who travels throughout the country speaking on a different college campus each night. His recent lecture at State University was clearly the result of extensive research and long hours of preparation. Storaska is a resounding success for two reasons: he talks to students about a relevant subject that no one else approaches, and he is an artist at keeping his audience involved in his lecture.

A portion of Storaska's success must be attributed to his unusual topic. Today, the subject of rape is pertinent to virtually everyone, yet almost no one will venture constructive information on the subject. Undoubtedly there are many specialized clinics that treat rape victims, but these clinics give advice only after the rape has occurred. People need the information before they are confronted by a rapist, and Storaska gives this information in a straightforward manner without trying to intimidate or scare his listeners. Students realizing the value of such information come to his lectures by the hundreds, certain that they will learn a great deal about coping with a rapist. Few are disappointed.

Storaska faces all of the problems of most speakers but with a few more besides. He must be conscious of the people who feel uncomfortable having rape so openly discussed, yet importantly, he must bring the subject out into the open where it can be most effectively dealt with. Storaska conquers both these problems through the use of humor. He sets his audience at ease early in the lecture with a comic description of French kissing. The initially nervous giggles turn to roars of laughter as inhibitions are forgotten. In a finely tuned balance, Storaska tempers his levity with seriousness, thereby keeping his audience entertained as he so very carefully instructs them in the most beneficial manner in which to react in a stress situation. Although there are periods of uncontrolled laughter in the room, everyone present realizes that rape is no joke and pays close attention as Mr. Storaska struts emphatically through the crowd. Constantly moving from stage to audience, Storaska uses humor and comic gestures to show just how ineffective "standard" methods of rape prevention really are. At one point he sends his listeners into bouts of laughter by beating on his chest like King Kong, all the while emitting cries that sound unmistakably like Tarzan. These actions may sound ridiculous, but very few persons listening will ever forget the lesson: that screaming and fighting are useless. Storaska makes point after point humorously, supporting each with authentic case histories. People laugh, but people remember.

Mr. Storaska has a difficult task each time that he faces a new audience. He has a relatively short time to tell people exactly what they will be faced with in a rape situation and how to deal effectively with the rapist. Storaska accomplishes these goals and, at the same time, manages to take the social disgrace out of rape. After lecturing to thousands of students annually for the past eleven years, Storaska is undoubtedly responsible for preventing quite a number of rapes and even some deaths that occasionally follow these assaults. Does not this thought alone warrant the standing ovation Frederic Storaska received at the end of his lecture?

student essay

Review of a Book

TIME PAST, TIME PRESENT

Time and Again, a novel by Jack Finney, incorporates the ingredients of a science-fiction adventure tale, a nineteenth-century melodrama of love and danger, and a pictorial social history.

By means of an elaborately conceived time-travel procedure (the science-fiction element), Finney is able to send modern-day commercial artist Simon Morley on a journey to the New York City of 1882.

One of Si's purposes while in the past is to discover the reason for the suicide of Andrew Carmody, grandfather of Si's twentieth-century girlfriend. A melodramatic tale of love and drama develops in the nineteenth-century setting when Si becomes the romantic rival of a larger-than-life villain, a blackmailer; both seek the hand of Julia Charbonneau. The blackmailer, Jake Pickering, also happens to be the one who provokes businessman Andrew Carmody to suicide. In discovering the blackmailing by eavesdropping, Si and Julia become trapped in a burning building; the couple makes a hair's-breadth escape from an upperstory window, their detective work complete. Ultimately, pursued by corrupt police, Si and Julia escape into the twentieth century. The moderately intricate narrative is genuinely gripping, even though the plot is full of gimmicks.

The two settings in time allow Finney the opportunity to moralize in the tradition of nineteenth-century popular novelists. Si makes numerous comparisons of current and past customs and attitudes, giving the book a strong element of social history. A nineteenth-century cab driver observes, "The way traffic is nowadays, it gets worse every day, you never know anymore." Si thinks, "New York wasn't really changed." At another point, Si sees a new invention in a display window. It is a typewriter. When the man standing beside him remarks that the new machine will become immensely popular, Si responds, "No, they'll never catch on; they lack the personal touch." In addition to many pictures of New York in 1882, *Time and Again* notes such customs as mail delivery five times a day; parlor games, such as *tableaux vivants*; and displays of ostentation and pride by the wealthy.

Although the narrative has its own merits, its larger purpose is to serve as a vehicle for the pictorial illustrations and social-history element of the book. And it is the social history that makes *Time and Again* truly worthwhile reading.

student essay

Review of a Movie

BARRY LYNDON

If William Makepeace Thackeray's literary reputation depended on so slight an offering as his novella *Barry Lyndon*, I doubt that generations of college students would have spent their time reading him. For those who do not know, *Barry Lyndon* is the story of an eighteenth-century shanty Irishman who would be rich. Upon assuming that position through a fortunate marriage, Lyndon becomes a womanizer *extraordinaire*, a debaucher, and a tyrant. In due course, he is seriously wounded by his stepson in a duel, his leg is amputated, he is separated from his family and fortune, and he leaves England for France. He is never heard of again.

In spite of the hackneyed and trite poor boy–rich boy–poor boy syndrome, writer, producer, director Stanley Kubrick (*Clockwork Orange*) has managed to make *Barry Lyndon* into an exciting and sensual film experience. It is not a "movie" in the accepted sense of the word: the characters are flat, bloodless, and one-dimensional; the conflict never approaches credible seriousness; the thematic concern is minimal. As compensation, Kubrick offers Kubrick. He offers hundreds of scenes in which his puppet characters prance at his will; he offers a dedication to detail that results in a staggering degree of period authenticity; he offers a sense of color that rivals the most graphic spectacles. We become so engrossed in the *pictures* of English and Continental life that we forgive *Barry Lyndon*'s shortcomings. We spend over two hours looking at costumes and scenery. And we give these externals our undivided attention because we are not especially interested in the characters or their problems.

It is Kubrick's sense of detachment from his characters that enables him to devote so much effort to cinematography. His direction is "cold": picture is heaped on picture, and the characters become almost incidental to his purpose. As stage props, Ryan O'Neal and Marisa Berenson do turn in yeomanlike performances. O'Neal has the wild-eyed look of the Irish zealot; Berenson, who appears only in the second part of the film, displays the necessary pallid and haunting demeanor of a wife wronged. But Kubrick never allows us to get close to his characters, and his detachment is infectious. We never feel for Lyndon, nor do we pine for his wife, and after his stepson (admirably played by Gay Hamilton) puts an end to his career by a well-placed bullet in the leg (the film's most ironic scene), we leave the theater humming some of the hauntingly beautiful music that is part of the production's effect.

Kubrick is no lightweight. He is the star of *Barry Lyndon*, and when he needs assistance, he knows where to get it. The score is adapted and conducted by Leonard Rosenman, who has woven throughout the movie's scenes Handel's "Sarabande," Mozart's "March from Idomenco," Schubert's "German Dance No. 1," and Vivaldi's "Cello Concerto in E Minor." Add to this traditional Irish refrains provided by "The Chieftains," and the sounds are striking.

With *Barry Lyndon*, Kubrick has brought a new dimension to the screen. It is a dimension that unabashedly suggests that movies are the director's province—that the director is really the star of the medium. As such, *Barry Lyndon* offers an alternate point of view to an art form sorely in need of it.

student essay

Review of a Concert

ROD McKUEN: BORING, BANAL BATHOS

You walk out of a Rod McKuen concert feeling glad to be alive. Now you know for sure that it's impossible to die of boredom. Otherwise you just would have.

On Saturday night (and again last night), McKuen sang, or muttered, his sad songs about sadness to a receptive, flashbulb-popping audience at the Kennedy Center Concert Hall. In essence, the performance was one long, protracted sensitivity greeting card.

McKuen has written a few nice numbers, and he included them on his program: songs like "The World I Used to Know" (abysmally arranged) and "If You Go Away," with a melody by the comparatively brilliant Jacques Brel.

Brel also collaborated on another McKuen song, "I'm Not Afraid," a pleasing melody that, however, bears a striking structural resemblance to a kiddie hit of the 50's, "The Chipmunk Song."

As for his poetry, Mr. McKuen writes two kinds: gibberish and slop. He read some of each to the audience, fingering casually through a stack of his best-selling books that sat on a stool next to his.

Most of the poems seemed to be about lovers saying goodby, although one concerned a homosexual whose cat ran away. Some were introduced as representing terribly personal and significant moments in the life of Mr. McKuen, and we were clearly expected to be very impressed with that.

If there is a McKuen mystique, it must derive from the new heroism of the antihero and the ersatz romance of the ersatz loner. How an audience can accept the sadistically prolific McKuen, who is by now at least a gillionaire, as some sort of rustic nomad, wandering highways with a backpack and a pocketful of appleseeds, is one of the cultural mysteries of our age.

His appeal is perhaps also based on the theory that within each of us there mopes a starsick sophomore waiting to be released. It takes the tight combination of banal imagery and masochistic bathos to do it. Mr. McKuen has lucked onto the surefire formula.

In addition to his songs, McKuen chatted and made a few wee jokes. He would offer a smutty remark and then, after the laughter, say, "Oh, I didn't mean that." After five minutes on the horrors of . Spiro Agnew . . . he said, "But I was only kidding."

The Concert Hall was full on Saturday night—but in certain real ways, it was never emptier.

Tom Shales, *The Washington Post*

THE TOPIC SELECTION PROCESS

There is an old folk tale that applies to the process of topic selection. After a long journey during which he'd had little to eat, a greedy merchant returned to his home and ordered a lavish feast. So delighted was he by the selection of food that he couldn't make up his mind with which delicacy to begin his feast. His servants found him dead of starvation the next morning. The point is that, in spite of the variety of your experience, you will derive benefit from it only insofar as you are able to use it. In order to write about the subject areas of your experience, you must translate these subjects into workable topics.

In most instances, deriving topics from your experience requires that you begin thinking about the general and then focus on the specific. Start, in other words, with a big stick and whittle it down until it has the shape and point you want. Thus, a general subject such as "smoking" may lead to the topic "how to buy a pipe" (exposition); "hunting" may lead to "why we should outlaw deer hunting in the Shoshone Mountains" (argumentation); "nature" may lead to "my escape from an enraged grizzly bear" (narration).

Because experience and perception differ from person to person, there is no one method that all writers use in their search for topics. Some writers may construct elaborate diagrams; others may doodle; still others may go through intense introspection while locked in a room. But whatever the mechanics of their search, they all proceed with the knowledge that the process of finding topics within experience is one of ever-narrowing focus.

The following suggestions indicate the basic progression required for narrowing subject areas into workable topics:

1. Select a *subject* that you know something about, one that, for whatever reason, you are interested in. If you have difficulty in making a selection, let your mind play freely—recall your primary and secondary experience and direct your thoughts by dividing your experience into specific areas: social, political, religious, and so forth. Or you may simply ask yourself, "What am I really interested in? What do I care about? Why? What do I know something about?"

2. Once you select a subject, no matter how general, focus your attention on that subject by breaking it down into its *components*. Components are simply parts of a whole. A stereo system, for example, is made up of a number of main components: an amplifier, a tuner, a turntable, speakers, and possibly a tape deck. Together, these components function as a whole—the stereo system. Bear in mind that individual components may then be further narrowed by breaking them down into

lesser components: for example, the turntable is made up of a tone arm, a record platter, a motor, and a needle, to name just a few. Naturally, some of these lesser components may be further broken down. You can see, therefore, that as you continue breaking subjects into major and lesser components, your focus narrows accordingly.

3. Items in your list of major and lesser components will trigger ideas, thoughts, recollections, emotions, and concepts that find their basis in your experience. For example, the general subject area "animals" may generate a list of components ranging from tigers to dogs. For whatever reason, you focus on dogs and break it down into lesser components, one of which is spaniels. The component spaniels, in turn, is further broken down into buying, feeding, grooming, and breeding. Each of these components may be still further narrowed—buying, for example, may lead to thoughts about buying a spaniel from a pet store or from a breeder. Naturally, this kind of focusing should continue until you have arrived at specific, related material suitable for your projected paper.

4. When you are ready to impose limitations on your material, you are ready to announce your *topic*. For example, the ever-narrowing focus in the above may lead to a paper on "how to groom a springer spaniel" (exposition and description) or "why you should buy a cocker spaniel from a breeder rather than from a pet store" (argumentation) or "the day my spaniel saved me from drowning" (narration). Remember that topic announces the focus and limitation of a subject.

The above suggestions indicate that the amount of focusing you must do depends largely on the type and length of your paper. Realize also that the interaction of your mind with your experience often leads to topics that earlier would have seemed remote from the general subject area you chose—"animals," for example, may eventually lead to "why we must abolish pet stores."

The following diagram was created by a student to illustrate how he applied the principle of ever-increasing focus to a subject area:

SUBJECT	NARROWING FOCUS	TOPIC
	primary——secondary—— college——teachers—— professors——administrators ——friends——books—— classes——sports——	
education	buildings——budgets—— sororities——fraternities ——grades——**grades**—— too much emphasis——too much pressure——memorize and regurgitate——learn	**Should we abolish the grading system in the American classroom?**

for grade rather than for
knowledge——grades measure
progress——help compete
against others——provide
incentive and motivation

In the above, you can see how the student began with a general subject; broke it down into components; found one component that triggered some ideas, notions, and questions; and evolved a topic that imposes focus and limitation on the original subject matter.

By focusing on another component of "education," we can create an entirely different topic from the same broad subject area:

SUBJECT	NARROWING FOCUS	TOPIC
education	primary——secondary——college——teachers——professors——administrators ——friends——books——classes——study halls——**study halls**——too many students——too much noise——too few teachers ——problems with discipline——impossible for student to concentrate ——waste of time	**Conditions in the high school study hall make studying an impossibility.**

The following diagram illustrates the creation of another entirely different topic from the subject of education:

SUBJECT	NARROWING FOCUS	TOPIC
education	primary——secondary——college——teachers——professors——administrators ——friends——books——classes——study halls——sports——buildings——budgets——sororities——**sororities**——excellent social life——chance to meet guys——feeling of belonging——help with studies——opportunity to make valuable professional contacts	**why I joined the Tau Tau Tau national college sorority**

The progression from subject to topic suggested above is basically the same for any subject area. For example, here is how a topic might be evolved from the subject of "music":

SUBJECT	NARROWING FOCUS	TOPIC
	opera——jazz——rock——	
	classical——blue grass	
	——mandolin——fiddle	**basic**
music	——banjo——guitar——	**guitar**
	guitar——six string——	**types**
	twelve string——folk	
	——classical——electric	

You should realize that the preceding examples show only the basic kind of progression that any writer must go through in order to focus on a workable topic. The mechanics of the progression are not important, and you may decide to originate your own system. Or you may find that you are able to select a topic without resorting to diagrams, doodles, or charts. But regardless of your process, remember that the progression is one of ever-increasing focus.

EXERCISES

1. Reexamine the list of components under "education" (pp. 40–41). If additional components occur to you, add them to the list. Focus attention on one component and create from it a topic suitable for a 500-word essay.
2. Create topics from each of these three general subject areas: nature, house, television.

Discovering Your Thesis   **4**

A thesis statement is the intellectual center of a paper. It offers a controlling generalization which informs your audience of the main idea that the paper will develop. A thesis is also a statement of intention. It lets the reader know the topic you will deal with, it imposes limits on that topic, and it suggests something of the paper's later development.

Your thesis may be expressed in a single sentence, or it may require more than one sentence if your topic is complex. Often, the thesis statement occurs in the introduction to an essay. (We shall have more to say about this on pp. 79–80.)

Consider, for example, the general subject "automobiles." Through the topic selection process, this subject may lead to the conclusion that many Americans today are driving foreign cars. And the generalization "Many Americans are buying foreign cars" is, in a rudimentary sense, a thesis. Similarly, generalizations such as "London is an interesting place to live," "The Old English sheepdog makes a good pet," or "Inflation is one of the nation's major problems" all qualify as theses insofar as each presents the reader with the main point behind the essay that is to follow.

In fairness to the reader, however, an *exact thesis* does more than simply toss out a generalization. None of the preceding examples accomplishes as much as it could. In fact, each immediately forces the reader to ask questions. "Many Americans are buying foreign cars" may lead to legitimate reader responses of "So what?" or "Why?" Most readers would want to know why London is interesting, what

makes Old English sheepdogs such good pets, and what kind of inflation the nation is suffering from. A thesis that omits vital information
—and forces the reader immediately to question—hinders communication because it breaks the reader's concentration.

OBJECTIVES OF A THESIS

If you have successfully completed the prewriting process to this
point, you should now be able to form a sound thesis statement. The
following section discusses what many writers agree to be the three
objectives of a thesis: (1) it indicates the *specific topic* you will deal
with; (2) it imposes *manageable limits* on that topic; (3) it suggests the
organization of your paper. Through the thesis, you say to the reader,
"I've thought about this topic. I know what I believe about it. And I
know how to organize it."

We can examine the earlier thesis on foreign cars in light of our
three stated objectives: specific topic, manageable limits, and organizational approach. The "comment" and "suggestion" that follow in each
case are designed to indicate the kind of thought process you might go
through to arrive at an exact thesis.

THESIS: Many Americans are buying foreign cars.

SPECIFIC
TOPIC

Comment:
Which foreign cars are they buying? For what reasons are they buying them? Is a person who buys a
$17,000 Jaguar motivated by the same reasons as a
person who buys a $4,500 Volkswagen?

Suggestion:
The topic should be more specific. Limit it to one
make of car (at least, in a short paper), say Volkswagen.

MANAGEABLE
LIMITS

Comment:
It seems unrealistic to deal with all the reasons that
motivate people to buy Volkswagens. Also, there
are differences in the various Volkswagen models.

Suggestion:
Focus on a few major reasons for buying one particular model of the Volkswagen—the Rabbit.

ORGANIZATIONAL
APPROACH

Comment:
Why are many people buying the Volkswagen Rabbit?

Suggestion:
List the specific reasons why people are buying the Volkswagen Rabbit so that the reader knows exactly what the paper is leading into, that is, how the paper will be organized.

Thus, the criteria of specific topic, manageable limits, and organizational approach enable us to sharpen the thesis, to make it more exact. Note the difference between the original thesis statement and the revised thesis statement:

ORIGINAL THESIS	REVISED THESIS
Many Americans are buying foreign cars.	Many Americans are buying the Volkswagen Rabbit because of its low price, fuel economy, and high resale value.

The revised thesis accomplishes the following: it deals with a specific topic (why some people buy a particular foreign car); it limits the topic to a manageable length (by focusing on economic factors and the Volkswagen Rabbit); it establishes the paper's organizational approach by indicating the order the discussion will have (three specific reasons for the Rabbit's popularity).

We can sharpen the three remaining theses in the same way:

ORIGINAL THESIS	REVISED THESIS
London is an interesting place to live.	Cultural opportunities, particularly theaters, art galleries, and museums, make London an interesting place to live.
The Old English sheepdog makes a good pet.	Endowed with a placid nature, an even temper, outstanding loyalty, and high intelligence, the Old English sheepdog deserves careful consideration if you are looking for a pet.
Inflation is one of the nation's major problems.	The nation's current inflation has had a serious effect on the housing industry. Because many people are no longer able to afford to buy single-family houses, builders are going bankrupt and consumers are forced into renting apartments, often at very high rates.

EXERCISES

1. Discuss the following questions with specific reference to the preceding three thesis statements:
   a. Explain the reasons for the changes in each of the revised thesis statements.
   b. Explain how each revised thesis satisfies the criteria of specific topic, manageable limitation, and organizational approach.
   c. The thesis on inflation differs from the other two theses. Explain these differences.
2. Revise the following weak theses:
   a. College administrators are impersonal.
   b. A good restaurant is hard to find.
   c. Drugs are dangerous.
   d. A career in public administration can be worthwhile.
   e. The kitchen is a hazardous room.
   f. People are often discriminated against by automobile repair shops.
   g. Drinking diet soft drinks can be advantageous to your health.
   h. Obscenity laws threaten all of us.
   i. Forced busing is a good way (or is not a good way) to solve the nation's racial problems.
   j. Butane lighters are more dangerous than matches.

ARRIVING AT A THESIS

To arrive at an exact thesis statement, it is helpful to ask yourself three basic questions that are really outgrowths of the strategy questions on pp. 17–19: (1) *What* is my point? (2) *How* will I present it? (3) *Why* is my point significant (often only implied in the thesis)? Answers to these questions will lead to creation of an exact thesis statement that will identify your topic, impose manageable limits on that topic, and suggest the organization of the body of your paper.

The following examples illustrate how a topic can be translated into an exact thesis statement by means of the three thesis questions:

TOPIC	QUESTIONS	THESIS
What to look for in a good stereo receiver	*What is my point?* To instruct the audience on the qualities to look for in a good stereo receiver.	If you are in the market for a good stereo receiver, you should select one that provides adequate wattage or power to drive your speakers, high usable sensitivity to capture
	How will I present it? By explaining the	

necessity for (1) appropriate wattage; (2) usable sensitivity; (3) frequency response.

Why is my point significant? It will help the reader select a good stereo receiver.

all the sounds from your listening source, and wide frequency response to capture distant radio stations.

TOPIC	QUESTIONS	THESIS
How the nation's political parties, contrary to democratic principles, give the voter no choice in the selection of the Vice-President of the United States	*What is my point?* To argue that a party's presidential nominee should not have what is, in essence, power to appoint a vice-presidential nominee; rather, a person running for the presidency should indicate prior to the national convention whom he wishes for a running mate. *How will I present it?* By explaining that the present policy makes the vice-presidency, in effect, an appointed, rather than an elected, office, and by also suggesting that this practice is unconstitutional. *Why is my point significant?* It calls attention to the need for election reform.	Both the delegates to national political conventions and the people voting in an election deserve a voice in deciding who will be their Vice-President. But since the tradition is simply to give the presidential nominee the power to appoint his running mate, neither the delegates nor the people have any say in the selection. Thus, the present process of selecting a vice-presidential nominee contradicts basic democratic principles, while it also violates the Constitution.

EXERCISES

1. Consider the following questions concerning the examples above:
   a. What topics, topic limitations, and organizational approaches are indicated in each example? Be as specific as you can.
   b. Outline the organizational approach suggested in the first thesis. How does it differ from that in the second thesis?
   c. Would the second thesis be better if developed as a brief or a lengthy paper? Why?

2. Choose a general subject and from it develop a topic and a thesis statement. Remember the *what, how,* and *why* questions that must be answered in order to arrive at an exact thesis. *Note:* It is not necessary or desirable to impose the mechanical formula "The purpose of my paper is" when you arrive at the point of actually writing your thesis.

THE VALUE OF AN EXACT THESIS

An exact thesis statement gives a paper *unity, precision,* and *emphasis. Unity* means that all the elements in a paper stand in support of the topic as indicated by the thesis. The thesis statement "Cigarette smoking endangers a person's health because it attacks both heart and lungs," is one that clearly states the paper's main point. It allows the writer to concentrate on the development of this one point and enables the reader to follow the progression of ideas.

An exact thesis also lends *precision* to a paper. *Precision* is exactness, the quality of avoiding ambiguity and vagueness. For example, the thesis "My new roommate is a very strange person" may confuse the reader because it gives no indication what makes the roommate strange. Ambiguous or vague words (such as *good, bad, nice, lovely, interesting, meaningful, exciting,* or *wonderful*) are only relative—they mean different things to different people. If you employ vague words in your thesis, you risk confusing and misleading your reader; you also risk confusing yourself because such words cannot suggest specific ways you might develop the body of your paper. Employ words and phrases in your thesis that can have only one meaning in the particular context. If you find that you absolutely must use a rather vague term, follow it immediately with an explanation: "My new roommate must be a very strange person *because* he paints himself a different color each night." An imprecise thesis can lead to an inexact, confusing paper. Precision, on the other hand, invites clarity.

Finally, an exact thesis—one that provides unity and precision—lends *emphasis* to a paper. It announces to the reader that the writer has given careful thought to the subject area and has control over the resulting topic. It indicates to the reader that the rest of the paper is worthy of his attention. Note that the following thesis statement is vague and generalized:

> The battle of the sexes is one of the many problems that men and women face.

The revised thesis is clear and precise:

Uncle Harry and Aunt Phoebe continually wage comic battles over her passion for shopping, his poker playing, her desire to find "culture," his love for country music.

By stating the main point of the paper clearly and with precise words, the revised thesis lends force to the entire paper.

EXERCISE

Examine the following thesis statements for unity, precision, and emphasis. Suggest ways for improving each.

1. The essential challenge facing the contemporary student in a world of disorder is to find a career that offers stability, security, and financial reward.
2. My roommate is a good person. I recall an occasion when he proved this to me.
3. Lacrosse is an exciting sport that offers a number of meaningful experiences to its participants.
4. The United Nations' willingness to be controlled by the demands of the Third World nations undermines its purpose as stated in its charter. In addition, it has proven itself incapable of dealing with disorders in Latin America and the Middle East.

Organizing the Composition 5

In order to fulfill its thesis, every paper needs a plan of organization. A thesis that has been well formulated will suggest a method of organization to you. When, in the prewriting process, you have arrived at a thesis statement, therefore, you will want to turn your attention to organizing the whole composition. As in other prewriting tasks, you'll find it helpful to make this step explicit.

In devising a working plan of composition, you may choose to employ an outline. An outline can enable you to see, shape, organize, and develop the material generated by your thesis and to make it concrete.

Outlines are particularly valuable for long papers involving complex topics. However, many writers use outlines—some in the most casual of forms—for anything they may write. If you decide to use an outline for your own essays, keep the following in mind:

1. Don't attempt to make an outline before discovering your thesis. Remember that an outline is a plan, not an idea.
2. View the outline as a means to an end; do not view it as an end in itself. The purpose of an outline is to help you accomplish what you intend to in a paper, not to produce a perfect outline.
3. Feel free to amend and improve the outline as you would any plan.

THE OUTLINING PROCESS

An effective thesis statement usually contains the main elements for an outline. As you examine your thesis, an organizational and developmental approach will begin to emerge. Assume, for example, that you have arrived at the following thesis statement:

> Many television commercials are disturbing because they are boring, insulting, or dangerous.

This is an exact thesis. It meets the necessary criteria: it clearly indicates the specific topic the writer will deal with; it imposes manageable limits on that topic; it suggests the organization of the resulting paper. In constructing this thesis, the writer answered the *what, how,* and *why* questions:

What is my point?	Many television commercials are disturbing.
How will I present it?	By showing that some commercials are boring, that some are insulting, and that some are dangerous.
Why is my point significant?	Television touches the lives of most of us.

Your first task in creating a workable outline from your thesis is to examine the thesis itself carefully. The main point, "Many television commercials are disturbing," must have points to validate it, and, in fact, there are three such points in the thesis: some television commercials are boring, some are insulting, and some are dangerous. You can now perceive the relation between your main point and its bases of support:

MAIN POINT	SUPPORTING COMPONENTS
Many television commercials are disturbing.	Some commercials are boring.
	Some commercials are insulting.
	Some commercials are dangerous.

The organizational approach for the outline and subsequent paper should now be apparent. Your main point depends on your developing the supporting components.

Your second task is to analyze each supporting component as specified in the thesis. Thus, you move to additional questions: What makes some television commercials boring? Why are some insulting? How can a commercial be dangerous? Questions such as these will enable you to discover the specific bases for your initial thoughts and attitudes on this topic. By questioning and answering, you can pinpoint organizational approaches that will support the thesis statement and develop the paper. The outline, dependent on the thesis and specifically on the method aspect of that thesis (*How* will I present my point?), begins to emerge and grow:

I. Introduction

    A. *Main point:* Many television commercials are disturbing.

    B. *Thesis statement:* Many television commercials are disturbing because they are boring, insulting, or dangerous.

II. Body

    A. Some television commercials become boring because of their frequency and triteness.

        1. Some commercials (cite examples) appear as many as three times in a thirty-minute program.

        2. The message employed in these commercials is often stated in clichés (cite examples).

Note that II A 1 supports and specifies one aspect (frequency) of point II A; II A 2 supports and specifies the other (triteness). Thus, there is coherence within the outlining process as one point or idea leads to another.

You can effectively employ the same basic process to develop the remaining two supporting components previously announced in the thesis: some television commercials are insulting; some television commercials are dangerous:

II. Body (cont'd.)

    B. Some of these same commercials that have become so tiresome are also insulting because of their blatantly illogical claims.

        1. We are asked to believe that product testimonials by "stars" constitute expert opinion (cite examples).

        2. We are exposed to commercials that, through association, suggest a particular product will enhance our glamour or sex appeal (cite examples).

As with points II A 1 and II A 2, point II B (some commercials are insulting) is supported by II B 1 and II B 2, which further specify that these same commercials are insulting "because of their blatantly illogical claims."

We can now deal with the last supporting component: many television commercials are dangerous:

II. Body (cont'd.)

    C. Some of these commercials are even dangerous.

        1. Some encourage the use of easy credit (cite examples).

        2. Some advocate poor diet practices (cite examples).

An almost limitless number of variations is possible with this or any outline. You could, for example, construct additional points, sub-points, and even sub-subpoints, depending on the topic's complexity and the paper's projected length. And you would most likely include a conclusion (which would be point III in the above outline). You could also use different forms for your outline. For example, you might use an outline that simply lists key words or sentences that identify the main components of the paper. Or you might use a full outline, like the one above, containing brief phrases instead of sentences for each of the points and subpoints.

Below is the finished outline. Note that a conclusion has been added. (We shall discuss writing a conclusion on pp. 126–132.)

TUBE TORTURE

I. Introduction

   A. *Main point:* Many television commercials are disturbing.

   B. *Thesis statement:* Many television commercials are disturbing because they are boring, insulting, or dangerous.

II. Body

   A. Some television commercials become boring because of their frequency and triteness.

      1. Some commercials (cite examples) appear as many as three times in a thirty-minute program.

      2. The message employed in these commercials is often stated in clichés (cite examples).

   B. Some of these same commercials that have become so tiresome are also insulting because of their blatantly illogical claims.

      1. We are asked to believe that product testimonials by "stars" constitute expert opinion (cite examples).

      2. We are exposed to commercials that, through association, suggest a particular product will enhance our glamour or sex appeal (cite examples).

   C. Some of these commercials are even dangerous.

      1. Some encourage the use of easy credit (cite examples).

      2. Some advocate poor diet practices (cite examples).

III. Conclusion

   A. *Recommendations:* What can be done about television commercials?

      1. Explore the advantages of public television and support public television with donations.

      2. Explore pay television.

      3. Encourage people to seek entertainment in books, radio, and records.

   B. *Prediction:* The continued abuse of the television viewers' intelligence will, I hope, result in a buyers' boycott.

A careful examination of this outline reveals a logical, specific, and unified writing plan. Points II A 1 and 2, II B 1 and 2, II C 1 and 2 arise from the *method* implied in the thesis statement (to show that commercials are boring, insulting, and dangerous). Thus, the components are directly subordinated to the paper's main point ("Many television commercials are disturbing").

THE PROCESS REILLUSTRATED

The importance of appropriate planning is illustrated by the following student thesis, outline, and resulting paper. As you follow the process, remember that an exact thesis statement will generate a precise outline which, in turn, will enable you to carry out your intention in the paper.

Thesis Statement

> The college homecoming has degenerated into a mindless autumn ritual, one motivated by financial exploitation and one which fosters reckless, lawless behavior.

Outline

I. Introduction

    A. *Main point:* The college homecoming has degenerated into a mindless autumn ritual.

    B. *Thesis statement:* The college homecoming has degenerated into a mindless autumn ritual, one motivated by financial exploitation and one which fosters reckless, lawless behavior.

II. Body

    A. Homecoming is motivated by financial exploitation.

        1. The college and local businesses unite to take the returning alumni's money.

        2. The returning alumni eagerly buy what the college and businesses are selling.

        3. To exploit the alumni further, both the college and the businesses inflate their prices.

    B. The result of homecoming is reckless, lawless behavior, which is most apparent during and after the traditional football game.

        1. During the game, many of the alumni are drunk and unsportsmanlike.

2. After the game, they become public nuisances, a threat to themselves and to the local populace.

III. Conclusion

A. *Restatement:* Summarize each supporting component in the thesis statement.

B. *Prediction:* The same events will happen next year.

Essay

HOMECOMING—A SHAM

Jubilant parades, formal dances, festive parties, enthusiastic speeches—all are presented to honor returning alumni. These form the myth of the American college homecoming. Although initially established by colleges and universities to promote school spirit and good fellowship, homecoming has become commercialized to such an extent that its meaning has been lost. The college along with many of the local businesses has assumed instead the role of retailer; the customer is the returning alumnus, eager to recapture, if only for a moment, his spent youth. Consequently, homecoming has degenerated into a mindless autumn ritual, one motivated by financial exploitation and one which fosters reckless, lawless behavior.

In his desire to recapture "the best years of my life," the returning alumnus becomes easy prey for the local and collegiate wolves. In return for publicity and perhaps a tax-deductible contribution to the athletic fund, the college allows the alumnus the nostalgia that comes with parades, beer blasts, wine parties, liquor on the quad, and, of course, the traditional football game against a "hated" rival. The local merchants, meanwhile, do a large business in everything from clothing and State U beer steins to loud pom-poms and dyed gardenias. The commercialization that underlies the cooperation between the college and the town also spreads to the alumnus, who judges his fun by the amount of money spent, who expects to stagger to his bed no earlier than 4 A.M., and who is disappointed if he doesn't wake up the following morning with a hangover. Loudly demanding his morning juice—a Bloody Mary—the alumnus doesn't flinch at the inflated prices on the local menus. The two-dollar "Sunrise Special" has suddenly become three-fifty; the fourteen-dollar motel room has jumped to twenty-four dollars; and a lukewarm dinner at the local greasy spoon costs the same as a lavish feast at the Ritz. The exploitation comes to a head with the Saturday afternoon ball game. Tickets, already high at seven dollars for other contests, suddenly are priced at ten. The program, the most obvious collusion between the college and the town, is packed with advertisements for

Doug's Drive-In, Hector's Hamburgers, Casper's Clothing, and the Hayloft Hotel ("special homecoming luncheon on Sunday, twenty-five dollars per couple"). The advertisers are, of course, full of spirit: "Good Luck, State U," "Whip the Whales," "Welcome Home, Alumni." And why not? As one local businessman candidly admits, "We figure that each out-of-town person will drop at least twenty-five dollars. Some spend hundreds."

These financial excesses are matched if not bettered by the extravagant emotions and behavior shown by the alumni and excused as "school spirit." Probably the football game best epitomizes drunken enthusiasm. The football game becomes a circus surrounded by screaming, chanting businessmen trying to recall the old fight song while swilling bourbon or scotch from their none-too-carefully concealed flasks. Growing progressively louder and more boisterous, these successful citizens from beyond the campus howl for the blood of the opponents, boo the officials, cheer banners that shriek "Kill the opposition!" and applaud every bone-jarring tackle made by State U. As one after the other files out of the stadium after the game, their "enthusiasm" expands into the town itself as they honk horns, scream from car windows, and head for the local watering hole to replenish their liquor. As if fearing an invading motorcycle gang, some townspeople lock their doors and shutter their windows, finding relief only in knowing that the next homecoming is a year away. But the unwary are trapped by drunken drivers, by sodden alumni falling out of cars, and by deafeningly loud cocktail parties.

The degeneration of homecoming thus becomes complete. In return for his money, the alumnus receives a weekend of mayhem encouraged by an institution of higher learning, and assisted by the local merchants. Ultimately, it is a well-struck bargain. The college and local businesses gain money and the alumnus regains his youth. If anyone suffers, it is only the serious undergraduate trying to study or the innocent townsperson seeking peace and quiet in his home. But everyone else is well satisfied. And next year, the ritual honoring school spirit, good fellowship, and returning alumni will begin anew.

In part, the success of this essay results from the student's exact thesis: his main point ("The college homecoming has degenerated into a mindless autumn ritual") is developed by supporting components ("Homecoming is motivated by financial exploitation" and "The result of homecoming is reckless, lawless behavior"). Each of these components guides the development of the paragraphs in the body of the paper, helping to ensure that each sentence in the finished paper is either directly or indirectly related to the thesis. (The components actually generate *topic sentences*, and we shall have more to say about the topic sentence in later chapters.)

Naturally, the movement from thesis statement to outline to essay is not static, and the above student essay reveals a number of modifications that took place somewhere between outline and finished paper. The student has, for example, decided that before explaining how the ritual of homecoming has degenerated, he should explain *what* homecoming has degenerated from. Therefore, he has led gradually into his thesis by depicting in his introduction some of the events traditionally associated with homecoming. In addition, sometime between arriving at his thesis and generating the outline, he has decided to focus specifically on the football game as a means of illustrating reckless, lawless behavior (note that he does not mention the game in the original thesis).

The process of outlining should conclude with the following checks:

- Do the major components adequately cover the topic as presented in the thesis?

- Are the components in the outline logically arranged?

- Does each component either directly or indirectly support the thesis statement?

EXERCISE

Examine the following student thesis, outline, and essay. Respond to the questions that follow.

Thesis Statement

Because of unscrupulous cutting practices in the redwood forests of California, the United States is in danger of losing one of the most impressive resources in its heritage—the giant redwood tree. Ineffective congressional action allows present cutting practices to continue, causing the destruction not only of the redwoods but of surrounding forests as well.

Outline

    I. Introduction

        A. *Main point:* The United States is in danger of losing one of the most impressive resources in its heritage—the giant redwood tree.

B. *Thesis statement:* Because of unscrupulous cutting practices in the redwood forests of California, the United States is in danger of losing one of the most impressive resources in its heritage—the giant redwood tree. Ineffective congressional action allows present cutting practices to continue, causing the destruction not only of the redwoods but of surrounding forests as well.

II. Body

A. Clear-cutting harvest methods are responsible for the loss of the giant redwood.
1. Clear-cutting creates ugly, barren areas.
2. Only one-fifth of the original redwood forests remains.
B. Congress has taken some action to protect the trees, but the slaughter continues.
1. Congress gave special powers to the secretary of the interior.
2. The legal provisions have so far been ineffective.
C. Clear-cutting also affects forests surrounding the redwoods.
1. Watersheds are being destroyed.
2. Flooding has become an important problem.

III. Conclusion

A. *Recommendation:* New, more stringent laws are needed if the redwoods are to be saved.
B. *Prediction:* Unless clear-cutting is prohibited, the redwoods face extinction.

Essay

LAST OF THE REDWOODS

Because of the unscrupulous cutting practices in the redwood forests of California, the United States is in danger of losing one of the most impressive resources in its heritage—the giant redwood tree. This truly majestic feat of nature has been in existence for over 150 million years, but only in the last century has its survival been so seriously threatened. Americans must all act together if we are to stop its annihilation. The senseless cutting practices used for felling the trees must be stopped immediately. Although the logging companies' cutting practices should have been restricted by the Redwood National Park Act of 1968, their methods have not changed, and they continue to endanger the very existence of the giant redwood trees and their surrounding forests.

The particular method used by logging companies to harvest the redwood is called clear-cutting. Clear-cutting is the process of choosing a particular site of trees and then leveling every tree in that area.

In the case of redwoods, these areas are usually from ten to forty acres. Cuttings of this type create large areas of ugly, barren land within a stand of trees. Because of clear-cutting, the redwood trees are rapidly becoming extinct. These beautiful trees, once covering millions of acres, now only exist in patches, barely a few hundred thousand acres.

In 1968, Congress finally recognized the redwood's precarious position by passing a long-overdue law designed to protect what was left of the great trees. The Redwood National Park Act of 1968 was drafted to protect the nationally owned areas of the redwoods from the adjacent logging operations that were scarring the environment and upsetting the forest ecosystem. The law authorized the secretary of the interior to: (1) enlarge the boundaries of the park by adding buffers of two thousand acres at strategic locations; (2) create a scenic route along portions of the Redwood Highway; and (3) protect the "timber, soil and streams" inside the park. The Redwood National Park Act should have partially controlled the logging operations around the park. Unfortunately, the secretary of the interior has failed to act on the provisions of the law, and the logging companies have kept right on cutting, often changing the park boundaries with their saws.

With their unchanged cutting practices, the logging companies are endangering the very existence of the redwood tree. Obviously, the clear-cutting of large areas in a forest kills many trees. What is not so obvious, although more damaging, are the effects of clear-cutting on the surrounding forest areas. One problem created by the massive overcutting of redwood stands is that, often, the trees being cut are desperately needed to provide cover for the forests' watersheds. These watersheds are essential to the redwoods because of the enormous amount of water that these trees need to survive. Without the cover that the trees provide, the watersheds and their surrounding areas not only lose much of their absorption ability but also suffer a great deal of water loss due to evaporation. Perhaps the most devastating effect of clear-cutting on the redwoods is soil erosion. After the efficient liquidation of an area of trees, nothing remains on the ground to trap and absorb the rain. Thus, when rain falls, it splashes on the bare ground, first loosening the soil, then forming puddles and gullies, and finally transporting a large amount of topsoil into nearby streams. This soil, called silt, accumulates at the bottom of streams and on the forest floor. Erosion of this kind has been serious enough in some redwood stands to cause flooding. Silt is also piling up around the bases of a large number of trees, reducing the infiltration of water into the soil. With their action, the logging companies are destroying the environment of the national park even without logging in the park. The redwood stands are already in a fragile state, and it is senseless to keep employing cutting practices that threaten the existence of this beautiful species of tree.

There is still some hope for the redwood trees. Environmentalists have successfully sued the Department of the Interior and have forced it to make reasonable efforts to protect the redwood parks from adjacent logging operations. This action will, I hope, encourage some stronger measures which are desperately needed. Although the government is beginning to see the need for protection of the redwoods, time is running out. Only if the watersheds are protected will the redwoods have a chance of survival. This means an end to the massive clear-cutting practices used by the logging industry. Even as the future of the redwoods begins to brighten, the trees keep on falling.

Questions

1. What are the major components by which the writer supports his main point?
2. Do the supporting components adequately cover the topic as presented in the thesis? Why or why not?
3. Are the components in the outline logically arranged? Why or why not?
4. Does each component either directly or indirectly support the thesis statement?
5. Does the body of the paper reflect the arrangement of the components as indicated in the outline?

EXERCISE

After careful consideration, select a topic, draw a thesis statement from that topic, and construct a detailed outline with components that support your thesis.

Finding a   6
Suitable Style

You may devise the best topic, thesis, and outline imaginable, but if you don't write for the proper audience, your writing will not communicate effectively. You need to tailor your presentation to a particular audience in a style that is suitable for that audience.

In preparing to address any audience, remember these points:

- Assume that the audience is intelligent.

- Use words, phrases, and constructions which are simple, clear, and unambiguous. (Ambiguity is lack of clarity that comes from a statement or word having more than one possible meaning in a particular context.)

- Provide support for all generalizations you use.

- Use current slang only if its meaning will be clear and appropriate to your audience.

- Employ only patterns of acceptable grammar and usage.

- Check your paper over carefully for errors—don't reduce your reader to proofreader.

EVALUATING YOUR AUDIENCE

The second strategy question emphasized that writing can be self-less, that a good essay does something to or for an audience. As the writer, you must determine what you want to do for your audience. To share an experience (narration) is to enlarge the audience's world; to explain an idea or process (exposition) is to give the audience knowledge it did not have; to question (primarily argumentation) is to challenge the audience's assumed position, to give it a different perspective. But whatever your reason for writing, you must interest your audience.

Central to your style, then, are two questions: (1) What am I attempting to do to or for my audience? (2) Who is my audience? Your answers to these questions will enable you to employ the most suitable style for capturing your audience.

Analysis of your audience can help determine how much supporting information you will need to provide, how appropriate or inappropriate technical terminology will be, and how formal or informal your language will be.

How much supporting evidence will your audience need?
Will technical terminology be appropriate?

If, for example, you attempt an expository essay on types of sailboats, much of what you say and how you say it will depend on the audience's knowledge of your topic. For a general audience, you probably would not refer to a "ketch" or a "sloop" without explaining the designs of these sailboat types, nor would you use highly technical sailing jargon. For an audience of sailing enthusiasts, however, you could legitimately assume a degree of expertise, and you could use technical boating terminology freely—in fact, your audience might feel insulted if you did explain "ketch" or "sloop."

Should your language be formal or informal?

There are different degrees of formality and informality. To capture the widest audience, strive for a style that is neither too formal nor too informal. The level of formality which you employ in a letter to a friend would differ markedly from the level which you would use in a history term paper; an obituary or letter of condolence would usually have greater formality than an editorial defending nude beaches.

Formality is usually marked by at least some of the following qualities: long, intricate sentences; frequent use of the passive voice; learned diction; and absence of the first-person singular ("I") point of view, for which the first-person plural ("we") or the third person ("one") is usually substituted. Informality usually has at least some of the following characteristics: relatively short, compact sentences; frequent use of the active voice; simple diction; and use of the first-person point of view.

The following paragraph is formal English. In it, the novelist Henry James is responding to a pamphlet on the art of fiction written by the English critic Walter Besant. James is addressing an audience of educated readers, particularly literary critics.

> It is of all this [heritage] that Mr. Besant is full when he insists upon the fact that fiction is one of the *fine* arts, deserving in its turn of all the honors and emoluments that have hitherto been reserved for the successful profession of music, poetry, painting, architecture. It is impossible to insist too much on so important a truth, and the place that Mr. Besant demands for the work of the novelist may be represented, a trifle less abstractly, by saying that he demands not only that it shall be reputed artistic, but that it shall be reputed very artistic indeed. It is excellent that he should have struck this note, for his doing so indicates that there was need of it, that his proposition may be to many people a novelty. One rubs one's eyes at the thought; but the rest of Mr. Besant's essay confirms the revelation. . . .
>
> "The Art of Fiction"

In the following paragraph from "On Becoming," written on an informal level, black revolutionist Eldridge Cleaver addresses what is largely an audience of black youths:

> I realized that no one could save me but myself. The prison authorities were both uninterested and unable to help me. I had to seek out the truth and unravel the snarled web of my motivations. I had to find out who I am and what I want to be, what type of man I should be, and what I could do to become the best of which I was capable. I understood that what had happened to me had also happened to countless other blacks and it would happen to many, many more.
>
> *Post-Prison Writings and Speeches*

In contrast with the intricate, complex structure of James's sentences, Cleaver's sentences are relatively short and simple. James uses learned words, such as *emoluments, reputed,* and *proposition.* Cleaver chooses words that are understandable even to a general audience. James writes in the third-person singular ("One rubs one's eyes"). Cleaver uses the first-person throughout his essay. James sometimes uses the passive voice; Cleaver always uses the active.

In general, you will probably wish to write on the informal level in order to be understandable to a wide audience. But highly informal language, including slang, dialect expressions, and abbreviations or symbols, such as "&" for "and," may only be appropriate in writing to a close friend.

EXERCISE

Examine the following excerpt from Mark Twain's *The Adventures of Huckleberry Finn* and respond to the questions that follow.

> You don't know about me without you have read a book by the name of *The Adventures of Tom Sawyer;* but that ain't no matter. That book was made by Mr. Mark Twain, and he told the truth, mainly. There were things which he stretched, but mainly he told the truth. That is nothing. I never seen anybody but lied one time or another, without it was Aunt Polly, or the widow, or maybe Mary. Aunt Polly—Tom's Aunt Polly, she is—and Mary, and the Widow Douglas is all told about in that book, which is mostly a true book, with some stretchers, as I said before.

Questions

1. What does Twain achieve through his sentence structure and diction?
2. What view of Huck Finn (the book's narrator) do we derive from the language Twain employs?

EXERCISE

Examine the following excerpt from James Baldwin's *Notes of a Native Son,* an account of ghetto life and social injustice. Repond to the questions that follow.

> On the 29th of July, in 1943, my father died. On the same day, a few hours later, his last child was born. Over a month before this, while all our energies were concentrated in waiting for these events, there had been, in Detroit, one of the bloodiest race riots of the century. A few hours after my father's funeral, while he lay in state in the undertaker's chapel, a race riot broke out in Harlem. On the morning of the 3rd of August, we drove my father to the graveyard through a wilderness of smashed plate glass.

Questions

1. The paragraph has a choppy effect from short sentences and from longer sentences broken up by many commas. Why do you think Baldwin desires such an effect?
2. Baldwin recounts the events matter-of-factly, yet the result of the paragraph is to arouse the reader's emotions. How does Baldwin achieve this result?

EXERCISE

The following excerpt is from Henry Adams' "The Dynamo and the Virgin," an autobiographical account of a nineteenth-twentieth–century American's initiation into the world of new science as presented at the Great Exposition of 1900. Notice that, although the selection is autobiographical, Adams refrains from using the first person ("I"), preferring instead to use the third person ("he") as narrator, in order to give a scientific or objective view of himself:

> Nothing in education is so astonishing as the amount of ignorance it accumulates in the form of inert facts. Adams had looked at most of the accumulations of art in the storehouses called Art Museums; yet he did not know how to look at the art exhibits of 1900. He had studied Karl Marx and his doctrines of history with profound attention, yet he could not apply them at Paris. Langley [American physicist and astronomer], with the ease of a great master of experiment, threw out of the field every exhibit that did not reveal a new application of force, and naturally threw out, to begin with, almost the whole art exhibit. . . . He led his pupil [Adams] directly to the forces. His chief interest was in new motors to make his airship feasible, and he taught Adams the astonishing complexities of the new Daimler motor, and of the automobile, which, since 1893, had become a nightmare at a hundred kilometers an hour, almost as destructive as the electric tram which was only ten years older; and threatening to become as terrible as the locomotive steam-engine itself, which was almost exactly Adams' own age.

Questions

1. Is Adams' style in keeping with his apparent objective? Why or why not?
2. What can you infer about Adams' audience from the style he employs?

PART TWO

The Development
Process

As the result of performing various prewriting tasks, you advance further into the writing process: you arrive at what we call the *development* process. Here the paper assumes a form as your thoughts take further shape.

Development follows closely on prewriting. Once the prewriting process yields a thesis statement, which in turn generates an organizational plan for the composition, the next step is one of expansion. You want to deliver what your thesis statement promises.

This part of the text discusses how to build the introduction, body, and conclusion of a composition in ways that develop your thesis intelligently. The development phase of the writing process involves constructing a network of paragraphs that present the main points in your thesis. The result is unified because each paragraph provides supporting information for one aspect of the thesis statement.

Part two discusses these aspects of the development process:

> constructing effective paragraphs
> employing methods of development
> ordering the material
> concluding the composition

Constructing Effective Paragraphs 7

The indention at the beginning of a paragraph is a great convenience in written communication. It gives the writer a way of signaling the reader that a new unit of thought is beginning. It also provides an excellent place for the reader to pause, if he wishes to, for longer than he usually pauses between sentences. Good writers shape their paragraphs so as to take advantage of these features. They pay particular attention to how each paragraph begins, how it ends, and how it announces its thought to the reader.

It is sometimes practical to think of the paragraph as a miniature essay, containing components similar to those of an essay. An effective paragraph proceeds from a central, controlling idea, just as an essay does. It follows a definite organizational plan, as an essay does. And it displays unity and coherence, as any piece of writing ought to. Like an essay but on a smaller scale, a paragraph is a single thought presented in an orderly manner.

It is, in fact, possible to have a one-paragraph essay. In such a case, the paragraph functions as a fully independent unit that announces and supports a central thesis. Generally speaking, however, an essay develops its thesis through more than one paragraph. Each paragraph serves as a semi-independent unit that develops one aspect of the thesis.

A useful way to gain control in developing paragraphs is by means of a convention known as the *topic sentence*. As its name implies, the topic sentence of a paragraph expresses one thought that other sentences in the paragraph develop and support. In turn, the topic sentences of the various paragraphs in a composition function together through their common relationship to the thesis statement. Much of the power of an essay stems from this support structure in which every paragraph contains a topic sentence that advances the central thesis in some way.

Paragraph Proportion

To a certain extent, paragraph breaks are influenced by considerations of length as well as content. An unduly long paragraph, although well unified, may need to be broken into two paragraphs so as not to tax the audience's attention. The length of each paragraph needs to be weighed in relation to the length of other paragraphs in the essay.

Someone writing a book of two hundred pages could reasonably ask an audience to read a fifteen-page introduction. In a two- or three-page essay, however, you may often achieve greatest impact with an introductory paragraph consisting of your thesis statement alone. In proportion to the other, longer paragraphs that follow, such an introduction thrusts the thesis forward for special notice. You might also use a fuller introductory paragraph containing a vivid example or quotation which leads up to the thesis statement. The thesis statement would then appear at the end of the introduction, thereby receiving a visual emphasis from the paragraph break that immediately follows it.

Develop paragraphs in the body of your paper so that they are long enough and provide information enough to convince the reader of the validity of your points. Normally, this may mean no fewer than four or five supporting sentences.

If, on the other hand, you have a statement which deserves special attention and it comes in the body of the paper, you may want to use a *paragraph fragment* for emphasis. For example, if you were writing directions for using a bottle of ammonia, you would wish your readers to know that the fluid is highly poisonous. Because this warning deserves all the emphasis you can give it, a separate, one-sentence paragraph would be appropriate. Similarly, if you wish to caution your audience to place the flange in front of the tweeter when constructing a musical yacht (which would fall apart if the flange were inserted behind the tweeter), you may decide to devote one proportionally brief paragraph to this advice.

Relatively brief introductory and concluding paragraphs usually help to emphasize the main points. But a series of relatively brief paragraphs in the body of the paper can distract readers from the main points. If the body of a 500-word essay has half a dozen or more paragraphs, the effect is like that of a series of choppy sentences: emphasis may be lost.

THE TOPIC SENTENCE

A topic sentence indicates the purpose of the paragraph and implies the relation among the sentences in that paragraph. When writing a topic sentence, keep in mind its three aims: (1) to announce the purpose of the paragraph, (2) to focus the reader's attention on one central thought that controls all the other sentences in the paragraph, and (3) to establish the overall plan and purpose of the essay (because each topic sentence is related to the thesis statement).

In order to announce their intention and to establish their control over the material in a paragraph, many writers place the topic sentence at the *beginning of the paragraph*. In the following excerpt from *Walden*, Henry David Thoreau employs a topic sentence to guide the content and development of the rest of the paragraph:

(1) *Let us spend one day as deliberately as Nature, and not be thrown off the track by every nutshell and mosquito's wing that falls on the rails.* (2) Let us rise early and fast, or break fast, gently and without perturbation; let company come and let company go, let the bells ring and the children cry,—determined to make a day of it. (3) Why should we knock under and go with the stream? (4) Let us not be upset and overwhelmed in that terrible rapid and whirlpool called a dinner, situated in the meridian shallows. (5) Weather this danger and you are safe, for the rest of the way is down hill. (6) With unrelaxed nerves, with morning vigor, sail by it, looking another way, tied to the mast like Ulysses. (7) If the engine whistles, let it whistle till it is hoarse for its pains. (8) If the bell rings, why should we run? (9) We will consider what kind of music they are like. (10) Let us settle ourselves, and work and wedge our feet downward through the mud and slush of opinion, and prejudice, and tradition, and delusion, and appearance, that alluvion which covers the globe, through Paris and London, through New York and Boston and Concord, through church and state, through poetry and philosophy and religion, till we come to a hard bottom and rocks in place, which we can call *reality*, and say, This is, and no mistake; and then begin, having a *point d'appui* [point of support], below freshet and frost and fire, a place where you might found a wall or a state, or set a lamppost safely, or perhaps a gauge, not a Nilometer, but a Realometer, that future ages might know how deep a freshet of shams and appearances had gathered from time to time. (11) If you stand right fronting and face to face to a fact, you will see the sun glimmer on both its surfaces, as if it were a cimeter [scimitar], and feel its sweet edge dividing you through the heart and marrow, and so you will happily conclude your mortal career. (12) Be it life or death, we crave only

reality. (13) If we are really dying, let us hear the rattle in our throats and feel cold in the extremities; if we are alive, let us go about our business.

Thoreau announces his main idea—the freedom that comes from living apart from civilization—at the beginning of the paragraph: *Let us spend one day as deliberately as Nature, and not be thrown off the track by every nutshell and mosquito's wing that falls on the rails.* From this, the topic sentence, the reader can assume that the remaining sentences in the paragraph relate to the main idea and that the substance of the entire paragraph reflects one specific thought unit. A close examination of Thoreau's paragraph reveals the unity and coherence:

TOPIC SENTENCE:	"Let us spend one day as deliberately as Nature, and not be thrown off the track by every nutshell and mosquito's wing that falls on the rails."
sentence 2:	examples of the joys of simplicity
sentence 3:	plea for simplicity and attack on those who "go with the stream" (those "thrown off the track")
sentence 4:	The unhurried and unregimented aspects of life are advocated by citing an example of regimented obligations.
sentence 5:	Man is free to pursue simplicity once he ignores obligations.
sentence 6:	Be bound by your love of simplicity.
sentence 7:	Ignore that which interrupts your life.
sentence 8:	Do not respond to civilization's commands.
sentence 9:	Interpret the commands of civilization for yourself in a new and fresh way.
sentence 10:	Find your rock bottom of reality "as deliberately as Nature"; don't be "thrown off the track" by "tradition," "prejudice," and so forth.
sentence 11:	After throwing off artificial ties and concerns, you are free to "spend" your days "as deliberately as Nature."
sentence 12:	Man craves reality (Nature), not artificiality.
sentence 13:	Avoid the "death" that the nondeliberate life brings; to live is to live "as deliberately as Nature."

Some writers prefer to lead gradually into the topic sentence and place it at the *end of the paragraph*. The reasons for such a strategy are (1) the abstract nature of the topic requires a variety of explanations and definitions before the writer can pursue his point; (2) the writer wishes to engage the reader's interest by asking a leading question or by citing a pertinent quotation; (3) the writer attempts to establish a dominant mood or tone by offering a surprising statistic or a startling anecdote before asserting his central point in the topic sentence. Whatever the reason for leading gradually into the topic sentence, the basic function of any topic sentence is still to announce paragraph purpose and sentence relationship.

The following paragraph is excerpted from Carl L. Becker's *Modern Democracy*. Here, the topic sentence is the *last sentence* in the paragraph.

(1) Democracy, like liberty or science or progress, is a word with which we are all so familiar that we rarely take the trouble to ask what we mean by it. (2) It is a term, as the devotees of semantics say, which has no "referent"—there is no precise or palpable thing or object which we all think of when the word is pronounced. (3) On the contrary, it is a word which connotes different things to different people, a kind of conceptual Gladstone bag which, with a little manipulation, can be made to accommodate almost any collection of social facts we may wish to carry about in it. (4) In it we can as easily pack a dictatorship as any other form of government. (5) We have only to stretch the concept to include any form of government supported by a majority of the people, for whatever reasons, and by whatever means of expressing assent, and before we know it the empire of Napoleon, the Soviet regime of Stalin, and the Fascist systems of Mussolini and Hitler are all safely in the bag. (6) But if this is what we mean by democracy, then virtually all forms of government are democratic, since virtually all governments, except in times of revolution, rest upon the explicit or implicit consent of the people. (7) *In order to discuss democracy intelligently, it will be necessary, therefore, to define it, to attach to the word a sufficiently precise meaning to avoid the confusion which is not infrequently the chief result of such discussions.*

EXERCISE

Outline Becker's paragraph, showing and explaining the relation between the topic sentence and the other sentences in the paragraph. Respond to the following questions:

1. Why does Becker gradually lead into his topic sentence?
2. What topics do you think might logically follow from this paragraph?

Some writers, when dealing with complex issues, may use *implied topic sentences*. For example, instead of using one awkward sentence to sandwich four key points, a writer will split his points into two or three sentences. At times, the major aim of the paragraph may be so obvious that a specific topic sentence is unnecessary. And at other times, a paragraph may be devoted entirely to an example or anecdote when the reason is indicated in a previous paragraph. It is not always possible to find one topic sentence in every paragraph.

In the following paragraph from *A Layman's Guide to Psychiatry & Psychoanalysis*, Eric Berne employs an example of a personality type which he subsequently analyzes:

> Mr. Krone had a good income, but he was miserly and lived on crusts in a tiny room on Railroad Avenue. Every day he had the same meals at the same time in the same corner, and every day he put his dishes back in exactly the same place. His mornings he spent fussing about in the bathroom, his afternoons calculating his expenses for the previous day, and his evenings going over his old ledgers from former years and looking through his collection of magazines.

The implied topic sentence for the paragraph may be stated, "Miserliness and obsessive ordering of the insignificant details of daily living characterize a certain type of immaturity." The specific details of the rather brief description serve to give the impression of excessive meticulousness as a habit of someone who is unable to enjoy life.

Implied topic sentences are valuable writing tools, especially for complex issues and perspectives. In general, writers become comfortable using the *explicit* topic sentence before attempting the *implied* topic sentence.

EXERCISE

Examine the following paragraphs for topic sentences. Explain the relation between the topic and supporting sentences in each.

1. (1) The dorm room presents a picture of last evening's celebration. (2) Twenty empty Budweiser cans are stacked in a precarious pyramid. (3) Three sweatshirts, a sweater, and my winter coat are piled onto the two coat pegs near the door. (4) Loud drips of water splatter into the crowded basin, which is clogged with half-submerged poptops, cigarette butts, a scarf, and someone's tube of lipstick. (5) Under the sink, a large, expended box of All detergent, which serves as a wastebasket, is stuffed to the top with crumpled beer cans and cigarette

butts and ashes. (6) Heaped before the closet door is an assortment of dirty underwear, damp washcloths, and two pairs of jeans.

student essay

2. (1) There is no wonder that this country has so many charms, and presents to Europeans so many temptations to remain in it. (2) A traveller in Europe becomes a stranger as soon as he quits his own kingdom; but it is otherwise here. (3) We know, properly speaking, no strangers; this is every person's country; the variety of our soils, situations, climates, governments, and produce, hath something which must please every body. (4) No sooner does an European arrive, no matter of what condition, than his eyes are opened upon the fair prospect; he hears his language spoke, he retraces many of his own country manners, he perpetually hears the names of families and towns with which he is acquainted; he sees happiness and prosperity in all places disseminated; he meets with hospitality, kindness, and plenty every where; he beholds hardly any poor; he seldom hears of punishments and executions; and he wonders at the elegance of our towns, those miracles of industry and freedom. (5) He cannot admire enough our rural districts, our convenient roads, good taverns, and our many accommodations; he involuntarily loves a country where every thing is so lovely.

St. Jean de Crèvecoeur,
Letters from an American Farmer

3. (1) We are now in a position to see the wonder and terror of the human predicament: man is totally dependent on society. (2) Creature of dream, he has created an invisible world of ideas, beliefs, habits, and customs which buttress him about and replace for him the precise instincts of the lower creatures. (3) In this invisible universe he takes refuge, but just as instinct may fail an animal under some shift of environmental conditions, so man's cultural beliefs may prove inadequate to meet a new situation, or, on an individual level, the confused mind may substitute, by some terrible alchemy, cruelty for love.

Loren Eiseley,
"The Real Secret of Piltdown"

4. (1) The room displayed a modest and pleasant color-scheme, after one of the best standard designs of the decorator who "did the interiors" for most of the speculative-builders' houses in Zenith. (2) The walls were gray, the woodwork white, the rug a serene blue; and very much like mahogany was the furniture—the bureau with its great clear mirror, Mrs. Babbitt's dressing-table with toilet-articles of almost solid silver, the plain twin beds, between them a small table holding a

standard electric bedside lamp, a glass for water, and a standard bed-side book with colored illustrations—what particular book it was can-not be ascertained, since no one had ever opened it. (3) The mattresses were firm but not hard, triumphant modern mattresses which had cost a great deal of money; the hot-water radiator was of exactly the proper scientific surface for the cubic contents of the room. (4) The windows were large and easily opened, with the best catches and cords, and Holland roller-shades guaranteed not to crack. (5) It was a masterpiece among bedrooms, right out of Cheerful Modern Houses for Medium Incomes. (6) Only it had nothing to do with the Babbitts, nor with any one else. (7) If people had ever lived and loved here, read thrillers at midnight and lain in beautiful indolence on a Sunday morning, there were no signs of it. (8) It had the air of being a very good room in a very good hotel. (9) One expected the chambermaid to come in and make it ready for people who would stay but one night, go without looking back, and never think of it again.

Sinclair Lewis, *Babbitt*

5.   (1) The history of kite flying goes back thousands of years in Eastern Asia. (2) In our country, such famous people as Alexander Graham Bell, the Wright brothers, and Benjamin Franklin were all kite buffs. (3) But for some odd reason—after the invention of airplanes—kites plunged in popularity, at least among adults, and only inspired sea-sonal interest in children. (4) Today it's a different story. (5) Kites are flying higher than ever, and the young in heart of *all* ages have caught the fever.

Better Homes and Gardens,
March 1975

6.   (1) Some people say it is a very easy thing to get up of a cold morning. (2) You have only, they tell you, to take the resolution, and the thing is done. (3) This may be very true; just as a boy at school has only to take a flogging, and the thing is over. (4) But we have not at all made up our minds upon it; and we find it a very pleasant exercise to discuss the matter, candidly, before we get up. (5) This, at least, is not idling, though it may be lying. (6) It affords an excellent answer to those who ask how lying in bed can be indulged in by a reasoning being,—a rational creature. (7) How? (8) Why, with the argument calmly at work in one's head, and the clothes over one's shoulder. (9) Oh—it is a fine way of spending a sensible, impartial half-hour.

Leigh Hunt,
"Getting Up on Cold Mornings"

BUILDING TOPIC SENTENCES FROM THE THESIS STATEMENT

As you attempt to organize your material clearly, you will find it helpful to build your topic sentences directly from your thesis statement. Planning your paragraphs in this fashion allows you to unfold your principal point neatly and gracefully.

Consider the following thesis statement:

> Bicycle riding through city traffic is a satisfying, though dangerous, means of transportation.

From this thesis statement you could logically build a topic sentence on each aspect of the central idea. Thus, your first paragraph would focus attention on the "satisfying" aspect of bicycle riding and your second paragraph on the "dangerous" aspect. A topic sentence for the first paragraph in the body of the paper might read:

> Commuting to work last summer, I found a satisfying way to get exercise while saving the expense of parking fees and gasoline costs.

This topic sentence is more specific than the thesis statement, but it does not provide the detail necessary to convince the reader. That is the function of the rest of the paragraph. It must develop the topic sentence through specific details about the rewards of exercise and the money that the rider managed to save. These specific details, by reinforcing the "satisfying" aspect of the thesis, will help persuade your reader that the topic sentence is valid.

The process of deriving topic sentences from the thesis statement involves:

- isolating the most important aspects of your discussion as expressed in the thesis statement

- incorporating each of those aspects in a separate topic sentence

- stating the topic sentence with precision that can lend emphasis, clarity, and reinforcement to the thesis

Sometimes you may find it necessary to *combine* more than a single aspect of the thesis into a single topic sentence. If, for example, you are discussing a complex subject such as energy conservation, you might first narrow the subject in order to cover it in 500 words, then go through the three steps listed above, and finally combine two or three ideas in a single topic sentence before offering supporting detail.

Consider how to narrow the subject. Narrowing energy conservation might bring you to the following topic: how to obtain high efficiency in automobile driving. You might begin with this thesis statement:

> Many simple methods are available to the consumer who wishes to conserve gasoline.

After giving this statement further consideration, you see that it doesn't express the different aspects of the topic that your paper will discuss. To be effective, the thesis must be more precise, yet general enough that it can still serve as a unifying, controlling idea. The same thesis, more precisely written, might look like this:

> The suburban consumer who wishes to conserve gasoline may take the following steps: (1) form a car pool; (2) consolidate trips whenever possible; (3) drive at moderate speeds; (4) avoid rapid starts and abrupt stops.

You now have four separate aspects of your thesis on which to build your topic sentences. The third and fourth aspects, however, are not broad enough for each to require a separate paragraph, so you decide to combine these aspects in a single topic sentence. On the basis of this thesis statement, your first topic sentence might read:

> Forming a car pool is often a simple, convenient means of conserving gasoline.

Your second topic sentence might read:

> Consolidating shopping trips with commuting or with other sorts of errands is another means by which the suburban consumer can conserve gasoline.

Your third topic sentence, combining aspects 3 and 4 of the thesis statement, might read:

> By driving at moderate speeds and avoiding rapid starts and abrupt stops, the suburban consumer may find that he is able to increase his gasoline mileage from two to five miles per gallon.

WRITING THE INTRODUCTION

Writing the introduction to a composition is finding the best way to present your thesis statement to your audience. In performing this task, you need to stand back from your thesis and try to see it from points of view that will be meaningful to the reader.

The opening paragraph of an essay often serves as introduction. It may consist of no more than the thesis statement, particularly if the paper is brief. Or it may include additional elements designed to arouse the reader's interest. Following are some of the main alternatives open to you as you plan an introduction.

Opening with a Broad Statement

One means of introducing your topic is to move from a broad statement on the nature of the general subject to a specific limitation of the topic in your thesis statement. The broad statement should be perceptive, perhaps thought provoking—certainly not self-evident or boring.

weak:
Some persons really have a sense of charity. My roommate, George, is one such person.

better:
Some persons find it harder to receive than to give. My roommate, George Strother, becomes quite embarrassed at any offer of aid to himself, yet he is exceptionally generous to persons in need. Last Christmas I visited George's home, and there I witnessed a truly self-sacrificing act.

Opening with a Quotation

A second means of introduction is to open with a quotation that is pertinent to your topic.

weak:
I get really frustrated whenever I have to register for courses at this university.

better:
H. L. Mencken defined "Puritanism" as "the haunting fear that someone, somewhere, may be happy." I think his observation applies very well to the philosophy of the clerks in the registrar's office at this university. These people seem to do their best to see that each student receives a totally frustrating schedule.

Opening with an Anecdote

An anecdote can provide an amusing and attention-getting opening if it is short and to the point.

weak:
Students aren't supposed to write in library books.

better:
When Samuel Taylor Coleridge borrowed books from Charles Lamb, Coleridge returned the books to Lamb enriched with brilliant notes in the margins. Well, things have changed. I wish the university library would heavily fine people who return books after having underlined the text mercilessly and written in their own marginal study notes—neither brilliant nor enriching.

Opening with a Statistic or Fact

Sometimes a statistic or fact will add emphasis or interest to your topic. It may be wise to include the item's authoritative source.

weak:
Many drunken drivers cause car accidents.

better:
According to the State Division of Motor Vehicles, fully half of all fatal automobile accidents involve a drunken driver. There are three ways in which you can help alleviate the problem: dissuade from becoming drunk those friends who must drive home; if they become drunk anyway, insist on calling a cab or on driving them home yourself; immediately report to the police the location of any drunken drivers you see on the road.

EXERCISE

Write four alternate introductions to the same subject, employing each of the above methods: (1) moving from a broad statement to the thesis; (2) using a relevant quotation; (3) using an anecdote; and (4) using a startling statistic or fact. In each introduction, present a thesis indicating what you will discuss, how you will discuss it, and why you are going to discuss it.

Employing Methods of Development   **8**

A variety of methods is available to you as you develop your thesis through the body of your paper. Effective writers consciously employ developmental methods that suit their subject and audience. They commonly select one method as their overall approach to the composition and then buttress it with other methods as they become needed.

Assume, for example, that you are writing a paper explaining the process involved in building a fire in a fireplace. Among the various methods of development, it would be reasonable for you to select the *process* approach—a method that serves any writer explaining any process, from assembling a functional college wardrobe to operating a nuclear reactor.

Other methods you might employ would play a secondary role to the overall approach of process. They might include *narration,* if you decided to present an account of a particularly frustrating day you spent attempting to construct a fire without understanding the process. They might include *illustrations/details/examples,* if you decided to mention the kinds of wood a proper fire demands. Here too you might employ *description* as you acquaint the reader with the different types of wood and their burning properties. One way of concluding such an essay would be to analyze the main reasons for the success of the fire. This approach would involve the *casual analysis* method of development. And, as we shall see in this section of our text, there are several other methods available as well.

The following student essay develops this thesis concerning the building and maintaining of a fire in a fireplace. Notice the process method predominating, with other developmental methods introduced from time to time.

FUELING THE FLAMES

For anyone fortunate enough to own a wood-burning fireplace, sitting in front of a healthy fire on a frosty winter afternoon provides a sense of luxury. Unfortunately, many fireplace owners do not understand how to build and maintain a successful fire and therefore either deny themselves the pleasure of a fire or else spend their time futilely attempting to raise a flame that has no chance of continuing success. Futility need not be the result if you **Thesis** master the three steps involved in having a successful **Statement** fire: preparing the fireplace, arranging the materials before igniting, and tending the fire.

I recall with amusement my first attempt at building a fire. We had recently purchased a home that featured a large fireplace. I couldn't wait for the first cold day of winter, and when it arrived, I charged out to the woodpile, grabbed an armful of unsplit logs, and raced back into the house. I dumped the logs on the carpet, threw **Narration and** some paper into the fireplace, and then placed four logs **Illustrations/** on the grate. I lit a match to ignite the paper. The paper, **Details/** of course, cooperated, but the logs seemed to be made of **Examples** stone. Try as I did they would not ignite. After three hours of lighting, relighting, and swearing, I surrendered and simply returned to the livingroom thermostat. A kind friend later patiently demonstrated how I could avoid a repetition of that first experience. Now I greet winter with a hearty fire.

The first step in building a fire is to prepare the fireplace and assemble the materials. Because fires require adequate ventilation, you must insure (1) that the fireplace surface is clear of debris and (2) that the chimney flue is open to permit necessary updraft for ventilation. **Process** After you have taken these steps, obtain a substantial newspaper (the Sunday *New York Times* is usually more than adequate) which can later be used for getting the flame started. Finally, make sure that you have an adequate supply (about three handfuls) of dry kindling wood (wood shavings, bark, and twigs will serve well), and an

Process equally adequate number of logs (about six, finally)—pine, maple, oak, ash, and birch are suitable fuels. Two notes of caution here, however: (1) the logs should be split to enable them to fire more quickly, and (2) they must be dry.

Process Once you have prepared the fireplace and assembled the materials, proceed to the second step—arranging the materials—as follows: rip the newspaper into sheets approximately the size of a book page (8½" × 11"), and roll or twist each sheet into a tight ball. Tightness here is important as the tighter the paper the hotter the resulting flame. Place the rolled-up paper balls under the fireplace grate (a runged-metal stand that holds the logs in place). Next, place the kindling in criss-cross fashion on the grate and directly over the paper balls. As you can imagine, the ignited paper balls will send flame upward to ignite the kindling. While the heat of the paper flame is quite low, the kindling, because of its greater mass, will produce a substantially hotter flame, one which has the necessary heat to fire the logs.

Process When you see that the kindling is burning well, place two logs on top of, and horizontal to, the kindling. Make sure that you leave half an inch of space between these logs for adequate ventilation. Depending on the type of wood you use, the logs should fire in five to fifteen minutes. When you see the flames take on a blue tint, you will know that your fire is now producing sufficient heat to enable you to place a third log on top of the first two. Again, however, remember to leave room for sufficient air to circulate between all three logs. From this point, you may replenish the logs in the fireplace to maintain even heat.

Causal Analysis and Restatement As you can see, the major principle involved in building a successful fire is a chain reaction of its components: the paper (low kindling point and low heat) ignites the kindling (slightly greater kindling point and heat), which ignites the logs (high kindling point and equally high heat). The flame is sustained by the wood and by the oxygen provided through ventilation. Like most chain reactions, the success of each step is dependent on the success of the one preceding it. So take care with each of the steps and you will be rewarded with all the pleasures of a fine blaze.

student essay

Notice how the writer of the previous essay uses a method of development that emphasizes a process because he is explaining how to do something. But notice too that, in order to capture his audience's attention and interest, he also uses narration to recount a past experience, employs illustrations/details/examples, provides accurate description, and concludes with a brief causal analysis, which restates the process.

Some developmental methods are more suitable for single paragraphs than are others; some are more suitable for entire essays; and some are equally suitable for paragraphs and entire essays. The following summary briefly indicates the primary function each method of development serves:

METHOD OF DEVELOPMENT	FUNCTION
illustrations/details/examples	provides supporting evidence within paragraphs
description	presents information and creates an impression within paragraphs and essays
narration	presents a story or sequence of events within paragraphs and essays
comparison/contrast	highlights similarities or differences within paragraphs and essays
analogy	clarifies complex subjects or processes within paragraphs
definition	limits and identifies a term within paragraphs and essays
classification	arranges a complex set of ideas or items within paragraphs and essays
process	explains how to do something within paragraphs and essays
causal analysis	explains and defines cause and effect relationships within paragraphs and essays
concession	acknowledges principal points of opposition argument, usually within paragraphs
generalizations	summarizes details or particulars in larger categories within paragraphs and essays
restatement	sums up main points or repeats for emphasis within paragraphs

Having learned through the prewriting process whether your main purpose is to explain, narrate, describe, or argue, you can decide which means is best suited to your topic. Base your choice on a thorough knowledge of the available methods, and select the method or combination that will offer you the greatest chance of success for developing your topic with emphasis and clarity. The following pages elaborate the various ways to develop a paper.

ILLUSTRATIONS/DETAILS/EXAMPLES

Every generality in an essay should be accompanied by sufficient evidence so that the reader will willingly accept what you are telling him. Most methods of development, in fact, incorporate illustrations/ details/examples. The obvious means of convincing someone of your point is to give him specific supporting evidence. For instance, if you are searching for an entertaining teacher, you may ask a student in Professor Zork's class if she shows that quality. If told yes, you are likely to ask for details: "What makes her so entertaining?" Upon hearing that, last Tuesday, Professor Zork showed slides and presented recordings of Robert Frost reading his poetry, you may well be convinced your informant is right.

You may find the following paragraph unconvincing because the detail needs to be more specific.

> Horseback riding can give a rider great pleasure. Riding through the autumn woods with its earthy smells and colors can invigorate even the most sluggish people. The crisp, clean air seems to wake up both horses and riders. The horses appear to prance as the cool air livens their spirits, and the riders joyfully chatter as they trot along through the woods enjoying the company of friends and the brisk ride. Although many people find joy in being with others as they ride, some find greater joy in riding alone. Racing across a wide meadow filled with fragrant flowers, or walking along a mountain stream enjoying the assorted sounds of the woods both give the rider a sense of being close to nature. The horse and rider can enjoy the ride and relax in the quieter surroundings. For some, there is a feeling of greater freedom by being alone. They have no pressures from work or problems to solve. They have a chance to be alone, to absorb nature, and to not have to think.
>
> *student essay*

This paragraph attempts to make believabie assertions about all persons who ever mounted a horse. To make the paragraph more convincing, the writer could have narrowed the topic, perhaps limiting it just to her own experience. Next, the writer might have asked herself specific questions to make the supporting detail more believable: Where are the autumn woods? Is it early autumn or late autumn? What are the "earthy smells"? What are the particular colors? What kind of "fragrant flowers"? Which particular stream? What are the specific feelings of the individual rider, the sources of her "great pleasure"? The revision of the paragraph shows how the questions can be answered, how the use of specific details can add interest and credibility.

> Horseback riding gives me a sense of relaxation and an opportunity to enjoy the mountains near my home in western North Carolina. Last October, as the maple leaves were at the height of their red brightness, I rode my pinto mare along the side of Brush Mountain. The air, which appeared from a distance as a blue haze, was free from the odor of car exhaust, which tainted the atmosphere in the valley below. And I could catch the aroma of pines and blue spruce, and of the moss growing in the yellow clay on the floor of the dense Jefferson National Forest. The rhythmic movements of the horse grew more rapid as I rode across a small meadow half-way up the mountain, and I felt calm and relaxed.
>
> *student essay*

EXERCISE

Examine the following questions on the preceding paragraph:

1. What are the specific details that help make the paragraph believable?
2. What is accomplished by the writer's identifying a specific locale, season, kind of horse, and so forth?

The *illustrations/details/examples* method of development involves the following tasks:

- Give your readers enough evidence so that they will be convinced of the reasonableness of your generality.

- Decide which senses—sight, sound, smell, touch, taste—you can best appeal to.

- Use *concrete* detail.

DESCRIPTION

Description necessarily incorporates the method of illustrations/details/examples. When developing an idea by description, you must first decide upon an impression you wish to create. You then sort out those details that will help establish this impression. For example, a salesletter written to impress potential buyers with the economic advantages of a particular model car will not overwhelm readers with descriptive details about the car's bucket seats, rhinestone-covered steering wheel, and fur-lined glove compartment. Rather, the writer will describe the efficient compression delivered by the copper head-gaskets, mention the computerized fuel-injection system, and dwell on the improved ignition system that requires infrequent servicing.

Having determined the impression you seek to create, you may appeal to one or more of the reader's senses in addition to his intellect. Details of sight, hearing, smell, perhaps even taste or touch can be effective if you wish to offer a convincing description of a scene or experience from nature.

The following passage offers a description and creates an impression:

> The most striking characteristic of the university's indoor stadium is its visual beauty. The artificial grass sparkles like a new carpet. Though soft to the eye, it is prickly to the touch, and if a runner slides on it, the grass burns and scrapes the skin. This man-made football field is one hundred yards long with an additional twenty yards for end zones. Large white numerals indicate each ten yards from goal to goal. Bordering the outside of the field is a track, one-sixth of a mile long. When the huge, bright lights directly overhead blaze down on the artificial grass at night, the turf resembles a large, flat, luminous piece of jade.

student essay

EXERCISE

Consider the following questions concerning appeals to the senses in the paragraph above:

1. In which sentence or sentences does the writer suggest an impression? How?
2. What visual details does the writer provide? What purpose do the visual details serve?
3. List the details of touch. What is their effect?
4. What is the effect of the comparison with jade?

In the paragraph about the stadium, the writer is relatively *objective*. He does not show a strong feeling for or against his subject, since he mentions both positive and negative features (the artificial turf is luxuriant, but it is "prickly"). You may find the following student essay to be a more *subjective* description, revealing more of the author's attitude.

GEOMETRY IN THE DEAN'S OFFICE

When I wanted to get permission to move out of a dormitory and into a private apartment with three friends, I was told that I would need the approval of the dean of students. The office as well as the physical appearance of the dean had so rigid an orderliness that I immediately sensed my request would meet with disapproval.

Dean Pullman's office was arranged for the visual satisfaction of a lover of geometry, not for the convenience of visitors. In the front half of the office were four straight-backed armchairs—all the joints were perfect right angles—two against opposite walls. And all of the chairs were at right angles to the dean's huge, rectangular desk. Once seated, I found it impossible to face him without turning awkwardly in the chair. So, twisting myself unnaturally in the hard wooden seat, I gazed first at his desk top. Each item on the desk was geometrically arranged. The smooth, dustfree, rectangular glass that covered his desk top had no papers on it, and I noticed that the telephone was not set at an angle but directly faced the dean. The five plastic buttons which controlled various phone lines were all protruding evenly. That not a one was depressed gave me the idea that the dean never used his phone, since to do so would require pushing a button and breaking the symmetry of the row. As if to give geometrical balance to the desk top, a dictionary (still wrapped in cellophane) was set on the other side of the desk, directly opposite the telephone. Behind the desk sat the dean himself.

Dean Pullman's personal appearance reinforced the impression of rigidity presented by the office. His thin gray hair was well oiled and combed straight back. Each strand looked cemented in place; no two hairs crossed. The expression on his face showed him to be a man with the verve of a Calvin Coolidge—forty years dead. The well-polished lenses of his silver-rimmed glasses showed no speck of dust before the clear gray eyes, which never blinked. I thought to myself that the taxidermist had done a good job. Below the glasses and around the corners of his mouth ran lines probably formed from years of scowling. His suit was a solid dark brown, and, even though he was seated, his coat was completely buttoned, yet it had been pulled and straightened so that no fold or wrinkle appeared in the part visible to a person seated across from his desk. His spotless white shirt looked starched, and a solid brown tie, which might have been made from the same material as his suit, lay flat and straight against the shirt front. He sat motionless, neither speaking nor nodding when I entered; his hands were symmetrically folded and rested on his desk top very lightly, as if he feared smudging the polished glass.

Dean Pullman turned down my request with only a monosyllable, "no." As I left his office, I imagined him rising to dust the chair I had sat in and straighten it ever so slightly. It was with intense gratification that I dropped a crumpled chewing gum wrapper in his doorway as I stepped out.

student essay

EXERCISE

Consider the following questions about the preceding essay:

1. What details show subjectiveness in the description?
2. Are you convinced that the writer's attitude is justified?
3. How is the description of the dean's appearance related to his assumed psychological outlook?
4. What details are offered in addition to those of physical description?

The process of development by *description* involves the following tasks:

- Determine the impression you want to create. (You may wish to establish two or three impressions, but your writing will be most effective if you are clear about which is most important.)

- Sort out the details that will support the impression(s) you want to create.

- If it will enhance the description, draw details from the other senses—hearing, smell, taste, and touch—in addition to sight.

NARRATION

When writing a narrative, you will often arrange facts in a chronological order. By explaining that A happened and then B happened and then C happened, you invite the reader to relive the experience as you discovered it. Sometimes, however, you may choose to rearrange the chronology to emphasize a special episode. For example, an account of a prisoner's fight to gain a new trial may start with his present circumstances in jail, then switch to the past to tell about his alleged crime, then return to the present to recount his many attempts to gain acquittal.

Keep in mind that many of the points made about description apply as well to narration. First, identify the idea or feeling you wish to present to the reader. Next, sketch out roughly the events of the incident or episode in chronological order—you may wish to draw details from the use of all the senses, if possible, not just that of sight. Finally, arrange the events in an order that will strengthen the idea or impression, and include only those other details which are necessary to give credibility to your account. For a particularly emphatic impression, you may hold the single most significant detail until the end.

The topic sentence—which openly states the impression you intend to make—may logically be presented at either the beginning or the end of the narrative. If placed at the end, the topic sentence may forcefully summarize and reemphasize the impression. Consider also that, with narration, the absence of a topic sentence can be highly effective if you present convincing details along the way, details that have been carefully selected to support the topic sentence you wish to imply.

The following paragraph is narration. Note how the details emphasize the impression of brutality.

> That autumn, late every afternoon, I watched the middle-aged woman across the street march into her front yard, leading a large, black, reluctant dog out for an obedience lesson. Dragging him by the collar into the grass strewn with dead leaves, she would first take five steps; the dog, partially being dragged and partially following voluntarily, stayed a pace behind. Then the woman executed a quick turn, shouted "Heel!" and, jerking the leash, brought the dog in step behind her. Back and forth. Back and forth. I watched as the sun, tinting the October sky with red, cast its fading light on the woman, the dog, and the dead leaves.
>
> *student essay*

Though the overall impression is left unstated, the narrator's selection of detail and choice of words (or diction) suggest that he senses death and a military authoritarianism in the scene. The narrator chooses to omit certain details: we learn nothing of the physical appearance of the woman; we know only her approximate age, which parallels the time of year (autumn) and time of day (sunset). Sunset, autumn, and middle age all suggest approaching death; the dead leaves, the blood-color of the sunlight, even the color of the dog (we get no other physical details about it other than its relative size) reinforce the impression of approaching death.

Notice that the writer omits other detail, telling nothing of the appearance of the house before which the scene takes place, how long the training session goes on, what the particular appearance of the dog is, how large the yard is, or where (geographically) the incident takes place. Diction adds to the feeling of destructive authoritarianism. Note "dragging," "march," "executed," "shouted," "jerking." Again, the writer creates an impression without directly stating it.

EXERCISE

Respond to the following with specific reference to the above narration:

1. Which senses are appealed to? Could the paragraph be more effective if other senses were employed?
2. Would some arrangement other than a chronological one be more effective?
3. With the intention of establishing an impression of *warmth* and *love* instead of *brutality*, rewrite the narrative of the dog training.

The following is a full-length narrative essay. The thesis statement, the last sentence of the introductory paragraph, indicates the dominant impression.

RAILROAD DAYS

Although my summer job on the railroad maintenance crew was a sort of physical torture, I regretted its coming to an end because I knew I would miss the friends I had made among my co-workers. My last day at work was physically difficult, but it had a charming close.

The three of us, Dave, Larry, and I, had spent the morning removing rotten railroad ties from the track bed, and in the afternoon we put in the new ties. The afternoon sun beat down on our bare heads and backs; perspiration dripped from my forehead onto the air hammer I was using to pound in new rail spikes. The racket from the hammer and air compressor combined with the heat to give me a headache, the pain jumping with the vibrations of the hammer. As I was driving the final spike late that afternoon, twice the air hammer slipped from the silver head of the spike and struck the top of my shoe, bruising my toes painfully. At 4:00 P.M., we left the work area to clock out. I felt dirty and tired. My shoulders ached from the strain of moving the ninety-pound air hammer from spike to spike.

From the office, after we punched out, we went across the street to the Oasis Bar, where they sold beer to us even though we were under age. Before we sat down at our regular table, Dave put a quarter in the juke box. As he had done each afternoon of the summer, Dave punched the set of buttons which brought the sounds of "I've Got a Tiger by the Tail" hammering into the darkened barroom. All of us were tired; all of us ached. Soon all of us were mildly drunk. But the beer was cold and the air conditioning felt good, and soon each of us began to speak of his immediate plans for going to college the following week. Slightly drunk and weary as we were, we each made a sentimental testimonial to the good fellowship we had enjoyed for three months and vowed to get together for a drink during Thanksgiving vacation.

I thought then that I would never see them again, and I haven't. But they did leave me with mellow memories of a time when I did the most physically tiring and demanding work I likely ever shall do.

student essay

EXERCISES

1. Respond to the following questions on the previous essay:
   a. How do certain details in the third paragraph parallel details in the second? Why may the writer have chosen to use parallel details?
   b. Would further detail in either the second or third paragraph make the impression (as stated in the introduction and in the conclusion) more convincing?
   c. From which senses does the writer draw his detail?
2. Narrate an incident in your experience, establishing one of the following as the dominant impression:
   a. irritation
   b. fatigue
   c. happiness
   d. surprise
   e. disappointment
   f. relief

The following are basic tasks in development by *narration:*

- Identify the feeling or idea you wish to convey through your narrative.

- Arrange the narrative events chronologically, selecting the details which will reinforce that feeling or
  idea.

- Include only those other details which you need to
  make the narrative credible.

- Determine whether you can gain greater impact by
  rearranging the chronology, perhaps placing the
  most important or interesting episode at the beginning or at the end.

COMPARISON/CONTRAST

One of the simplest yet most effective methods of development is comparison/contrast. It is especially useful for defining and
describing. If your material is suited to this method, you have two
basic means of employing it. You might first discuss qualities of Subject A, and then discuss qualities of Subject B, taking care to treat the
strikingly similar or distinctively different qualities of A and B in the
same order. Or you might wish to make alternate statements (again
carefully arranged so as to be parallel) on A, then on B; A again, then
B again; and so on. The comparison/contrast method is usually used in
combination with another method, such as generalizations, description, analogy, classification, or illustrations/details/examples. Whatever combination of methods is used, the material needs to be
arranged so as to highlight the most significant similarities and/or differences, at the beginning or at the end of your paper.

The next essay is an example of the first type of comparison/contrast
(combined with illustrations/details/examples). Notice how the items
in the second paragraph are presented in the same order as those in
the first:

THE ALGER-FINLEY PROVIDENCE

Horatio Alger, Jr., and Martha Finley, two very popular novelists
of the late nineteenth century, both believed that virtue is revealed
by the ability to become rich; their heroes, however, are basically
different. Alger's acquire their fortunes actively and Finley's acquire
their fortunes passively.

Alger often writes about an impoverished boy who earns his way
to fortune through honesty and pluck, with occasional help from
Providence. Ragged Dick, for example, begins as a New York boot-
black who barely earns enough to pay for occasional lodging at the

semicharitable Newsboys' Lodging House—usually Dick sleeps in an alley or on a hard bench of the Brooklyn Ferry. One day, however, Dick obtains the job of giving a tour of the city to a young man of education and wealth. Dick decides to follow the example of his new acquaintance: he buys some books and begins a program of self-education and follows a rigorous savings plan with his shoe-shine earnings. Providence comes to his aid by causing a rich man's son to fall into the river; this gives the hero an opportunity to demonstrate that he has "pluck": Dick rescues the boy. He is rewarded with $10,000 and a position as a clerk in the wealthy man's firm. He gets more opportunities for advancement from a former shine customer, who enrolls him in Sunday school. By the end of the book, the hero possesses a small but growing fortune.

Finley, on the other hand, shows her chief heroine, Elsie Dinsmore, passively acquiring a fortune which, through no effort of the heroine, continues to grow, as Elsie continues to show virtue to relatives who persecute her. Elsie, at first, lives as a Cinderella in a wealthy southern family. She is a belabored child in a house where a variety of cruel cousins and cruel grandparents treat her as a servant, assigning her cleaning chores and making her wear hand-me-down clothes. Horace, her father (her mother has died), one Sunday demands that Elsie play a worldly tune on the piano; though loving and faithful to the tyrant, the child refuses to—as she sees it —set her father's commands above God's. From this experience grows the conversion of Horace to Christianity. Soon, Elsie's father begins to requite the love and affection she has offered him, though the other children continue to bully and insult her. Before long, Elsie finds that she is an heiress. She acquires her mother's Louisiana plantation; a large fortune from her father; and, upon her marriage, the fortune of Edward Travilla, her husband, who subsequently dies, making her sole owner of their joint wealth.

The essential difference between Alger's Ragged Dick and Finley's Elsie Dinsmore lies in Finley's only implying the relationship between virtue and prosperity and Alger's openly exhorting readers to virtue in order that they may gain riches. Both writers seem foolishly idealistic in this respect, basically denying that there may exist millions of virtuous persons who remain poor all their lives.

student essay

EXERCISE

Respond to the following questions with reference to the above essay:

1. Identify the *comparison* between Alger and Finley introduced in paragraph one.

2. Identify the *contrast* between Alger and Finley introduced in paragraph one.
3. Explain, with specific reference to paragraph two, how Ragged Dick acquires his fortune "actively."
4. Explain, with specific reference to paragraph three, how Elsie Dinsmore acquires her fortune "passively."
5. In the last paragraph, the writer notes that Alger and Finley "seem foolishly idealistic" because they deny "that there may exist millions of virtuous persons who remain poor all their lives." What is the justification for such a view? Explain with specific reference to paragraphs two and three.

The following essay is an example of the second type of comparison/contrast, that of alternating statements on A and B.

THE ALGER-FINLEY PROVIDENCE

Horatio Alger, Jr., and Martha Finley, two very popular novelists of the late nineteenth century, both believed that virtue is revealed by the ability to become rich; their heroes, however, are basically different. Alger's acquire their fortunes actively and Finley's acquire their fortunes passively.

Honesty and pluck are characteristics of both Alger's heroes and Finley's heroines. Ragged Dick, one of Alger's early heroes, earns an honest living by blacking boots in New York City; Dick's struggles are of an economic nature. Elsie Dinsmore, the chief heroine in Finley's works, shows not only honesty but also courage by refusing, upon her widowed father's demand, to play a worldly tune on the piano one Sunday; Elsie's struggles are chiefly emotional, rather than economic. Dick bends his efforts toward making money by emulating the saving and study habits of a young man who had once hired Dick as a tour guide of the city, and the Alger hero also shows pluck in rescuing the son of a rich man from drowning. Elsie's pluck, on the other hand, shows in her ability to endure the bullying and insults of her cousins and the servant chores assigned to her by cruel grandparents.

Providence, in both Alger and Finley, rewards virtue with money. Ragged Dick's emulation of the saving and study habits of the boy with whom he tours New York leads to Dick's rapid advancement in the firm of the father of the boy Dick saved from drowning, and the father gives a $10,000 reward to Dick at the same time. More chances for advancement come from a former shine customer who has Dick enrolled in Sunday school. By the conclusion of the novel, the hero possesses a small but growing fortune. Elsie Dinsmore likewise enjoys a flow of Providential gold. For enduring her father's curses on her refusal to play worldly tunes on Sunday, she wins not only his conversion to Christianity but his estate as well. The heiress also gets her deceased mother's Louisiana plantation and a fortune from Edward Travilla, her subsequent husband, who later dies, making her sole owner of their joint wealth.

Though Finley only implies the relationship between virtue and prosperity, Alger openly shows it. Both writers appear foolishly idealistic in this respect, for they implicitly deny that there may exist millions of virtuous persons who remain poor all their lives.

student essay

EXERCISE

Consider the following questions with reference to the above essay:

1. Identify the *comparison* between Alger and Finley in paragraphs two and three.
2. Identify the *contrast* between Alger and Finley in paragraphs two and three.
3. Now compare the two essays. Which one is the more effective? Why?
4. Both essays employ illustrations and details to fill in and support their arguments. Are the illustrations convincing? Do they effectively establish the points?
5. Is it fair to generalize about *all* the works of Alger and Finley and then cite examples from the lives of only two characters?
6. Are there places in the development where the detail could be more specific, more effective? Examine, for instance, such phrases as "bullying and insults" and "chances for advancement."

The *comparison/contrast* method of development involves the following basic tasks:

- Determine the points you wish to emphasize.

- Identify points of comparison (the similarities).

- Identify points of contrast (the differences).

- Choose the method of discussion that suits your subject matter (treat all of topic A, then all of topic B, or use alternating treatments of A and B).

- Arrange the material to highlight the most significant similarities or differences at the beginning or at the end of your discussion.

ANALOGY

The main function of analogy is to clarify. It is effectively used in combination with comparison/contrast. By employing analogy, you offer the reader a simple means of understanding complex subjects or processes. Analogy, in effect, is comparison. Remember, though, that there usually are differences, as well as similarities, between the items being compared, and because of the differences, analogy is *not valid for proving* a point. But it is very useful for clarifying one.

The first task in developing an analogy is to determine the impression you wish to create about your subject. The writer of a flier on behalf of a candidate for political office might wish to characterize the candidate's opponent as "invidious"—someone who unjustly creates ill will. After selecting a subject (such as a form of sport) that offers some parallel to the political campaign, the writer of the flier might select an aspect of the sport that illustrates "invidiousness"—details that depict colorfully, in terms that a wide audience can understand, the characteristic that the writer wants the audience to see in the opponent. The writer might draw an analogy from another sort of contest, a baseball game, and argue that stealing a political point is like stealing a base:

> Though it is legal to steal a base, it is unsportsmanlike to spike the shortstop. When my opponent refers to me as "a man who would rather breathe fresh air than see his neighbor have a job," then he is spiking me and stealing the political issue. He is trying to draw off the support of union members who should be able to have both clean air and a job.

The following analogy was made by a member of the Federal Trade Commission:

> Overregulation benefits no one. . . . Government cannot protect everybody from everything. There will be bears in the woods. It is wiser to accept that fact and proceed with appropriate caution than to employ a scorched-earth regulatory policy which gets rid of the bears by getting rid of the woods and leaving everybody with a serious erosion problem.

Though the analogy presents a concrete picture of the problem of the government agency, its usefulness ends at pointing to the problem. It is not an argument supported by logic—at least, as it stands here. No facts, figures, or case histories are presented to convince the reader who does not agree with the writer at the outset. But the analogy is useful and may be analyzed thus: the woods are equivalent to the marketplace in which the consumer walks; the bears are the persons or products which threaten the well-being of the consumers. Government regulations, applied too widely, bring "scorched earth" (the ruining of the marketplace or economic system). The "serious erosion problem" is equivalent to the destruction of opportunities to develop the economy and the marketplace (the "woods"). Such destruction, however, would rid the consumers of the "bears" (the threats to their well-being).

An analogy is useful for clarifying a point, a process, or an abstraction. It should be kept simple, concise, and self-contained. An analogy does *not* prove a point but rather clarifies one. Therefore it should never dominate a paper.

EXERCISES

1. Develop an analogy for two of the following:
   a. McDonald's and a church building
   b. a baby and a pickle
   c. a car and a monster
2. Create the basis for an analogy for each of the following:
   a. a textbook and _____
   b. the speaker at your high school commencement and _____
   c. a professor and _____
3. Develop a paragraph for each of the analogies in exercise two.

Using *analogy* involves these tasks:

- Decide on the impression you wish to give your reader about your subject.

- Think of another subject that lends itself to comparison with your subject.

- Find areas of likeness between the two subjects.

- Draw the comparison between the subjects.

DEFINITION

To develop an essay or a paragraph by definition is to examine the meaning of a term at some length. For this term, you select what is for your audience the most pertinent *class* (a set or group having at least one common characteristic) to which the term belongs. This is especially important when the term to be defined is a subjective one, such as "patriotism." A thesis statement for a definition essay—or a topic sentence for a definition paragraph—involves specifying (1) the *term* to be defined, (2) the *class* to which the term belongs, and (3) the *differentia,* a statement of the attributes or characteristics that the term possesses. The differentia distinguishes the term from other terms which fall into the same class that you have designated. Consider, for example, this definition: "An ear is an organ of hearing." The *term* is "ear"; the *class* is "organ"; the *differentia* is "of hearing." The definition is developed by amplifying the differentia, by carefully describing the details that separate the term from the other terms that fall into the same class.

Often, definition is combined with one of the other methods of development discussed in this part, such as narration, which may give an example of how the concept is illustrated or applied. For instance, a definition of "puritanism" may begin with the term-class-differentia formula: *"Puritanism* is a *belief* in *strict moral or religious conduct."* The definition could then be developed by a brief narrative of two pertinent episodes from the biography of the Puritan preacher Jonathan Edwards. Other useful means of defining are by using analogy or comparison/contrast with another, similar term in the same class. For example, a definition of "liberty" may be developed by using an analogy with plane geometry, describing an optical illusion that parallels one person's idea of freedom with another's view of restraint, the opposite of freedom.

The one-sentence definition is useful in technical papers for a general educated audience, as in the following:

> We must analyze the poetry of the Provençal practitioners of the *trobar clus,* a form of poetry employing symbols and allusions not known or understood by anyone but the poet himself. In doing so, let us give special attention to prosody (patterns of rhyme and accent).

Dictionaries provide definitions using the term-class-differentia format. *The American Heritage Dictionary,* for instance, defines "gargoyle" as "a roof spout carved to represent a grotesque human or animal figure, and projected from a gutter to carry rainwater clear of the wall." The *term* is "gargoyle"; the *class* is "roof spout"; a gargoyle is distinguished from all other roof spouts by its being "carved to represent a grotesque human or animal figure, and projected from a gutter to carry rainwater clear of the wall" (the *differentia*). Further development of the subject may logically follow. If you have a 500-word limit, you might specify the restrictions on the subject as follows: "Romanesque gargoyles are of special interest to readers of horror fiction"; or,

"Gargoyles have practical uses, such as frightening children from the grounds of a mansion." In the first case, development by illustrations/ details/examples or analogy could be combined with definition. In the second, narration could be employed.

The following paragraph uses definition. Notice how the writer has stated the term, class, and differentia, and then elaborated upon the differentia in order to make his definition clear and emphatic.

> A dream is a subconscious depiction of a fear or wish, and it may employ "displaced" or substituted objects, settings, and persons for the ones with which the dreamer is really concerned. When a man learned that an older friend, John, had died while traveling in another state, he had the following dream the next night: While visiting his Uncle Joe, the dreamer discovers that Uncle Joe is living in John's house (but John himself has no actual presence in that house during the dream). After a drink and some pleasant conversation, Uncle Joe ascends the stairs into the dark. Before long Uncle Joe reappears; he shakes hands and bids goodbye to the dreamer, leaves the house, and enters a blue car that is being driven by someone else. The blue car slowly drives off into the darkness. At that point the dreamer awoke. The following morning, on reflection, the dreamer became convinced that his dream was associated with his fear that his father would soon die. The displaced objects led him to this conclusion: there were stairs in his father's home, but not in his uncle's nor in the house of his friend John. The dreamer's father, not John or Uncle Joe, owned a blue car. Other details in the dream reinforced the dreamer's belief that the events depicted this fear: the darkness suggested death, and the car's departure suggested both John's traveling and a journey to meet death.

student essay

EXERCISES

1. Respond to the following questions about the preceding paragraph:
    a. Identify the term, class, and differentia in the definition.
    b. What method of development has been combined with the definition?
2. Write a definition paragraph or essay on one of the following subjects:
    a. eccentricity
    b. a miser
    c. a virtue
    d. electrical (or some other kind of) engineering
    e. poverty
    f. carelessness

When employing *definition,* keep the following in mind:

- Whether you use *narration, analogy,* or any other means of development in conjunction with definition, you must at some point state *term, class,* and *differentia.*

- See that your definition is sufficiently elaborate, that the term you are defining is clearly distinguished from other terms in the same class.

CLASSIFICATION

The development of a thesis by classification can be useful for arranging a complex set of ideas or items that share some common feature. Whether it is library books, antiques, or cats that you are attempting to arrange, the first step is to examine the items to be classified and then choose—with an eye to the quality or element that is likely to be most useful or relevant to the audience—the *basis* for the classification. The basis will help you determine the categories into which you will group the items being classified.

In selecting your categories, you must be careful not to pick categories that overlap. For example, you might decide to classify toads on the basis of their size and color. These two qualities might then lead to the following categories: red, green, large, and small. But now consider a giant green toad. This toad would not fit into any *one* category because the categories overlap. In order for the classification to be useful, the categories must be mutually exclusive. Therefore, you might decide to classify toads on the basis of size alone and group them into three categories: large, medium, and small. In addition to providing mutually exclusive categories, the basis of the classification should be such that it can be applied to *all* items in the set. Every item should fit into a category, and there should be no leftovers.

It is important to select the basis of classification that will be of the greatest use to your audience. For example, if you classify teachers for the benefit of other students, you might base your classification on *ability to dispense information,* or you might base your classification on *ability to entertain.* These are useful classifications. It would also be possible to classify teachers on several other bases, such as height, color of hair, age, or weight, but for your particular audience these classifications would be far less useful. A commodity such as supermarket meat might be usefully classified according to the type of animal from which it derives, the amount of fat it contains, price per pound, amount of bone per pound, and so on. A group such as a tribe of cannibals could be classified according to sharpness of teeth, preference for certain cuts of meat, or size of jaws. U. S. Presidents might be classified on the basis of number of vetoes cast, amount of federal assistance provided for education, or number of federal programs proposed.

The following essay employs classification to help distinguish the various types of dairy science students.

OPTIONS IN DAIRY SCIENCE

On the basis of curriculum, dairy science students may be classified as (1) production-management majors, (2) pre-vet majors, or (3) science majors.

One curriculum option, production management, is for students who are interested in the various aspects of dairy production, allied agri-business industries, extension, and various other positions. Students who graduate from this option of study find a wide variety of jobs open to them. Some of these jobs are managing herds and dairy farms, working with feed and artificial insemination, operating equipment companies, and working as county agents and breed fieldmen. This option is the most flexible of the three because it allows seventy credits of electives. Students are able to choose the electives best suited to their needs and interests. More dairy science students choose this option, and about seventy-five percent of those students who graduate from this option go on to farm-related jobs.

Another course of study which dairy science students can choose is the pre-vet option. This is for those students who wish to become veterinarians. The pre-vet option does not have the flexibility that production management does because students in pre-vet have more required courses to take. They must take a number of courses in organic chemistry and physics and they must take almost all of the courses given by the veterinary and animal-veterinary science departments. Since there is no veterinary school in this state, these students are restricted in where they can go to finish their study in order to become veterinarians. Only a certain percentage of pre-vet students are accepted into veterinary school, and the grade requirements for these schools are very high. This fact alone discourages many students from entering this course of study. However, with the anticipation of this university's getting a veterinary school, more and more students are choosing the pre-vet option.

Some dairy science students prefer the science option. This course of study is for those who plan to go to graduate school or who plan a career in quality control, laboratory work, or research product development. The science option is very restrictive, too. Students must take many courses in chemistry, mathematics, physics, microbiology, and zoology. These courses give students a wide background for further study in many areas. And because of its wide variety of study, students in this option can change to one of the other options during their third or fourth year more easily than can students in one of the other options. Science students would not have to pick up courses they had missed, as students in one of the other options would. Only a few students choose the science option, however.

Dairy science students have, then, three options of study to choose from: production management, pre-vet, and science. Production management is the option most students choose because of its flexibility and because of the job opportunities it offers. Students in pre-vet, of course, plan to go on to veterinary school. And the science option is for students who want to go on to graduate school or who plan to pursue a career in research. Students in the science option can change most easily to one of the other two options because of the variety of courses they are required to take.

student essay

The writer explains the basis of the classification in the opening paragraph, the thesis statement. The basis is logical, and the classification is complete—all the options of study are covered. Each of the main paragraphs is then developed by means of *definition* and *comparison/contrast*.

The following selection shows how a single paragraph may be developed by classification. It is excerpted from an expository essay on parlor games.

Board games may be classified on the basis of the element of chance each involves: (1) those which are almost entirely matters of luck, (2) those which are largely based on skill, and (3) those in which chance and skill play approximately equal roles. In the first group are such games as Ludo, Candyland, and Chutes and Ladders. In the second group are such games as chess, checkers, and Masterpiece. The third group, those in which chance and skill operate equally, includes Chinese checkers, Monopoly, and *Milles Bornes*.

student essay

EXERCISE

Think of three or four means of classifying students in the curriculum you have chosen or may choose. On what basis could you classify students who have not yet chosen a curriculum? In each case, consider your audience to be your peers. What basis of classification would be most useful for such an audience?

The process of *classification* involves the following tasks:

- Determine the group of items to be classified.

- Choose the classification basis most useful to your audience.

- Be certain that the categories of the classification system are mutually exclusive.

- Be certain all items in the group can fit into the classification system.

PROCESS

A process paper or paragraph concentrates on *how* something is done. When you develop by process, you may wish to enumerate the major (if not also the minor) steps involved. If a particular order of steps is essential, provide proper warnings. An important consideration with process development is that of how much your audience knows about your subject. If your audience is not well informed on the subject, your discussion will have to be detailed. If, however, you are addressing a well-informed audience, you may employ technical terms that are in its vocabulary and use less explanatory detail than you might otherwise have to.

Certain processes, such as constructing a music box, are fundamentally the same under any circumstances. For such processes, you may wish to use the second-person point of view ("These are the steps *you* follow."). Other processes, however, may vary according to the individual circumstances of members of your audience. For example, an explanation of how to organize a local political campaign will have to allow for varying circumstances from town to town, city to city. Such a process can most effectively be presented as a case history, written from a first-person point of view ("These are the steps *I* followed to organize the campaign for reelecting Mayor Dunning.").

You can simplify your audience's job if you group a series of many small steps into two or three major ones. For example, a discussion of how to raise a healthy St. Bernard could present the following main steps: (1) provide adequate space for the dog; (2) be certain the animal has a proper diet; (3) see that the dog receives preventive medical care. Each of the three main steps involves a series of smaller steps, and a knowledgeable writer could easily devote a full paragraph to each of the three items.

Suppose you decide to write a brief process paper entitled "How to Develop a Flea Circus for Fun and Profit" for an audience of novices. The thesis statement (addressed to a participating audience) could begin with some encouragement and suggest the paragraph divisions to come:

> You can obtain seven hours of spectator pleasure each week and supplement your income by $50,000 a year by operating a flea circus.

You could then develop the material into paragraphs that deal with the two major steps: (1) how to obtain fun and (2) how to obtain profit. The first main paragraph might read as follows:

> By constructing two simple, inexpensive pieces of circus equipment for your fleas, you can obtain an hour of pleasure each day watching the antics of these tiny performers. First, stand a bicycle upside down; then glue bottle caps (flat side down) to the outer circumference of the rear tire. Be certain to use the rear and not the front tire since the rear is connected to the peddle and chain, and you can cause the tire to rotate by turning the peddle with your hand. The bottle caps can serve as seats, and your rear bicycle tire becomes a ferris wheel for fleas. A second item for your flea circus can be an elephant ride. Find a stray dog and spray-paint it gray. Next, tie a two-foot length of garden hose to the dog's nose. Spray-paint the hose gray also. An old, toothless dog is best because it may be feeble enough to cooperate willingly and it cannot bite you if it resists being painted. Having erected the ferris wheel and prepared the "elephant," loose ten or fifteen fleas near the equipment. In just a few minutes the fleas will, with no training or encouragement from you, begin riding the ferris wheel and elephant. Your only task will be to crank the bicycle tire by means of the peddle and enjoy the spectacle.
>
> *student essay*

This paragraph establishes the pleasurable aspect promised in the thesis statement. Several smaller steps are included in the main step, how to obtain fun. A subsequent paragraph, dealing with profit, could describe the various steps involving advertising the attraction, setting admission prices, paying the overhead, and investing the net profit.

The following full-length essay also shows the combining of smaller steps into larger ones; this time, however, the audience is observing.

HOW TO AVOID PICKING UP THE CHECK
WHEN DINING OUT

In these days of tight money, I sometimes find it necessary to dine out at the expense of an unsuspecting friend. What is difficult about such a venture is getting away with it while keeping the friendship intact. There are three basic steps I follow: (1) locating a friend who is reasonably affluent so that I don't suffer from pangs of conscience; (2) selecting an elegant restaurant so that I can continue to cherish the dining experience in lean days to come; (3) getting my friend to pick up the check.

In order to determine if one of my friends can afford to treat me to dinner, I follow him to a store in which he plans to make a purchase by check. As he is filling out his check stub, I peer over his shoulder to determine his checking account balance. If, however, this is impossible, I arrange to have myself invited to his home. Although the home-inspection procedure is a less satisfactory means of determining his affluence than is peering into his checkbook, I can adequately gauge his wealth by the furnishings, and especially by the size of his color television screen (21 inches and up is a positive sign), or by examining the selections in his wine rack. (If the rack contains some Dom Perignon, Mums, Rothschild, or the like, I can assume that he is in better financial shape than I am.) If both of these ploys prove unworkable, I engage him in a conversation about credit card companies. If he admits to having a Diner's Club card, a Carte Blanche, or an American Express card, I can assume that he will at least be able to charge a fine dinner.

After I have selected my host, I must choose an appropriate restaurant. This I do by inquiring of friends who dine out often or by reading gourmet reviews (since I live in a metropolitan area). Another method of choosing an appropriate restaurant (which is more effort than the above two methods) is to tour restaurants myself and read the menus. Many fine restaurants place their menus in outdoor glass display cases, but sometimes I have to go inside and explain to the maître d' that I wish to see the menu prior to bringing a group of twenty to the restaurant the following week. I also determine a restaurant's quality by examining its wine list, entree selections, specialties, and service. Money is no object.

Now I am ready to invite my friend to dinner. I meet him at the restaurant and begin by ordering two or three drinks for each of us (the drinks are to dull his wits—and his suspicions). I enjoy a fine meal of several courses, being liberal with the wine selection and ordering as many tantalizing pastries and glacés as I desire, and I make sure to have at least one after-dinner drink. In order to get my friend to pay, I proceed in the following manner: (1) during the dinner conversation, I reveal that I am in a financial bind, but that I expect my fortunes to increase in the near future; (2) I talk about the unexpected expenses I have had lately; (3) I discuss in depth the profound friendship that I enjoy with my host. When the check arrives, I look the other way. If my conversational ploy has succeeded, my friend will feel a moral obligation to pay the whole check. If not, more drastic steps are in order. The most obvious is to begin a frantic search for my missing wallet. If, however, I feel a desire for the dramatic, I feign a sudden epileptic fit or heart seizure. Naturally, my friend will rapidly pay the bill prior to assisting me to the car. With luck, he will be too embarrassed to request the money upon my recovery.

In order to follow the three steps of selecting a friend, locating a good restaurant, and duping my host, I must overcome any moral sensibilities I sometimes harbor. As the poet says, "The enjoyment of the culinary art is man's most noble and most ennobling duty."

student essay

EXERCISES

1. Respond to the following questions with specific reference to the preceding essays:
   a. How are smaller steps subordinated to the main steps?
   b. Is there a method of development other than process in the essays?
   c. Has necessary information been overlooked in either of the selections? Does any undefined jargon appear?
   d. Does any of the smaller steps require elaboration?
2. Develop a process paper on one of the following subjects:
   a. how to care for a certain kind of animal
   b. how to prepare a certain kind of dinner
   c. how to visit the dentist courageously
   d. how to quit smoking
   e. how to improve your skills at a certain sport
   f. how to build or maintain a certain piece of mechanical equipment

---

These tasks apply to the *process* method of development:

- To make the process simple to follow, organize the many small steps involved in the process into a few main steps.

- If your audience is to see itself as a participant in the process, use the second person ("you"); if the circumstances of the process vary from person to person, give a case history of your own performing of the process, using the first person ("I").

- Define any technical terminology that may be unfamiliar to your audience.

- Be sure to provide all essential information.

CAUSAL ANALYSIS

Causal analysis is a method of development that reveals and discusses a cause-effect relationship. Consider this statement, for example: "Continual interference by adults in children's squabbles results in many children's being unable to solve their own problems." The statement points up first a cause and then its effect, as does the following: "Exposing your skin to smoke from burning poison ivy can bring on a rash." Either of these cause-effect statements may be developed by citing examples, statistics, or case histories.

There are different types of causes, and sometimes cause-effect assertions need to be qualified. The declaration, for example, that "cigarette smoking causes lung cancer" is not true in the case of all smokers. Many smokers never contract lung cancer at all. But the assertion, "Cigarette smoking *can cause* lung cancer," is supported by clinical evidence; thus, it is a statement of *sufficient* cause. Other sorts of causes are termed *contributing*. For instance, the observation that a certain mine cave-in resulted from shoring with rotten timbers may state a contributing, rather than a sufficient, cause. Rotten timbers along with the instability created by a fault vein that shifted above the mine caused the cave-in. Similarly, the assertion that "Mary's poor vision caused her to stumble" may point to only one of several contributing causes, such as icy sidewalks and poor coordination.

The following is an example of cause-effect development. The writers also use exposition in presenting the reasons for the development of tornadoes.

Rising air, like air flowing toward a *Low*, moves spirally in a counterclockwise manner, thereby causing extremely low pressure in the center of the rising column. The lower the pressure, the stronger the winds, the greater the gyratory action in the updraft and the more intense the low pressure becomes. The lowering pressure cools the air rapidly to below the dew point; as a result, a cloud develops in conformity with this chimney of low pressure; hence, the characteristic funnel-shaped cloud. . . . The very low pressure (as low as 23 inches recorded at Minneapolis in August, 1904) causes buildings to explode when the funnel cloud reaches the ground, and the terrific velocities of the wind—perhaps as great as 500 miles per hour— usually prostrate every standing object in the tornado's path.

Clarence E. Koeppe and George C. De Long,
Weather and Climate

EXERCISE

Respond to the following with specific reference to the above paragraph:

1. Identify the cause-effect relationship asserted in the topic sentence.
2. Does the above paragraph make use of sufficient or contributing cause?

Examine the cause-effect logic in the following selection from a magazine article:

"CAN'T ANYONE HERE SPEAK ENGLISH?"

"The Americans," Walt Whitman wrote in the 1850s, "are going to be the most fluent and melodious-voiced people in the world, and the most perfect users of words." The line was more hopeful than prophetic. Today, many believe that the American language has lost not only its melody but a lot of its meaning. Schoolchildren and even college students often seem disastrously ignorant of words; they stare, uncomprehending, at simple declarative English. Leon Botstein, president of New York's Bard College, says with glum hyperbole: "The English language is dying, because it is not taught." Others believe that the language is taught badly and learned badly because American culture is awash with clichés, officialese, political bilge, the surreal boobspeak of advertising ("Mr. Whipple, please don't squeeze the cortex") and the sludge of academic writing. It would be no wonder if children exposed to such discourse grew up with at least an unconscious hostility to language itself.

Much of the current concern about language is only a pedant's despair. Some of the preoccupation masks a cynical delight in the absurdities that people are capable of perpetrating with words. No one worries very much about the schoolmarm's strictures against "ain't" and "it's me." Connoisseurs savor genuine follies, like those of the new priests of thanatology, who describe dying as "terminal living," or the Secretary of Health, Education and Welfare who explained a $61.7 million cut in social services as "advance downward adjustments." But whatever mirth there may be in these and other buffooneries, euphemisms, pomposities, tautologies, evasions and rococo lies, they are also signals of a new brainlessness in public language that coincides with a frightening ineptitude for reading and writing among the young.

Some linguistic purists wrongly fear slang and neologisms; these are the life signs of a language, its breath on the mirror. The danger now is something that seems new and ominous: an indifference to language, a devaluation that leaves it bloodless and zombie-like. It is as if language had ceased to be important, to be worthy of attention. Television undoubtedly has something to do with that. With its chaotic parade of images, TV makes language subordinate, merely a part of the general noise. It has certainly subverted the idea of reading as entertainment. A recent study by A. C. Nielsen Co. found that Americans watch a numbing average of 3.8 hours of TV per day.

Part of the devaluation of language results from a feeling that somehow it is no longer effective. Samuel Johnson's society pinned its faith on language; Americans attach theirs to technology. It is not words that put men on the moon, that command technology's powerful surprises. Man does not ascend to heaven by prayer, the aspiration of language, but by the complex rockets and computer codes of NASA.

The indifference to language is also a result of Viet Nam and Watergate. An accumulation of lies inevitably corrupts the language in which the lies are told. After an American bombing raid in Cambodia, a U.S. Air Force colonel complained to reporters: "You always write it's bombing, bombing, bombing. It's not bombing! It's air support." The classic of the war, of course, came from the American officer who explained: "It was necessary to destroy the village in order to save it." In Nixon's White House, concealing information became "containment." "I was wrong" or "I lied" became "I misspoke myself." And so on. Abuse of power is usually attended by abuse of language. Viet Nam and Watergate, along with later revelations about the FBI and CIA, have encouraged a cynical, almost conspiratorial view that public words are intended to conceal, not to transmit, the truth.

Time, August 25, 1975

EXERCISES

1. Consider the following questions about the above article:
   a. Are sufficient causes for language decay brought out? If so, what are they?
   b. Are contributing causes brought out? If so, identify them.
   c. Do you accept the statements of cause-effect logic? Why or why not?
2. Discuss each of the following as a *sufficient* or as a *contributing* cause:

 a. Charlie wore blue jeans to church because he wanted to irritate his mother.
 b. The President allowed 100,000 refugees into our country because of his humanitarian principles.
 c. This kitchen is hot because :hirty people are packed into it.
 d. Coach Smith produces winning basketball teams because he has ten years of major league experience.
 e. Radial tires improve gas mileage.
 f. Doctors usually charge high fees to recoup the high cost of their education.
 g. The haystack burned because lightning struck it.
 h. Alcoholism causes marriages to fail.
3. Develop a paragraph on one of the above by combining causal analysis with narration, analogy, description, comparison/contrast, or illustrations/details/examples.

Development by *causal analysis* involves these tasks:

- Be certain the cause-effect relationship indeed exists.

- Identify the cause as contributing or sufficient.

- Provide supporting evidence by using narration, description, or another appropriate means of development.

- If you use an analogy for clarification, do not mistake it for supporting evidence.

CONCESSION

Concession is a means of development that acknowledges the main points of the arguments opposing your own. It usually forms only a small portion of a larger piece of writing, and it is usually most effective when it comes early in the piece. If you graciously acknowledge the logical points of your opponent's argument, you may engage the sympathies not only of those who are already on your side but also of those who are undecided. You may even gain the ear of your opponent. Concession has an important function in the process of persuasion. Enumeration of the opposing arguments, in a fair and unslanted presentation, can help you to present the arguments concisely and can help the audience to grasp the issues more easily.

Nearly any controversial issue—be it abortion, busing, defense spending, or gun control—does have sound arguments on both the pro and con sides. If you fail to acknowledge the well-founded arguments of the opposition, you risk alienating an intelligent and well-informed reader.

Examine the following introductory paragraph:

> Many so-called environmentalists are determined to destroy the American automobile industry through a lot of unreasonable demands that only show that they don't know what they are talking about.

Here the writer is obviously unwilling to concede that those opposing his position may be well-intentioned and may have valid points to present. As a result, he presents himself as biased and narrow-minded. Moreover, his dismissal of the opposition as "environmentalists" who make "a lot of unreasonable demands" succeeds only in muddying the issue because he fails to state specifically what those demands are or how they pose a threat to the automobile industry. Finally, the writer's charge that the "so-called environmentalists . . . don't know what they are talking about" further confuses the reader because the writer has not explained the opposition view.

In the following introductory paragraph, the writer uses concession to suggest his fair and studied approach to an issue. By enumerating the environmentalists' demands, the writer focuses attention on the specific points of contention:

> A growing number of environmentalists have insisted that the American automobile manufacturers drastically reduce the size and weight of their cars. Such reductions, they argue, would lead to greater fuel economy on our highways, thereby helping to solve our gasoline shortage, easing oil imports, and generally strengthening the national economy. Well intentioned as the environmentalists may be, and valid as their insistence on energy conservation doubtless is, they need to consider the impact their proposals would have on the nation's largest economic union, the automobile producers and consumers.

student essay

EXERCISES

1. Compare the diction, or choice of words, in the preceding two examples. What, for instance, does the first writer achieve with reference to "so-called," "environmentalists," "destroy," "unreasonable demands," "they

don't know what they are talking about"? In the second example, what does the writer achieve by acknowledging that the opposition may be "well intentioned," and that "their insistence on energy conservation" is "valid"?

2. Choose a current issue, such as gun control, welfare, or abortion, and draw up a list of pro and con arguments. Take one side on the issue and write an introductory paragraph employing concession.

In developing by *concession*, perform these tasks:

- Identify the main points of the opposition argument.

- Acknowledge those points that are logically valid.

- Word your acknowledgment in a fair, unemotional manner.

GENERALIZATIONS

A generalization is a statement concerning or applied to a set of things, ideas, or instances. For example, "Dogs make dangerous passengers in automobiles" is a generalization. The statement applies to an entire set of creatures in a certain circumstance.

Though specific details are usually necessary for convincing an audience, a few types of writing do not require that all generalizations be supported. In report or plot summaries and in abstracts of articles or discussions, you can assume that your reader already has some specific knowledge of the subject matter. The objective in these types of writing is more to provide general information than to persuade. When summarizing someone else's material, it is helpful to make an outline by extracting the thesis and topic sentences; if the topic sentences are implied rather than openly stated, formulate the topic sentences yourself.

The following illustrates the generalization method of development. The writers maintain a smooth flow from sentence to sentence, not allowing choppiness—a danger in this method—to set in.

> Drama begins in make-believe, in the play-acting of children, in the ritual of primitive religion. And it never forsakes its primitive beginnings, for imitative action is its essence. When an actor appears on stage, he makes believe he is someone other than himself,

much as a child does, much as primitive people still do. Thus like play-acting and ritual, drama creates its experience by doing things that can be heard and seen. "Drama," in fact, comes from a Greek word which means "thing done." And the things it does, as with play-acting and ritual, create a world apart—a world modelled on our own, but one which has its own charmed existence.

Robert Scholes and Carl H. Klaus, *Elements of Drama*

The above paragraph discusses the general nature of all drama. Though a paragraph on such a broad subject is necessarily abstract as well as general, notice that it attempts to give the reader a concrete foothold with the generalized example, "When an actor appears on stage . . ."

The following paragraph is also developed by generalizations; it deals with a related topic, "play," but as a psychological rather than as a purely dramatic concept. The paragraph serves the function of summarizing various theories.

Psychology and physiology deal with the observation, description and explanation of the play of animals, children, and grown-ups. They try to determine the nature and significance of play and to assign it its place in the scheme of life. The high importance of this place and the necessity, or at least the utility, of play as a function are generally taken for granted and form the starting-point of all such scientific researches. The numerous attempts to define the biological function of play show a striking variation. By some the origin and fundamentals of play have been described as a discharge of super-abundant vital energy, by others as the satisfaction of some "imitative instinct," or again as simply a "need" for relaxation. According to another it serves as an exercise in restraint needful to the individual. Some find the principle of play in an innate urge to exercise a certain faculty, or in the desire to dominate or compete. Yet others regard it as an "abreaction"—an outlet for harmful impulses, as the necessary restorer of energy wasted by one-sided activity, as "wish-fulfillment," as a fiction designed to keep up the feeling of personal value, etc.

Johan Huizinga, *Homo Ludens*

The writer manages to cover several theories of psychology and physiology in a single paragraph, smoothly connecting the theories by comparing and contrasting them and by employing such connectives as "by some," "by others," "or again," "according to another," "some find," "yet others regard." (Additional discussion of *transitions* appears in the treatment of *parallelism* in chapter 13.)

EXERCISE

Select one of the following subjects and, by using the generalizations method of development, construct an essay (approximately 500 words) that provides general information about that subject. Remember to look for comparison/ contrast connections and to employ appropriate transitional phrases and words:

1. theater
2. television commercials
3. abstract art
4. a kind of music
5. novels
6. a campus

Development by *generalizations* involves the following tasks:

- Cover all the main points and as many subpoints as space permits.

- Employ transitional phrases and words.

The process of developing a summary of someone else's material is similar:

- Examine the material for ideas, concepts, and information.

- Outline the material.

- Cover each point as thoroughly as possible within the limits of space available.

- Employ transitional phrases and words where necessary.

RESTATEMENT

As a method of paragraph development, restatement (like generalizations) is a means of summing up main points. When used carefully, it is also a device for emphasis and clarification.

The process of restatement has the following steps: (1) succinctly present the basic, abstract idea in the first sentence; (2) provide a brief series of undeveloped examples that make the abstraction concrete; (3) with proper diction variety, conclude the paragraph with a restatement of the abstraction. Step one, for example, could be an abstract statement such as the following:

> Some men have consciously chosen an isolated life.

Step two (restating the abstraction concretely) might then consist of this:

> A poet of the last century might have gone into the forest to be isolated because the separation from society helped him develop theories about the individual's relationship with his God. Some have willingly rejected society in order to explore man's ability to rely on himself. Others, such as J. D. Salinger, have gone into isolation for reasons the public has not yet discovered.

The third step, restatement of the abstraction, might then be:

> When a life of isolation is a choice of the individual, the pain of loneliness need not follow from that choice.

Examine the following paragraph:

> Insist on yourself; never imitate. Your own gift you can present every moment with the cumulative force of a whole life's cultivation; but of the adopted talent of another you have only an extemporaneous half possession. That which each can do best, none but his Maker can teach him. No man yet knows what it is, nor can, till that person has exhibited it. Where is the master who could have taught Shakspeare? Where is the master who could have instructed Franklin, or Washington, or Bacon, or Newton? Every great man is unique. The Scipionism of Scipio is precisely that part he could not borrow. Shakspeare will never be made by the study of Shakspeare. Do that which is assigned to you, and you cannot hope too much or dare too much. . . .
>
> Ralph Waldo Emerson, "Self-Reliance"

EXERCISES

1. Consider the following with specific reference to Emerson's paragraph:
   a. What abstract thought does Emerson present?
   b. When is it first evident?

    c. How is the abstraction made concrete?

    d. How is the abstraction finally restated?

2. Develop a paragraph of restatement, employing the three-step process.

The *restatement* method of development involves these tasks:

- Present the main abstract idea succinctly in the first sentence.

- Provide a series of undeveloped examples to make the abstraction concrete.

- Restate the abstraction.

Ordering the Material

9

Try to keep an open mind about matters of organization throughout the writing process. Don't assume that the order in which ideas first occur to you, or even the order you plan upon at the conclusion of the prewriting process, is necessarily the best order for presenting the topic to your audience.

As you consider how to arrange the points in your composition, ask yourself what arrangement promises to emphasize the most important points. Ask yourself also what arrangement will best convince your audience that your thesis is valid.

When considering alternative arrangements, examine your material from these five points of view: the *chronological,* the *spatial,* the *chronological and spatial combined,* and the *inductive* and *deductive.* Each of these five approaches to organization will suggest a different order of development, both for entire papers and for paragraphs within papers.

CHRONOLOGICAL ORDER

If you use a chronological order of development, you need to ask, "In what order did (or do) these events actually take place?" Your developmental order, then, will be the order in which the events, or the steps in a process, occurred in time.

The following example is an account of a natural disaster in a rural African village as recalled by a man who witnessed it. The author allows the unfolding of events in their natural order to shape his narrative.

When I was a schoolboy a locust invasion came to my home area. An elderly man who was a neighbour and relative of ours, burnt a "medicine" in his field, to keep away the locusts. Within a few hours the locusts had eaten up virtually everything green including crops, trees and grass, and then flown off in their large swarms. Everybody was grieved and horrified by the great tragedy which had struck us, for locust invasions always mean that all the food is destroyed and people face famine. Word went round our community, however, that the locusts had not touched any crops in the field of our neighbour who had used "medicine." I went there to see it for myself, and sure enough his crops remained intact while those of other people next door were completely devastated. I had heard that a few people possessed anti-locust "medicines," but this was the first person I knew who had actually used such medicine and with positive results.

John S. Mbiti, *African Religions and Philosophy*

The chronology established in Mbiti's account simply follows the events as they unfold: (1) the precautions that the elderly man takes against the locusts; (2) the locust attack; (3) the results of that attack; (4) the effect of the attack on the villagers; (5) the report that the elderly man's fields have been spared; (6) the narrator visiting the man's fields and confirming that the reports are true.

Chronological progression may have variations. For example, instead of arranging events strictly in time sequence, you might emphasize the most important by presenting it first, then provide the chronological background events, and finally discuss the outcome or conclusion of the incident (see also "Narration," pp. 89–93). The following paragraph is taken from a student essay arguing that riding a motorcycle may be safer than driving a car; notice that conclusions and statements of analysis precede and follow the narrative itself:

The exposed position of the cyclist seems to make him more vulnerable to injury and accidents, but his extra alertness and his protective clothing allow the skilled bike rider to walk away from otherwise disastrous incidents. I was riding in my neighborhood at 35 miles per hour when, unexpectedly, a driver pulled out in front of me and blocked the entire street. I slammed on my brakes, causing the bike to skid, stood up for better control, avoided the car but smashed into the curb. To save my bike I thrust myself toward the street, forcing the bike to land on the grass. I rolled the entire width of the street, yet, protected by my helmet and clothing, I got up immediately to turn off my cycle—a 35-mile-per-hour spill with no injury. The maneuverability and small size of the bike enabled it to avoid a collision that could well have been fatal if I had been driving a car. I concluded that bikes can execute seemingly minor miracles which enable them to avoid accidents. Furthermore, the apparently vulnerable situation of a cyclist actually gives him greater visibility since, unlike the motorist, he has no blind spots, no obstructions, and a much higher line of vision.

The writer *begins* his account with a conclusion about the experience that he has yet to unfold: the motorcycle rider's "extra alertness and his protective clothing allow [him] to walk away from otherwise disastrous incidents." He then provides the chronology of events that form the basis for his conclusion. Finally, he ends the paragraph by elaborating on the meaning of the first sentence.

SPATIAL ORDER

The spatial order of development involves giving a physical description from a certain vantage point. For example, a view of a city may start from the tops of the buildings and progress downward to the street, as it catalogs detail after detail. Or it may begin at the street and move upward to the tops of the buildings. Similarly, a view of a person may begin with a description of how she appears from half a block away and then describe her changing appearance as she walks nearer and nearer. Or it may begin with a close-up view and describe the person as she walks farther and farther away. As with chronological development, spatial development allows emphasis of the significant aspects of a person, object, or scene as they appear to you.

The following example of the spatial order of development is from Frank Norris's *McTeague*, the story of a dull, brutish dentist:

When he opened his Dental Parlors, he felt that his life was a success, that he could hope for nothing better. In spite of the name, there was but one room. . . . There was a washstand behind the screen in the corner where he manufactured his moulds. In the round bay window were his operating chair, his dental engine, and the movable rack on which he laid out his instruments. Three chairs, a bargain at the second-hand store, ranged themselves against the wall with military precision underneath a steel engraving of the court of Lorenzo de' Medici, which he had bought because there were a great many figures in it for the money. Over the bed-lounge hung a rifle manufacturer's advertisement calendar which he never used. The other ornaments were a small marble-topped center table covered with back numbers of *The American System of Dentistry*, a stone pug dog sitting before the little stove, and a thermometer. A stand of shelves occupied one corner, filled with the seven volumes

of *Allen's Practical Dentist*. On the top shelf McTeague kept his con-
certina and a bag of bird seed for the canary. The whole place ex-
haled a mingled odor of bedding, creosote, and ether.

Norris presents the room exactly as it would appear to someone opening the door. The view begins with the "washstand behind the screen
in the corner" and proceeds in a circular fashion around the room. The
description of the room then has a vertical order, beginning with the
"steel engraving of the court of Lorenzo de' Medici" and concluding
with the various objects on McTeague's "stand of shelves." By empha-
sizing the careful arrangement of the room and the objects it contains,
Norris is able to suggest much about McTeague's nature, personality,
and taste.

One of the most famous passages in literature is Herman Melville's
description of Captain Ahab in *Moby Dick*. Viewed through the eyes
of Ishmael, the narrator, Ahab takes on a frightening aspect:

> There seemed no sign of common bodily illness about him, nor of
> the recovery from any. He looked like a man cut away from the
> stake, when the fire has overrunningly wasted all the limbs without
> consuming them, or taking away one particle from their compacted
> aged robustness. His whole high, broad form, seemed made of solid
> bronze. . . . Threading its way out from among his grey hairs, and
> continuing right down one side of his tawny scorched face and neck,
> till it disappeared in his clothing, you saw a slender rod-like mark,
> lividly whitish. It resembled that perpendicular seam sometimes
> made in the straight, lofty trunk of a great tree, when the upper
> lightning tearingly darts down it, and without wrenching a single
> twig, peels and grooves out the bark from top to bottom, ere run-
> ning off into the soil, leaving the tree still greenly alive, but
> branded. . . .
>
> So powerfully did the whole grim aspect of Ahab affect me, and
> the livid brand which streaked it, that for the first few moments I
> hardly noted that not a little of this overbearing grimness was owing
> to the barbaric white leg upon which he partly stood. It had pre-
> viously come to me that this ivory leg had at sea been fashioned
> from the polished bone of the sperm whale's jaw.

Melville employs spatial development. Ishmael begins with Ahab's
general aspect—"a man cut away from the stake"—and then supports
his impression by directing attention to Ahab's head where he notices
"a rod-like mark, lividly whitish." The development moves vertically,
from top to bottom, and concludes with a description of Ahab's leg,
"fashioned from the polished bone of the sperm whale's jaw." The
spatial order of development aids Melville in comparing Ahab to a tree

that has been struck by lightning. Just as Ahab has been branded by the "rod-like mark" that runs the length of his frame, lightning darts down the tree trunk and "grooves out the bark from top to bottom . . . leaving the tree still greenly alive, but branded."

CHRONOLOGICAL AND SPATIAL ORDER COMBINED

Employing a combination of chronological and spatial development lets you stress the perspective of the narrator in relation to the unfolding of events. You can alternate description and narration, proceeding first spatially, then chronologically, then spatially, and so on.

In the following passage from "Araby," a narrative about first love, James Joyce uses a combination of the chronological and spatial modes of development:

> When the short days of winter came dusk fell before we had well eaten our dinners. When we met in the street the houses had grown sombre. The space of sky above us was the colour of everchanging violet and towards it the lamps of the street lifted their feeble lanterns. The cold air stung us and we played till our bodies glowed. Our shouts echoed in the silent street. The career of our play brought us through the dark muddy lanes behind the houses where we ran the gauntlet of the rough tribes from the cottages, to the back doors of the dark dripping gardens where odours arose from the ashpits, to the dark odorous stables where a coachman smoothed and combed the horse or shook music from the buckled harness. When we returned to the street light from the kitchen windows had filled the areas. If my uncle was seen turning the corner we hid in the shadow until we had seen him safely housed. Or if Mangan's sister came out on the doorstep to call her brother in to his tea we watched her from our shadow peer up and down the street. We waited to see whether she would remain or go in and, if she remained, we left our shadow and walked up to Mangan's steps resignedly. She was waiting for us, her figure defined by the light from the half-opened door. Her brother always teased her before he obeyed and I stood by the railings looking at her. Her dress swung as she moved her body and the soft rope of her hair tossed from side to side.

The young narrator uses vertical progression, moving from the houses "grown sombre" to the "everchanging violet" sky. Horizontal progression presents "the muddy lanes," "the dark dripping gardens," and the "odorous stables," outlining the physical confines of the boy's world. Simultaneously he presents a chronology of events: the boys dashing from the street to the lanes behind the houses to the back doors of the gardens to the stables and then back to the street, where they watch first for the boy's uncle and then for Mangan's sister. And when she appears, Joyce subtly combines the chronological with the spatial: the boys leave their "shadow" and walk up the steps to the door, where the narrator stands "by the railings" looking at "her figure defined by the light," her dress swinging, and "the soft rope of her hair tossed from side to side."

INDUCTIVE ORDER

Rather than relying only on the chronological or spatial method for arranging your material, you may also employ either the inductive or deductive order of development. Both are particularly suitable for exposition and argumentation, for they stress specific evidence and the conclusions drawn from that evidence.

With inductive development, you first present the evidence and then provide the main point (the conclusions drawn from the evidence) at the end. In the following excerpt from *Dombey and Son*, Charles Dickens uses induction to stress his criticism of industrial "progress." (In the first line, "earthquake" is used figuratively, not literally.)

> The first shock of a great earthquake had . . . rent the whole neighborhood to its center. Traces of its course were visible on every side. Houses were knocked down; streets broken through and stopped; deep pits and trenches dug in the ground; enormous heaps of earth and clay thrown up; buildings that were undermined and shaking, propped by great beams of wood. Here, a chaos of carts, overthrown and jumbled together, lay topsy-turvy at the bottom of a steep unnatural hill; there, confused treasures of iron soaked and rusted in something that had accidentally become a pond. Everywhere were bridges that led nowhere; thoroughfares that were wholly impassible; Babel towers of chimneys, wanting half their height; temporary wooden houses and enclosures, in the most unlikely situations; carcases of ragged tenements, and fragments of unfinished walls and arches, and piles of scaffolding, and wildernesses of bricks, and giant forms of cranes, and tripods straddling above nothing. There were a hundred thousand shapes and substances of incompleteness, wildly mingled out of their places, upside down, burrowing in the earth, aspiring in the air, mouldering in the water, and unintelli-

gible as any dream. Hot springs and fiery eruptions, the usual atten-
dants upon earthquakes, lent their contributions of confusion to the
scene. Boiling water hissed and heaved within dilapidated walls;
whence, also, the glare and roar of flames came issuing forth; and
mounds of ashes blocked up rights of way, and wholly changed the
law and custom of the neighborhood.

In short, the yet unfinished and unopened Railroad was in progress; and, from the very core of all this dire disorder, trailed
smoothly away, upon its mighty course of civilization and improvement.

While Dickens does use the spatial order of development to catalog the
chaos that the building of a railroad imposes on "civilization," he is
also working inductively. He cites specific evidence of the railroad's
destructive effect on society in the first paragraph, and, based on that
evidence, he concludes in the second paragraph that the "progress"
usually associated with the railroad is really nothing but "dire disorder."

DEDUCTIVE ORDER

Equally effective for exposition and argumentation is the deductive
order of development in which you first set forth your conclusion and
then follow it with the premises of your argument and the support for
those premises. The following paragraph, from an essay arguing for
reform in the judicial system, is an example of deductive development:

Some juveniles who commit crimes against the elderly are quickly
arrested by the police and just as quickly released by judges to
return to the streets and commit more crimes. In the past week, two
juveniles, one 14 and the other 16, were arrested for mugging and
raping an 84-year-old woman. Because of their youth, they were
released on $500 bail that same evening. They were arrested the next
day for mugging a 93-year-old man. In another instance, a gang of
five teen-age prostitutes set upon an elderly West German ambassa-
dor, knifed him, and fled with his money. Arrested near the scene of
the crime, the prostitutes were charged with juvenile delinquency,
and they were released the same evening to the custody of their
parents. Three of these girls were arrested one month later for the
robbery and murder of a retired social worker.

student essay

In the above paragraph, the initial sentence presents the conclusion; the evidence (specific examples) that supports this conclusion follows in the next six sentences.

EXERCISES

1. Write a paragraph narrating either a happy or an unpleasant event in your life. Use the chronological order of development, after placing the most important fact first.
2. Write a paragraph describing a favorite room; use the spatial order of development.
3. Combine the chronological and spatial ordering schemes to develop a paragraph describing your first meeting with a person who became important to you. Use narration, if you like, as well as description.
4. Use the inductive order of development to present an analysis of the characteristics of the person in exercise 3 above.
5. Use the deductive order of development to discuss the benefits you find in one of the ways you spend your leisure time.

Concluding the 10 Composition

The conclusion is your last opportunity to put your thesis across. A good conclusion offers readers a way of viewing the composition as a whole. It eases the audience out of the piece while offering final affirmation of your thesis. Each word should contribute to the impression you wish to leave with your audience.

If the thesis has been well sustained by the body, a relatively short paper may need no separate conclusion. Do use a conclusion with longer papers, however, and with short ones that are complex—such as a process discussion involving many steps. A conclusion, like an introduction, should be of suitable length in proportion to the rest of the composition. It is handy to confine it to a single paragraph, though a conclusion can also be effective when introduced in the middle of the final paragraph.

STRATEGIES FOR CONCLUDING

When deciding upon the form a conclusion ought to take, it is useful to review your purpose, the thesis you set out to establish. Following are six strategies you may find it useful to explore as ways of concluding your paper. They include the *summary*, the *prediction*, the *question*, *recommendations*, the *quotation*, and various *combined strategies* from among the above, which often overlap.

With a Summary

Summary is the simplest—and potentially the most effective—

means of concluding. If your essay is primarily argumentative, a summary conclusion enables your reader to recall the main points of your position. Summary also works effectively with expository writing; for example, you might list the steps in a process you have just explained in order to reinforce the reader's memory. If a piece of writing is relatively lengthy, a summary conclusion can effectively reemphasize points established many pages back in the text. As these examples show, summarizing places the points of an argument, exposition, or lengthy discourse in a simple, coherent perspective for the reader. The process of writing a summary involves (1) drawing out the topic sentences from the foregoing paragraphs and (2) restating them with appropriate transitions and subordination of the less important ideas.

Note the coherence with which sociologists Nena and George O'Neill summarize their complex discussion of "trust" in their chapter on that subject:

> Trust, then, open trust, has nothing to do with expecting or doing specific, predetermined things in marriage, but rather with sharing the knowledge of your immediate desires and needs with your mate, living for now and not for yesterday or tomorrow, living not the life that somebody else has laid out for you in terms of role expectations, living instead for your own self through shared communication and growth with your mate's self. Trust then is freedom, just as Robert said in his interview with us—the freedom to assume responsibility for your own self first and then to share that human self in love with your partner in a marriage that places no restrictions upon growth, or limits on fulfillment.
>
> *Open Marriage*

The reader who has read through the O'Neills' chapter will find his memory refreshed by the conclusion since its generalities carry with them the associations of the supporting detail which preceded. Notice the transitions from thought to thought consist of contrasts: "nothing to do with . . . but rather with . . . ," "for now . . . not for yesterday . . . ," and so on. The example of Robert's interview is grammatically subordinated to the more important definition of trust.

The summary of a shorter piece of writing may be correspondingly briefer. The concluding summary of a 500-word narration concerning a frustrating trip to see a legislator simply restates the main impression:

> The frustration I felt after waiting three hours to see Senator Flush resulted not so much from the boredom of having nothing to read but seven-month-old *Newsweek* magazines but more from seeing him slip out the side door of his office after his secretary had told us that he was not in. He had been there the whole time.
>
> *student essay*

With a Prediction

Prediction is an effective means of concluding a narrative or a cause-effect discussion. If the body of the paper is a statement of events or conditions, the conclusion may suggest or predict what the results may or will be in the situation discussed or in similar situations. "If these conditions are allowed to continue, then . . ." or "If you follow the above three steps, you will find that . . ." A brief paper on a certain aspect of ecology might conclude as follows:

> If the citizens of this country continue failing to adhere to the 55-mile-per-hour speed limit, they may expect eight percent higher traffic fatalities this year as opposed to last, a two percent decrease in the amount of heating oil available next winter, and a three percent rise in utility rates and oil-produced commodity prices.

> *student essay*

The process of developing a prediction conclusion requires making certain that (1) the facts you presented in your paper are correct and (2) you have established yourself convincingly as an authority on your subject. Also, your cause-effect line of reasoning should be logically sound (see chapter 12).

In "Democracy and Anti-Intellectualism in America," Richard Hofstadter uses prediction to reassert his position:

> This world will never be governed by intellectuals—it may rest assured. But *we* must be assured, too, that intellectuals will not be altogether governed by this world, that they maintain their piety, their long-standing allegiance to the world of spiritual values to which they should belong. Otherwise there will be no intellectuals, at least not above ground. And societies in which the intellectuals have been driven underground, as we have had occasion to see in our own time, are societies in which even the anti-intellectuals are unhappy.

With a Question

Closing with a question lets your reader make his own prediction, draw his own conclusion. For example:

> If the so-called "fair-trade" laws are not abolished, will the consumer be able to absorb another two percent increase in the cost of living this year?

Or

> If abortions are allowed after the fetus is more than twenty-six weeks old, shall we not consider this an act of murder?

Or

> Which, then, does the public find more valuable, the rights of the fetus to life, or the rights of the mother to have the say-so about what happens to her own body?

You can adapt a question conclusion to fit two types of audiences. If you are addressing persons who already agree with your position, a rhetorical question (one that assumes knowledge of the answer the reader would give) can serve to arouse additional enthusiasm for your position. The first of the two questions above on the subject of abortion is slanted in such a way (by the "not") that the writer anticipates his audience responding "Yes! We should consider this an act of murder!" The second of the questions on abortion may work best with an audience whose sympathies are uncertain or with an audience whose position opposes your own. Notice that you cannot tell from the question alone which position the writer holds; ideally, the writer's attitude on the question has been apparent from the material preceding the conclusion. Having presented your attitude reasonably, without emotion, you can hope to have two effects on your audience: (1) those strongly opposed to your views have at least allowed themselves to reconsider the question; (2) those who were unsure can now make the decision to agree with your views.

With Recommendations

A recommendations closing is one that stresses the actions or remedies that should be taken. For example, an argument opposing Ace Oil Corporation's plan to use its high profits to purchase Buffalo Brothers' Circus might conclude with a call for a letter campaign to Senator Basketsweat, whose committee oversees policies of energy development. A discussion of the failure of the school board to appropriate adequate money for the education of retarded children might conclude with a request that the board follow the principles of the State Education Act.

George Orwell, a noted British author, includes near the closing of his "Politics and the English Language" six specific recommendations for improving the use of the language:

Afterwards one can choose—not simply *accept*—the phrases that will best cover the meaning, and then switch round and decide what impressions one's words are likely to make on another person. This last effort of the mind cuts out all stale or mixed images, all prefabricated phrases, needless repetitions, and humbug and vagueness generally. But one can often be in doubt about the effect of a word or a phrase, and one needs rules that one can rely on when instinct fails. I think the following rules will cover most cases:

(i)   Never use a metaphor, simile or other figure of speech which you are used to seeing in print.

(ii)   Never use a long word where a short one will do.

(iii) If it is possible to cut a word out, always cut it out.

(iv)   Never use the passive where you can use the active.

(v)   Never use a foreign phrase, a scientific word or a jargon word if you can think of an everyday English equivalent.

(vi)   Break any of these rules sooner than say anything barbarous.

These rules sound elementary, and so they are, but they demand a deep change of attitude in anyone who has grown used to writing in the style now fashionable.

Shooting an Elephant and Other Essays

With a Quotation

Since a quotation may summarize, predict, question, or call for action, you may use a quotation within a conclusion (or as the entire conclusion) for nearly any kind of paper, from argument to narrative.

Suppose you were writing an essay on the philosophy of Horatio Alger. You might end the essay effectively by quoting Tom Nelson, Alger's hero in *The Young Adventurer*, since Nelson's words typify the author's philosophy. Tempted to keep a money-filled wallet he has found, Tom thinks, "It wouldn't be honest . . . and if I began in that way I could not expect that God would prosper me."

A concluding quotation can also make an appeal to authority (see chapter 12) especially forceful. If in your writing you cite the views of an expert in the field that your paper discusses, the direct words of the expert, if clear and not too technical for your own audience, may make a stronger impression than your own summary of the expert's views. In the following conclusion (which is largely summary), psychologist Thomas Harris uses a quotation by the philosopher Will Durant to give authority to Harris's own philosophy:

We cannot produce responsible persons until we help them un-
cover the I'M NOT OK—YOU'RE OK position which underlies the
complicated and destructive games they play. Once we understand
positions and games, freedom of response begins to emerge as a real
possibility. As long as people are bound by the past, they are not
free to respond to the needs and aspirations of others in the present;
and "to say that we are free," says Will Durant, "is merely to mean
that we know what we are doing."

I'm OK—You're OK

A paper discussing the poor qualifications of certain modern political leaders effectively emphasizes party leaders' attitudes by concluding as follows:

In *Plunkitt of Tammany Hall*, William L. Riordan records the
thoughts of the corrupt politician, George Washington Plunkitt, on
the subject of education and political leadership: "Most of the leaders are plain American citizens, of the people and near to the people,
and they have all the education they need to whip the dudes who
part their name in the middle and to run the City Government. We
got bookworms, too, in the organization. But we don't make them
district leaders. We keep them for ornaments on parade days."

student essay

With Combined Strategies

Combinations of the above kinds of conclusions provide a variety of
additional choices. For instance, if you have discussed a problem, you
may end with *recommendations,* suggestions of ways to improve conditions. If the problem you discuss is abortion, you may conclude with
a *quotation* of recommendations by an authority in medicine or soci-
ology. If you are writing on the need for environmental protection,
you may use *prediction, recommendations,* and perhaps also *quotation* or
question.

The process of devising a conclusion is best determined by the
answer to the questions, "Who is my audience?" and "What type of
conclusion will best sway my audience to my way of thinking?"

**Ways to conclude an essay vary according to the
writer's purpose and the form of writing used:**

- If the purpose is to explain and make clear (as in

exposition), consider concluding with a summary, a quotation, recommendations, or a combination from among these types.

- If the purpose is to give an account of an action or a series of actions (as in narration), consider concluding with a summary, a quotation, or both.

- If the purpose is to portray a person, place, or object, or a combination of persons, places, or objects (as in description), consider concluding with a summary, a quotation, or both.

- If the purpose is to present a course of reasoning (as in argumentation), consider concluding with a summary, a quotation, recommendations, a prediction, a question, or a combination from among these types.

ARRIVING AT A TITLE

Titling an essay well makes the essay more effective. A title announces your topic simply and briefly, and it also may suggest your attitude toward your topic. But a title need not be mysterious or clever, highly imaginative or comic. Wit may—depending on your subject—be appropriate, but concentrate primarily on giving the reader enough straightforward information on your topic so that he will want to read further. A reader who approaches your paper with indifference may be put off by a title that is too mysterious or cute.

A title may be ineffective through inappropriate tone, as when a serious subject receives a comic or light-hearted title. Some titles appear strained because they contain words that are rarely used, or because of rhymes or distractingly heavy alliteration (repetition of the same initial sound in two or more words). Other titles may be weak because they are vague. Whether simple or imaginative, an effective title suggests clearly and simply the general nature of your thesis.

EXERCISE

Examine the following thesis statements and accompanying titles, deciding which titles are inappropriate. Explain why you find them inappropriate and suggest a better title for each thesis statement.

THESIS STATEMENT	POSSIBLE TITLES
Although many cooks think of soup as uninteresting—something to be dumped out of a can—the best cooks fully understand the art and rewards of creating a savory potage.	Supping Soups A Good Potage Is No Mirage Soup's On!
Weight gain is a matter of metabolism.	The Futility of Dieting Hey, Fatso! Meatballs and Metabolism
Thousands of Americans waste thousands of dollars because they are not aware of the services of the Rent-a-Coffin Corporation.	Live Like a Pauper, Die Like a King Death: A Serious Inquiry into the Practices Regarding Funerals
There are five steps to disassembling a lobster for easy eating.	Dinner Dissection How to Dismember a Lobster
Getting caught shoplifting was one of the most fortunate things that ever happened to me.	Stop, Thief! Sweating a Snatch Rehabilitating Shoplifters
The U.S. government should not limit production of highpower automobiles.	Vrooom! Conservation by Legislation Bringing Ecology to General Motors

PART THREE

The Revision Process

The final aspect of the writing process is *revision*. During revision, you stand back from your work to see whether it effectively communicates the thesis you intended, in a manner that will suit the intended audience.

Like prewriting, revision is a part of the writing process that you should never omit. Some short papers may require only a single draft, which is then polished and prepared in final form. Other papers may need several drafts in order to flow smoothly and logically. Generally speaking, the longer and more complex the paper, the more revision it deserves. However, *all* writing benefits from conscientious revision.

Even if you revise frequently as you write, there should come a time when you put the work aside and then return to it, trying to imagine that you are reading someone else's work. Your first consideration should be whether the material establishes clear organization and sufficient, convincing development. Then additional shaping and polishing are in order.

Following are four central aspects of the revision process. These tasks, indeed, are important throughout written communication. Think of the revision process not as a last-minute task but as an integral part of the writing process.

considering your language

reviewing your logic

improving your sentences

checking mechanics

The revision process as a whole is illustrated in Appendix A. There a student essay appears in three progressive drafts, affording a unified view of one paper being strengthened by revision.

Considering   **11**
Your Language

Let us look now at the medium that writers use to guide readers: the medium of language. The language of written communication, of course, is words. At one level, your writing is simply a quantity of words, one following another. Indeed you cannot communicate with your audience except through choice and arrangement of words. Readers cannot see your facial expression or hear your tone of voice. They cannot visualize what you are visualizing unless you guide them.

Effective writers therefore strive for good *diction*, the best choice of words. Revising for diction should be an ongoing part of the writing process at all times. Moreover, language should be considered again before the work is submitted to its intended audience.

Your message will be communicated emphatically and persuasively if you present it in language that is simple, fresh, specific, and honest. Be sensitive to ideas and attitudes that your audience may associate with a given word (its connotations), and use words that work well together.

SIMPLICITY

In written communication, not only does every word count but every ineffective word hurts. Avoid cluttering your writing with words that lack precision. Have no fear of saying things simply, in language suitable for your audience. From your experience as a reader, you know that it is difficult to understand writers who are vague or wordy or otherwise clumsy with language. As you learn to handle language with greater control, you will appreciate how the "right word" is worth looking for, while three or four poor substitutes cannot really do the job.

When seeking to determine whether your language is suitable for its intended audience, ask yourself two questions: "Have I used words that express my idea clearly and that my audience will be likely to understand?" and "Have I chosen words because they communicate my idea, not because they show my audience how much learning I have?"

Using the Common Word

If you write about "equitation" instead of "horseback riding," you may be saying to your audience, "You can see how smart I am by the big word I know, and some of you are going to have to guess what my topic is or else wait until you have read a third of my paper to find out." Similarly, the psychologist who wrote the following sentence could easily have restated it in nonjargon so that it would be comprehensible to a general audience:

> The technique of paired comparisons of plastic forms in testing oral stereognosis . . . has apparently eliminated problems of intersensory contamination inherent in earlier methods.

Revised:

> By placing two plastic objects of different shapes in a person's mouth, I can objectively test the person's ability to recognize objects by sense of touch.

A first step in the process of revising for simplicity is to select the common word that most accurately conveys the concept under discussion. Use technical terminology only if there is no precise, common-word substitute, and define the term the first time you use it unless you are writing for an audience of experts.

Writing with Economy

A second step in revising for simplicity is to substitute, whenever possible, a single word for a phrase—so long as the substitution does not make it more difficult for the audience to understand what you are saying. That is, delete unnecessary words. An employer who responds to a job application by writing, "It has come to my attention that your missive of 29 July seeks to ascertain the potentiality of your becoming an employee with our corporation," is an employer who is likely to scare off the applicant rather than interest him in the job. In revising the letter, the employer could have written more economically—and more effectively—"I have received your letter of application."

Substituting Active for Passive

A third step in revising for simplicity is to consider substituting the active voice for the passive. *Voice* is not the same as *tense*, which indicates whether something happened in the past, present, or future. Rather, voice has to do with whether the *subject* (usually the first noun element in the sentence) *acts* or *is acted upon*, whether the subject *performs* the action or *receives* the action. For example, "Horace hits the ball" is in the active voice; Horace, the subject, the first noun in the sentence, performs the action. However, the passive statement, "The ball is hit by Horace," has the subject, the first noun in the sentence, being acted upon. The active statement has the greater simplicity: not only is the same amount of information presented in four words instead of six, but the writer is forced to present *all* the information. That is, had he used the passive, he might simply have stopped after writing, "The ball was hit." The reader would have to guess at the *agent* (who did the hitting?).

Sometimes, however, you may find it useful to employ the passive for the purpose of variety or to give special emphasis to the person or thing which receives the action. For example, "Duane was hit in the face by the bat" properly emphasizes the victim rather than the agent. Often, though, substituting the active voice for the passive will give your prose a greater degree of simplicity, action, and directness.

FRESHNESS

Effective writing is writing that sounds fresh, rather than trite. You need not be gifted with a colorful imagination to develop freshness— though such an imagination may serve you well at times.

Avoiding Clichés and Fixed Phrases

To achieve freshness, your first step is to check for clichés and fixed phrases. Clichés consist of common expressions, platitudes (flatly uninteresting observations), adages, and bits of folk wisdom so commonly used that they have become tiresome. Some examples are the following: "I'm so hungry I could eat a horse"; "as big as a house"; "as flat as a pancake"; "a sight for sore eyes"; "nip in the bud"; "the grass is always greener on the the other side of the fence." It is important to use fresh expressions not just because worn-out ones may bore your reader but also because overused expressions are often imprecise. For example, the politician who says that union members will have to "bite the bullet" to help get inflation under control is not identifying exactly the sacrifices he expects the union members to make. Suppose, however, that the same politician were to say, "XYZ Union members will have to hold their wage demands below seven percent if they want to help get inflation under control." In the second case, precise and useful information comes to the listeners' attention.

Examples of fixed phrases are "due to the fact that," "in the event that," "at this point in time," "in terms of," "in all likelihood." See if such phrases are needed at all or if shorter substitutes can serve just as well. "Because" is a ready substitute for "due to the fact that"; "if" can be used instead of "in the event that"; "now" or "then" can replace "at this point in time"; "regarding" or "as to" substitute for "in terms of"; "probably" is a less wordy way of saying "in all likelihood."

Using Figurative Language Appropriately

Your writing can be more vivid if you use appropriate figurative language—language that provides a comparison, describes something as if it were some *other* thing. Your ability to see likeness in unlike things can give your reader a new perspective. Through reliance on sensory experience, you can add interest, freshness, and perhaps even humor to your writing. In addition, because figurative language relies on association, it is economical.

Be careful not to overuse figurative language, however. Unless it is used sparingly, figurative language may distract the reader. And in some situations, such as those in which the reader wants only simple, straightforward facts, figurative language may be inappropriate.

Among your resources are, fundamentally, four kinds of figurative language: *metaphor, simile, personification,* and *allusion.*

Metaphor

A metaphor is a comparison of things that are apparently dissimilar. It provides comparison without using "like," "as," or other words that announce a comparison is being used.

Her ears are flags.

The university is an octopus wrapping its tentacles around my checkbook.

Simile

A simile compares two apparently dissimilar things, softening the comparison by using the qualifiers "like" or "as." Instead of saying "A *is* B" (metaphor), the simile says "A *is like* B" (or "A is *as* B").

> He returned her dropped handkerchief as if it were a wet diaper.

> The petshop owner's voice wheezed and whined like that of an asthmatic guinea pig.

Personification

Personification is a figure of speech that is particularly useful for emphasis. To personify is to speak of an abstraction or nonhuman thing as if it were a person. Personification appears, for example, in the clichés Father Time and Mother Nature. Personification can effectively endow nonhuman things or abstractions with human characteristics, as in the following:

> The automatic dishwasher gargled, then spit the sudsy water into the sink.

> The wind reached its chill fingers between the buttons of my coat.

> Bright pink walls shouted at us as we entered the lounge.

Allusion

An allusion acts as a kind of metaphor. It is an implied comparison of something with an historical or literary subject or event. For example, a reference to a political candidate "meeting his Watergate" assumes that the audience will associate Watergate with political crimes and humiliation. To explain that someone's powers of oratory are "Churchillian" is to suggest that the person has the exceptional speech gifts of a Winston Churchill. An allusion should remain in the realm of knowledge that your audience is likely to possess; avoid using allusions which might be too specialized or obscure.

> My employer, Mr. Higgins, is another Ebenezer Scrooge.

> He is a good composer, but he is not a Beethoven.

> The Zerlon Company's machine is the Edsel of typewriters.

> My grandmother's attic resembles a creation from the mind of Edgar Allan Poe.

The Mixed Figure of Speech

Mixed figurative language, which gives the reader two or more dissimilar images in rapid succession, should not be used.

> The professor, a mean old bear of a man, roared directions at the students in a voice as clear as a bell.

This sentence suggests to the reader an absurd image of a bell-shaped bear roaring like a lion; the mixed figure causes distraction from the point the writer is attempting to make. While figures of speech can make writing more vivid, it is far better to make a literal statement than to use figurative language that does not present a distinct image consistent with the writer's intention.

SPECIFICITY

By employing specific, precise diction, you can achieve both freshness and clarity. One noted scholar of the English language, S. I. Hayakawa, states that language offers various means of conveying substantially the same information; these means may be seen as a ladder of abstractions. The following sentences range from *abstract* to *concrete:*

1. I like beauty.
2. I like beautiful things.
3. I like beautiful flowers.
4. I like beautiful roses.
5. I like long-stemmed American Beauty roses.
6. I like the long-stemmed American Beauty roses arranged in a vase in the window of Mrs. Murphy's living room.

At different times, each level may be appropriate. Levels five and six are most effective as supporting development, yet level six is the more specific because it refers to certain flowers and to no other ones. By presenting supporting information on the sixth level, you will be using *concrete* detail, which will make your writing precise, emphatic, and interesting.

But the six-step ladder has, so far, taken care of only the noun in step 1, "beauty." There are also different degrees of *intensity* for the verb, "like." And when you are striving for true precision, you can analyze "like" in a similar manner, questioning yourself as follows: "Precisely how did I feel when I saw those roses last Saturday? Did I want to bring my friend to see them also? Did I want to stand looking at the flowers for ten or fifteen minutes? Or did I simply admire them in passing and hurry on home for lunch?" You might then turn to a college dictionary and examine the list of synonyms under the "like" entry: "love, enjoy, adore, savor, relish, fancy, dote." (Most dictionaries provide synonym lists under the entry for the most commonly used of the word's synonyms.) Having determined the various shades of meaning—and, in particular, the different levels of intensity—of each of the verbs, you may decide to declare, "I *adore* the three long-stemmed American Beauty roses in the window of Mrs. Murphy's living room." By selecting "adore," you will convey the notion of extreme fondness.

Verbs often have synonyms that suggest varying degrees of intensity; adjectives and nouns usually have synonyms with varying degrees of abstraction. The revising process calls for careful examination of diction if you are to select the words that most accurately and appropriately reflect your meaning.

HONESTY

Effective writing involves honesty. This is not to say that a criminal or accomplished liar cannot also be a successful writer. Being honest in choosing your words—as well as your concepts—means being honest with yourself. Is a statement such as "I enjoy living in the dormitory because everyone there is friendly" really honest? (In most dorms there are at least a few people whom it would not be accurate to characterize as "friendly.")

Revising for honesty involves identifying *overstatement*, points which you have exaggerated or idealized. Take particular care in developing such topics as a religious experience, a kindly grandparent, university food, a death or funeral (mourners tend to idealize the character of the deceased), a favorite car, a sports performance in which you starred—any topic about which you have strong likes or dislikes, any topic about which society has formed strong attitudes (patriotism, motherhood, communism).

DENOTATION, CONNOTATION, AND SLANTED DICTION

Words have both denotative and connotative meanings. Denotative meanings are dictionary definitions of a word. Connotative meanings are the associations that culturally or personally accompany a given word. For example, "mother" may connote warmth and security for you; but for some person whose mother tied him to a playpen for his first five years of life, "mother" may well carry associations of frustration and fear. Generally, though, choose words according to the public, or cultural, connotations that they will be likely to carry for an audience.

Examine the way that connotation operates in the following statements, which convey essentially the same denotative information:

1. John is scatterbrained.
2. John is muddle-headed.
3. John is disorganized.
4. John is unsystematic.

Slanted diction is word choice that suggests a strong bias in the writer's attitude toward his subject. Notice the bias (indicated by italicized words) in the following paragraph:

> The *octopus* oil industry, in its attempts to retain the tax *loophole* of the depletion allowance, has shown once again that it cares more for its own profits than for *justly* bearing its *fair* corporate share of the tax *burden*. The *crafty* leadership of three companies recently appeared before a Senate tax reform committee and, accompanied by a *crew* of *slick* lawyers, *overwhelmed* the legislators with a *barrage* of charts and graphs portraying large expenses involved in oil exploration. The "large expenses" were, however, a *pale shadow* compared to the size of the companies' annual profits.

Examine the more nearly neutral or positive substitutes for the italicized words and phrases:

octopus—highly developed
loophole—benefit
justly—properly
fair—appropriate
burden—obligation
crafty—informed
crew—several
slick—able
overwhelmed—persuaded
barrage—large number
pale shadow—small

Diction that carries highly emotional connotations has a place in rhetoric, but it must be combined with believable supporting detail. Believable supporting detail can make an emotional topic move an audience; exaggerated supporting detail may cause the topic to slip into the pit of *sentimentality* (indulging in an emotion for its own sake). There is genuine feeling—not sentimentality—in the way John Malcolm Brinnin concludes his description of the death of his friend, Dylan Thomas, a noted poet.

In Dylan's room nurses were dismantling the oxygen tent and clearing away other instruments. He had stopped breathing, one of them told us, while she was bathing him. As she was about to turn him over on his right side she had heard him utter a slight gasp, and then he had become silent. When the nurses left us alone, Liz sat down in the chair in which she had watched all the nights of his dying. Dylan was pale and blue, his eyes no longer blindly searching but calm, shut, and ineffably at peace. When I took his feet in my hands all warmth was gone; it was as if I could feel the little distance between his life and death. Liz whispered to him and kissed him on the forehead. We stood then at the foot of his bed for a few very long minutes, and did not weep or speak. Now, as always, where Dylan was, there were no tears at all.

Dylan Thomas in America

Whisper, kiss, gasp—these and other words carry connotations of strong emotion. But the emotional diction in the passage combines with believable detail—the nurses dismantling the oxygen tent and clearing away the instruments, Liz sitting down in the chair, the narrator holding the poet's feet, the two of them standing silently at the foot of the bed. The combination of specific detail and emotional diction makes the passage convincing and moving. Compare the Brinnin passage with the account below, which because of exaggerated detail seems sentimental and unconvincing.

To punish her daughter, a mother refused to kiss the girl at bedtime. The weeping child finally fell asleep that gray morning, and she never woke again, never! Grief is unavailing now! She lies in her little tomb. There is a marble urn at the head, and a rose bush at her feet; there grow sweet summer flowers; there waves the grass; there birds sing their matins and their vespers; there the blue sky smiles down today, and there lies buried the freshness of my heart.

Adapted from *Ladies Home Journal,* as recounted in S. B. Shaw,
Touching Incidents and Remarkable Answers to Prayer

EXERCISES

1. Rewrite the paragraph on the oil industry (p. 144), slanting the material as *favorably* as you can.
2. Examine each of the following sentences for wordiness, floweriness, and pomposity. Restate each briefly and simply.
   a. In terms of grading, he is an easy teacher.
   b. He was ill-disposed to reject the potential career proffered by the agency.

    c. Her hair was like the finest gossamer, and her almond eyes strayed to catch the fading pink on the sky's last-illumined billows.

    d. After perusing the library's various and multifaceted tomes, I have, I believe, arrived at the inescapable conclusion that it is indeed worthy of my donation of $10,000.

    e. On the basis of having examined your missive, I feel compelled to do everything in my power to ease your financial encumbrance.

    f. In terms of the school budget, and with regard to the fact that those of us assembled at this time and place are passionately interested in and committed to our children's educational well-being, we find it incumbent upon ourselves to pledge that we will judiciously, meticulously, and honestly administer the duties and responsibilities which we have with all due regard taken.

    g. The inebriated clerk misappropriated the company's funds.

3. Identify which of the following sentences are in the active voice and which are in the passive. Rewrite the passive sentences in the active voice and the active sentences in the passive voice; determine which voice is more effective in each case.

    a. The audience liked the play.

    b. The speech was delivered to Congress by the President.

    c. She showed concern by taking the dog to the vet.

    d. He played the piano well by the age of six.

    e. A criminal stole money from the bank.

    f. He was loved by his mother.

4. A *mixed* figure of speech combines two or more images in a way that appears incongruous or awkward. Describe the problem that occurs in each of the following:

    a. His jowls, which gave him the appearance of a bloodhound, swung like hammocks when he walked.

    b. He was on the road to recovery even though the doctor's diagnosis wasn't even in the ballpark.

    c. The policemen treed the criminals, who were like sitting ducks on a pond.

    d. The old battle-ax gave sugar-coated advice.

    e. His voice, soft as silk, cut through the air like a knife.

5. Below is a list of clichés and fixed phrases. Write a substitute for each cliché or phrase that clarifies it or makes it more fresh or more precise.

    a. quiet as a mouse

    b. solid as a rock

    c. fell like a ton of bricks

    d. equally as good as

    e. in the same boat

    f. center around

    g. in connection with

    h. in back of

  i. kind of different

  j. pretty as a picture

  k. the fact of the matter

6. Restate plainly or develop a new metaphor for each of the following adages:

  a. A bird in the hand is worth two in the bush.

  b. A rolling stone gathers no moss.

  c. Still waters run deep.

  d. A stitch in time saves nine.

  e. Toe the line.

  f. If it had been a snake it would have bitten you.

7. For each of the following abstractions, construct a list of words ranging from the less abstract to the concrete:

  a. vehicles

  b. sports

  c. plants

  d. music

  e. beverages

8. Find synonyms for the following verbs and arrange each list of synonyms according to intensity:

  a. hate

  b. run

  c. injure

  d. play

  e. see

9. Describe how each of the following statements is an exaggeration that needs qualifying:

  a. Sunsets are beautiful.

  b. Politicians are crooks.

  c. The sea is man's ally.

  d. Man is loneliest in a crowd.

  e. No man is an island.

  f. Universities are cultural centers.

  g. Classical music is better than rock.

10. Write out the denotative meaning of each of the following words and then list several connotations of each:

  a. politician

  b. manhood

  c. freedom

  d. intellectual

  e. scientist

  f. snake

11. Explain how connotation is or is not appropriate in the following figures of speech:

  a. The naked man hung from the tree, looking like a peeled grape.

b. The bridge builder's career spanned decades.

c. The exquisite dinner had more aromas than a locker room.

d. The punch tasted like the water from a defrosted refrigerator.

12. Construct a statement personifying each of the following:
    a. winter
    b. passion
    c. thirst
    d. mountains
    e. a telephone
    f. a typewriter
    g. the sun
    h. a piano
    i. dawn
    j. the ocean

13. Construct both a simile and a statement of allusion to describe each of the following:
    a. a friend's face
    b. a wartime disaster
    c. a football team's victory
    d. a favorite aged relative
    e. a high school teacher
    f. a new record
    g. your hometown
    h. a fraternity or sorority party
    i. a political campaign
    j. a movie

Reviewing Your Logic   **12**

Much of writing is proving a point—whether your thesis is one that takes a stand on a controversial issue, such as gun control, or one that examines a less emotion-laden topic, such as the procedures a police officer follows in making a report of an investigation. Whenever you attempt to convince an audience of a thesis, you will wish to appear reasonable. If your points are not convincing, readers are not likely to respect your thesis. Skillful reasoning may even enable you to gain the ears of readers who initially oppose your thesis.

The most effective arguments in written communication are those in which each point is firmly buttressed by supporting evidence that the reader will accept. Logic, then, is part of the writing process because no writer can afford to appear illogical.

This discussion aims to make you aware of key ways in which reasoning can go astray. It explores certain common *fallacies* (illogical appeals) committed by writers and others who undertake persuasion. Sharpening your ability to recognize illogic will gradually help you to avoid fallacies in your own thinking and writing. It will also help you to spot them in your own writing plan and, barring that, to catch them during the revision process.

Appeal to Force

Appeal to force is a common technique of persuasion. In written communication this fallacy is usually more subtle than "Hand over your wallet or I'll put a .22 slug in you!" Though it may be a compelling argument, an appeal to force is not a *reasonable* one. For example, the student who argues that dormitory regulations must be altered because if they aren't he will lead a student riot is using such an appeal, though there may be a dozen valid (logical) reasons he could have used. Yet another example is the "logic" of the person who demands that certain books be banned in a school and accompanies the demand with a threat to bomb the school building. War, obviously, is the ultimate appeal to force, and conflicts that might have been settled by reasonable, positive approaches may continue until one of the sides is humiliated or destroyed.

Abusing the Opposition

If you argue that Senator Faust should not be reelected because he is divorced, or because he flunked out of law school, or because he is a jerk, you are abusing the opposition. Name calling is unfair. There may well exist many logical reasons why the senator should not be reelected, such as his failure to cast any vote in the Senate during the first two years of his term, and these reasons should be the basis of your argument. As with the appeal to force, abusing the opposition may take subtle forms. Diction with negative connotations needs careful handling. Think, for example, of the connotations suggested by "the *crafty* man," "the *impersonal* city," "the *snakelike* railway."

Circumstantial Attack

Closely related to abusing the opposition is the fallacious means of persuasion that uses the circumstances of the opponent to discredit his argument. When you argue that a former oil company executive should not be appointed to the Federal Energy Commission because he would surely favor the needs of his cronies in the oil industry, you are using circumstantial attack. Former conditions of employment are irrelevant to a person's present honesty or dishonesty. If, on the other hand, you have a letter written by the executive which clearly shows that he intends to use his position to increase corporate profits, you have a valid reason for denying him the appointment. A similar use of circumstantial attack is the following: The president of the Sanitation Workers Union calls for higher wages; the opposition replies, "The president's claims are unfounded—he is only arguing for a pay raise because he is the union leader." There may, in fact, be valid points raised in the president's argument, and those points may fail to get consideration because of the circumstances (in this case, the position) of the man who argues for them.

Appeal to Authority

An authority is an expert—a person with extensive professional knowledge—in some field. The appeal to authority becomes fallacious if you use the expert's opinion to reinforce an argument concerning some field *outside* the expert's area of expertise. For example, a commercial showing a baseball player urging an audience to buy a certain brand of coffee maker is using an invalid appeal to authority. If, however, the baseball player were to testify to the merits of a certain brand of glove, his opinion would legitimately carry some weight, even if one argues circumstantially that the manufacturer is paying the player to testify so. In another instance, assume that a medical doctor is running for mayor. People who are used to taking the doctor's advice on matters of health may unconsciously transfer their respect for his medical expertise to the area of political issues. Here, the illogical appeal to authority is unstated. Yet a good doctor can make a good mayor. He must provide evidence that he is as capable and knowledgeable about political issues as he is about medicine.

Appeal to the Masses

Closely related to the appeal to authority is the appeal to the masses. With this appeal, you attempt to persuade your audience that because "everybody" is doing something, buying something, or believing something, the audience should also. This argument can take such forms as the following:

> Because most other large cities have imposed an income tax, Gotham should too.

> Sonex sells more stereos than any other brand. Shouldn't you own one?

The appeal to the masses is also known as the "bandwagon approach." Sometimes you can literally see this metaphor in operation: witness the soft-drink commercial showing a haywagon loaded with happy people drinking the "in" brand cola, or the political campaign parade with the candidate actually riding a bandwagon crowded with his supporters. The bandwagon approach appeals to man's urge to be part of the group, but it offers no legitimate reasons for his doing so.

Appeal to Pity

Though appeal to pity is often as persuasive as the appeal to force, it equally violates reason. It is argument by way of the tearduct rather than by way of the brain. Charities commonly use the appeal to pity as a means of persuasion; often this appeal is directed at the audience's sense of guilt as well. As part of a drive to raise money for a starving nation, you are urged to forgo a meal a week and send the money saved to an organization that shows you pictures of fly-covered toddlers gnawing chicken bones. The same message could more logically appeal to humanitarian principles. It can be acceptable to play on your audience's emotions in certain circumstances, as long as you do not bypass the reasoned argument.

Argument from Ignorance

Another irrational method—one that does not rely on manipulating the audience's emotions—is the argument from ignorance. Such an argument states that something is true because it has not been shown false. For example, just because the Better Business Bureau has received no complaints about Dick's Used Car Company does not mean that Dick always deals honestly. It is likewise invalid to argue that Mr. Queezenberry is a good bus driver because you have never heard otherwise.

Begging the Question

Begging the question is a type of reasoning that presents a conclusion without providing any basis for that conclusion. Instead, the conclusion—stated in different words—is presented as the reason for the conclusion. (This fallacy is sometimes called *circular argument*.) If you write that "the United States has the strongest defense of any country because it has the mightiest nuclear arsenal," you are presenting an argument that, instead of offering proof for its conclusion, simply states the conclusion in another form. This argument contains no information that the audience can use as grounds for agreeing with you. Such circular reasoning can be deceptive, because the restated conclusion normally appears in wording quite different from the originally stated conclusion. Another example is the following: "Sonex FM radios give you better sound than any other brand. No other radio on the market today has tonal quality superior to that of the Sonex." Again, the conclusion receives no support—the argument contains no evidence beyond that which is contained in the conclusion itself.

Complex Question

A question based on an implied assumption also violates sound logic. "Is the nation going to continue harboring Communists?" assumes that the nation is now doing so. "Have you given up smoking?" assumes that the listener is, or has been, a smoker. Notice that these two questions require a "yes" or "no" answer which implicitly acknowledges the truth of the assumption. But these questions are less dangerous than one that might be asked of an innocent man in court: "Have you discontinued your illegal gambling practices?"

Complex questions may also be planted in the guise of adjectives: "Does Smith still play a *lousy* game of golf?" not only asks if Smith still plays golf but also assumes that Smith used to play the game poorly.

Hasty Generalization

One of the most common reasoning errors in student writing is hasty generalization. Here a conclusion is reached on the basis of an isolated or exceptional case. This is the fallacy committed by the person who declares:

> I met the nicest woman in Mobile, Alabama. People are always more friendly in the South.

> That curt bus driver in New York didn't surprise me. City people are never helpful.

> After hearing the Chinese delegate's speech, I realize that all Communists want to overthrow America.

These statements are invalid because they assume that what is true under a particular condition is true under all conditions. You have only to think of one contradictory example—an unfriendly gas-station attendant in Grits, Georgia; a Philadelphia hotel clerk who stood in the rain to hail a taxi for a stranger; a Communist peasant in China who cares about nothing more than working on the communal farm— and the conclusion in each case becomes false. You can identify hasty generalizations by thinking of exceptions to statements with such open or implied absolutes as "never," "always," "no one," and "everyone."

Sweeping Generalization

The counterpart of hasty generalization is sweeping generalization —applying a general rule to a particular case which may be the exception to that rule. Examine the following:

> I have tested thirty Ace photocopiers, and each gave clear reproductions. This thirty-first one, therefore, will also make clear reproductions.

The writer has tested a sufficient number of machines so that his conclusion ought to be valid. However, it will not be valid if a workman dropped the thirty-first copier while loading it onto the truck, and each reproduction the copier makes looks like a butterfly. The error of logic lies in not allowing for a possible exception. The conclusion should have a degree of qualification: "The thirty-first one, therefore, will *probably* make clear reproductions."

Irrelevant Conclusion

The error of irrelevant conclusion appears in a shift in the issues, as in the case of this argument:

> More nuclear power plants should be built because the nation has growing energy needs.

The real issue is that of how growing energy needs should be met or whether ways to decrease energy needs should be sought. To deal with the issue requires analyzing the various kinds of energy resources and setting up guidelines (such as safety, efficiency, cost) for finding the best answer to the problem. Another way to meet the issue would be to examine the practicality of reducing energy needs.

Similarly, an irrelevant conclusion appears in the following argument:

> Capital punishment is an effective crime deterrent because the public is fascinated by it.

The issue shift assumes that anything that fascinates the public will deter members of the public from committing crimes punishable by death, when in fact public fascination has nothing to do with crime deterrence.

False Cause

The error of false cause occurs in statements which suggest that events are causally connected when in fact no such connection may exist. The human ability to commit this error is what has led doctors at times to prescribe sugar pills for some patients. The woman who chronically complains of backache takes the medication (actually, sugar pills) the doctor has prescribed. Feeling better, she attributes the cure to the pills, when in fact it is her own psychological powers—her faith in the "medicine"—that have cured her.

Similarly, people are often persuaded by arguments containing the error of false cause, such as the following:

> More women have full-time jobs today than in 1967. In the past ten years, teen-age drug use has steadily increased. It is therefore clear that teen-agers are taking drugs because their mothers are away from the home working.

> Environmental pollution has become a serious problem since Senator Frump was elected, so if you're concerned about the environment, you should vote for his opponent.

These arguments assume that, because two events occur at about the same time, one event is caused by the other. Actually, there may be no causal connection whatsoever between the two events.

The Either-Or Dilemma

Not allowing for exceptions or for alternatives can create a logical dilemma for your audience, as in certain either-or statements. Such a dilemma appears in a common slogan of the 1960s: "America—Love It or Leave It." There is an obvious third choice for the person who neither loves America nor wishes to leave it: stay and try to change matters. But the "(either) love it or leave it" declaration ignores alternatives.

There are a variety of such illogical commands: "Put up or shut up"; "Sink or swim"; "Like it or lump it." Each statement has an assumed "either" at its beginning; each ignores other alternatives.

EXERCISE

Identify the faulty logic in each of the following items:

1. A person should never drive while intoxicated. If he gets caught, he'll receive a $500 fine.
2. You'll get the best deal on a new car from us. We're the largest volume dealer in four states.
3. Don't vote for that man. He has shifty eyes.
4. If you don't give me a passing grade, Professor Jones, I won't be able to graduate and get that teaching job that my high school offered me.
5. The vice-president of the corporation wants to get the federal grant just because it will put him in line for a promotion.
6. If you had seen the fire that destroyed the Smiths' house, you would not hesitate to buy our $50,000 homeowner's insurance policy.
7. Every visitor to Washington should dine at the Sans Amour; after all, the leaders of Congress lunch there.
8. Our candidate for president of the student council is the best for the job because she advocates the best programs.
9. The supervisor must really like Joe's work. I've never heard him criticize Joe at all.
10. John is nice to his aunt only because he expects to inherit a pile of money from her.
11. Are you still drinking too much?
12. She was born under the sign of Taurus, so it's no wonder she blew the deal today.
13. Never trust anyone over thirty.
14. Every country boy dreams of living in New York.
15. The Engineering Department is noted for its teaching excellence; therefore, Professor Headly over there must be a fine teacher.

16. The Germans make outstanding cars, so this German car must be outstanding.
17. All right-thinking people will reject the evil that is socialism.
18. Ladies and gentlemen of the jury, you cannot believe Mrs. Jones's testimony in this murder trial. Ten years ago she was convicted of driving under the influence of alcohol.
19. Use Brand X toothpaste or lose your teeth.
20. Joe Namath uses Brand X. Shouldn't you?
21. Today's university professors are expected to spend much of their time publishing. Therefore, you shouldn't go to college because your teachers will be more interested in their publications than they will be in you.
22. All the other kids are doing it—it's okay for me to.
23. Thousands of happy and contented families are already enjoying their own Brand Y swimming pools.

Improving   13
Your Sentences

The writer who strives for clarity will tailor his sentences with care, trying to shape each sentence so that it conveys its unit of meaning efficiently. That is why a clear and convincing essay is often the product of two or more revisions. Sentences continue to improve as they are reworked. (Writers too improve as they continue to manipulate sentences.)

Even when you are satisfied with that second, third, or fourth draft, it will be worthwhile to read your work over at the sentence level. Look for awkwardness in sentence construction that obscures your meaning. Root out the faulty grammar that lets a sentence say something you don't intend. Make your sentences work for you (1) to emphasize what you want to emphasize, (2) to keep the logical relationship among your concepts clear, and (3) to avoid distracting your reader with usages that are unconventional.

The entries that follow concern some of the main ways in which sentences can be strengthened for presentation to an intended audience. Not all of them will be of equal importance in the writing of a particular individual. The discussion here reflects a conservative view of what is acceptable written English in forums where people write for an educated, nontechnical audience. For clarification of any terminology about grammar that appears in these pages, consult Appendix C.

POINT OF VIEW

A writer has the option of presenting his material from various points of view: the first person ("I" or "we"), the second person

157

("you"), or the third person ("he," "she," "it," or "they"). Here *point of view* is used only in the sense of *person*; don't confuse *point of view* with *viewpoint*, which suggests "attitude" or "feeling."

Perspective

In order to maintain continuity, many writers use a single point of view, or perspective, throughout an entire discourse. Though point of view can shift within an essay—or even a paragraph—a single perspective should always be maintained within a single sentence. Writing informally from personal experience, you may use the first person, "I" and "me." (If you employ the highly general third-person point of view, "one," you may unintentionally sound pompous in an otherwise informal discourse.) If you shift from "I" to the audience's point of view, "you," you may not only distract your reader but place him in a perspective that he finds difficult to accept.

For example, the following sentence, which shifts point of view from first person "I" to second person "you," not only is distracting but also places the reader in an awkward position:

> What *I* learned from my last beer party is that *you* should never hide out in a girl's closet.

Many writers restrict use of the "you" point of view to a process paper, in which they wish to draw the audience into a sense of participation in working through a process together (see p. 104). They also restrict the "one" point of view to formal reviews and reports, in which a feeling of formality is appropriate.

Direct and Indirect Discourse

Another aspect of point of view in which it is important to maintain continuity is the use of either direct or indirect discourse. Direct discourse is a direct quotation—as in "He asked, 'Are you going?' " By contrast, indirect discourse is restatement from the perspective of the listener—"He asked if I was going." Notice the awkward shift in the following sentence:

> My friend *asked me to go* on vacation with him and *would I share* expenses.

This sentence would be clearer if amended to either of the following:

> My friend asked me to go on vacation with him and to share expenses.

(Both parts of the request are in indirect discourse.)

> My friend asked, "Will you go on vacation with me and share expenses?"

(Both parts of the request are in direct discourse.)

SENTENCE VARIETY

To maintain a smooth prose style—one that will not bore or distract the reader from your message—provide variety both in the structure and in the length of consecutive sentences.

Order of Sentence Elements

The usual order of English sentence elements is subject-verb-object or subject-verb-complement, as in the following simple sentences:

> We enjoy going to ballgames.
> S   V   O

> You easily can vary sentence beginnings.
> S   V   O

> The preacher frightened the congregation.
>   S   V   O

> John is a fine policeman.
> S   V   C

Here are some variations of the pattern:

> Going to ballgames is something that we enjoy.
>   S   V   O

> Sentence beginnings easily can be varied.
>   S   V

> It was the congregation that the preacher frightened.
> S V   C

> To know John is to know a fine policeman.
>   S   V   C

The following are complex sentences:

> I visit my aunt whenever I go to New York.
> independent clause   dependent clause

<u>She takes her teddybear</u> <u>wherever she goes.</u>
    independent clause   **dependent clause**

<u>John teaches from the text</u> <u>that Professor Jones wrote.</u>
    independent clause   **dependent clause**

Variations:

<u>Whenever I go to Chicago,</u> <u>I visit my aunt.</u>
    dependent clause   **independent clause**

<u>Wherever she goes,</u> <u>she takes her teddybear.</u>
    dependent clause   **independent clause**

<u>The text</u> <u>that Professor Jones wrote</u> <u>is the one</u> <u>that John teaches from.</u>
independent   **dependent clause**   **clause**   **dependent clause**

Consider which elements would lend themselves to subordination (see p. 162). Then vary your arrangement of clauses accordingly.

To vary sentences, use different conjunctions instead of repeating the same one. For example, in this passage the conjunction "but" is used three times:

> He was a thoughtful man, *but* he knew that he lacked the objectivity a psychologist could provide. He tried to find time to consult a professional analyst, *but* his schedule was simply too tight. The man decided to wait for his problem to go away, *but* the problem only got worse.

Note the improvement when the conjunctions are varied:

> He was a thoughtful man, *but* he knew that he lacked the objectivity a psychologist could provide. *Although* he tried to find time to consult a professional analyst, his schedule was simply too tight. The man decided to wait for his problem to go away; *however,* the problem only got worse.

Variety can be achieved by alternating sentence beginnings. For example, open some sentences with the subject of the sentence, others with a prepositional phrase, still others with an infinitive or participial phrase or with a dependent clause. Combining clauses, instead of stringing the information out in several sentences, helps too. Examine the following paragraph and its revision:

> I found strange customs in the country of Floristan. I was told by a native of that country that some tribes swore by salt. I was also told that other tribes swore by snuff. Each tribe swore by what it considered the most sacred thing. They had great regard for their oaths.

Their economic system was also unusual. Every article of exchange was called money. Besides this they had no currency at all. Hoes were in great demand, and axes were also. The best currency was rum, and cotton goods were valuable too. Articles of exchange had no regular value. This gave traders a great chance for extortion. Rum in Floristan led to all manner of crime.

A sameness in the sentences makes the above passage tedious. Now consider this revision:

In the country of Floristan I found strange customs. I was told by a native of that country that some tribes swore by salt and others by snuff. Each tribe, in fact, swore by what it considered the most sacred thing, and the natives had great regard for their oaths. Also unusual was the economic system of Floristan: not only was every article of exchange called money, but there was, besides this, no currency at all. Although hoes, axes, and cotton goods were in great demand, the best currency was rum, which led to all manner of crime. Because articles of exchange had no regular value, traders had a great chance for extortion.

COORDINATION

Coordination is the linking of similar elements within a sentence. For coordination to be correct (1) the proper coordinator must be used and (2) the coordinated clauses must be of equal importance.

Coordinating conjunctions indicate a special relationship between two independent clauses. "And" indicates that two related clauses are of equal value and complementary in meaning:

I'm going to buy her a dress, *and* she can wear it on Sunday.

"But" indicates that two related clauses are of equal importance but contrasting in intention:

I'm going to buy her a dress, *but* she can't wear it on Sunday.

"Or" indicates an alternative or choice between the concepts in clauses that are of equal value:

I'm going to buy her a dress, *or* she will buy one herself.

"Nor" is the negative counterpart of "and." Like "and," "nor" introduces a clause of equal value with the first, but "nor" indicates negation of that clause. When the second clause is introduced by "nor," "not" or "neither" must appear in the first clause:

> I cannot buy her a dress, *nor* can I pay for her dinner.

When a coordinating conjunction links two independent clauses, a comma normally precedes the coordinating conjunction. But examine the following:

> I'm going to town *and* coming home by five o'clock.
>
> I'm going to town *but* not coming home until suppertime.
>
> I'm going to town *or* to the country.
>
> I'm going neither to town *nor* to the country.

No comma precedes "and," "but," "or," "nor" in these statements because the sentence elements which follow the conjunctions are not independent clauses. Note that other sentence elements, such as words and phrases, may be linked by coordinating conjunctions, as in the sentences above.

SUBORDINATION

The purpose of subordination is to show, within the same sentence, the importance of one thought in relation to another. (You may also wish to consult the discussion of transitions, pp. 164 and 185.) Subordination may be carried out by the following methods.

Begin the less important clause with a subordination-marker word:

although	unless	as
though	whether	when
since	so that	where
because	before	while
if	after	until

> I wanted to attend the dance. I couldn't get a date.
>
> *Although* I wanted to attend the dance, I couldn't get a date.

Use "who," "which," and "that" clauses:

> I bought the book at the university bookstore. It is having a sale.
>
> I bought the book at the university book store, *which* is having a sale.

Use clauses that contain a nonfinite verb form, such as "going to the store" and "to go to the store":

> We always eat in a Chinese restaurant when we go to a game.

> When *going* to a game, we always eat in a Chinese restaurant.

If a subordinate clause uses a subordination-marker word and precedes the main clause, it is normally followed by a comma:

> *Although* I like hamburgers, I can't afford to eat them.

> *Since* he's not here yet, why don't we leave?

> *If* you don't like the man, you shouldn't vote for him.

> *Wherever* they found termites, they sprayed insecticide.

PARALLELISM

At times you may find that you can make a sentence flow more smoothly and provide extra emphasis by placing certain clauses, phrases, or words conveying concepts of equal value in parallel grammatical form. Parallelism is a logical requirement for items in a series.

Grammatical Class

The process of making individual words parallel involves placing them in the same grammatical class. For example, to convey information about your favorite pastimes, you might state:

> My pastimes include *photographing* wild flowers, *playing* the bassoon, and *jogging* in the park.

Here you have used parallelism of verb phrases, with each verb in the participial (*-ing*) form. Another means of stating this information (though less specifically) would be to use parallelism of nouns:

> My pastimes include *photography, music,* and *jogging.*

With parallelism, you achieve both emphasis and smoothness.

Repetition

Sometimes parallelism consisting of repetition can lend emphasis to a statement or to a series of statements. For example, you might give the following explanation for getting home late:

> On the way home, I had to stop at the hardware store, the post office, and the bank.

Using parallelism with repetition of the preposition "at," you can state the same sentence more forcefully:

> On the way home, I had to stop *at* the hardware store, *at* the post office, and *at* the bank.

Yet another option, for even greater force, would be the following:

> On the way home, *I had to stop* at the hardware store, *I had to stop* at the post office, and *I had to stop* at the bank.

Observe that repetition may also apply with subordinate clauses:

> I thought *that* he had caught the ball, *that* we had won the game, and *that* we were the new champions.

Repetition should be used sparingly, however, if it is not to lose its emphasis.

Transitions

Understanding parallelism when using transitional and contrastive pairs such as "either . . . or," "not only . . . but also" can help you maintain smooth and logical syntax. For example, the following statement violates parallelism:

> He not only set his racing car on fire, but also he blew up his house.

For the clauses to be parallel, the "but also" in the second clause should immediately precede the verb, as "not only" does in the first clause:

> He not only set his racing car on fire but also blew up his house.

The clauses can also be made parallel by moving "not only" to the beginning of the first clause:

> Not only did he set his racing car on fire, but he also blew up his house.

Compare the following statement with the examples above:

> He will either go to the bar or to the hotel lobby.

"Either" precedes the main verb "go" and the prepositional phrase "to the bar"; "or," however, precedes only the prepositional phrase "to the hotel lobby." Correct parallelism would move "either" to follow the verb "go":

> He will go either to the bar or to the hotel lobby.

Another way to achieve parallelism would be to add a verb following "or":

> He will either go to the bar or go to the hotel lobby.

There is additional discussion of transitional devices on p. 185.

Logical Categories

Logical categories are a necessity in parallelism. Consider this sentence:

> The best sportsmen are *Russians, Canadians,* and *Jews.*

The categories in the series—Russians, Canadians, and Jews—are not parallel: some Russians and Canadians are also Jewish. The writer has illogically mixed nationalities and religions in the same series. For the categories to be logical and parallel, the sentence should be revised as follows:

> The best sportsmen are Russians, Canadians, and Jews of all nationalities.

Comparisons

Comparisons employing "more . . . than" require parallel constructions. It is wrong, for example, to say:

> I find *more* enjoyment in listening to Beethoven.

This is an incomplete statement; necessary for logical completion is a parallel "than" complement:

> I find *more* enjoyment in listening to Beethoven *than* in listening to The Purple Pits.

All comparisons, not just those employing "more . . . than" must be stated fully. For example, it is illogical to state:

His views on foreign policy oppose the *President*.

It is the President's views that are being opposed, not the President himself. Logically, the statement should read:

His views on foreign policy oppose the *President's*.

SENTENCE COHERENCE

Check to see that modifying words, phrases, and clauses are placed as closely as possible to the word, phrase, or clause being modified. Normally, the modifier immediately follows the term modified, but sometimes it is necessary for the modifier to precede the term modified.

Misplaced Modifiers

The following sentences contain misplaced modifiers:

Upon finding his watch, Gordon ran to his car, drove rapidly to school, and arrived at the class without pants on.

Judas is the most interesting person in the poem as a character.

The unfortunate thing about John is his habit of breaking down doors under the influence of alcohol.

The woman called a physician with the flu.

The baby liked being carried by Phyllis with the bottle in her mouth.

Bruce only loved his wife.

Sometimes misplaced modifiers do no more than read awkwardly; at other times they cause confusion, sometimes amusing confusion. In either case, the process of correcting misplaced modifiers involves placing the modifying phrase as closely as possible to the term modified. Here are the sentences corrected:

Upon finding his watch, Gordon ran to his car; drove rapidly to school; and arrived, without pants on, at the class.

(The original sentence reads as if the class—not Gordon—had no pants on.)

As a character, Judas is the most interesting person in the poem.

(The original sentence reads as if the poem itself were the character.)

> The unfortunate thing about John, when he is under the influence of alcohol, is his habit of breaking down doors.

(The original sentence reads as if the doors were under the influence of alcohol.)

> The woman with the flu called a physician.

(The original sentence reads as if the physician, rather than the woman, had the flu.)

> With the bottle in her mouth, the baby liked being carried by Phyllis.

(The original sentence sounds as if Phyllis were drinking from the bottle. If the point to be made is that one certain baby as opposed to another liked being carried by Phyllis, the sentence should be written, "The baby with the bottle in her mouth liked being carried by Phyllis.")

> Bruce loved only his wife.

(The original sentence conveys the idea that the only thing Bruce did was love his wife; the revised sentence limits the category of those he loved to his wife alone.)

The last example points up the care that is necessary with such modifiers as "only," "just," and "merely." Consider the different meanings conveyed by repositioning "only" in the following sentences:

> He only ate a bowl of chili for breakfast.
>
> He ate only a bowl of chili for breakfast.
>
> He ate a bowl of chili for breakfast only.

Dangling Modifiers

A second problem of coherence results from dangling modifiers. A dangling modifier is one that does not clearly and logically refer to some word in the sentence. The following are examples:

> After two martinis, the waiter brought us menus.
>
> Watching for cars, the road looked safe to cross.

Having arrived at the shore, the sun warmed John's chilled skin.

While watching television, the news of the general's death startled us.

Being new to the job, the boss assigned Joe to break me in.

To cook in the Chinese manner, a bottle of peanut oil must be kept handy.

Here are the sentences corrected:

After we had had two martinis, the waiter brought us menus.

(The original sentence reads as if the waiter had the martinis.)

Watching for cars, the children believed the road looked safe to cross.

(The original sentence indicates that the road is watching for cars.)

Having arrived at the shore, John felt the sun warm his chilled skin.

(The original sentence has the sun rather than John arriving at the shore.)

While watching television, we were startled by the news of the general's death.

(The original sentence has the news watching television.)

Because I was new to the job, the boss assigned Joe to break me in.

(The original sentence indicates that the boss is new to the job.)

To cook in the Chinese manner, keep a bottle of peanut oil handy.

(The original sentence requires the bottle of peanut oil to do the cooking.)

Squinting Modifiers

A third kind of incoherence comes from placing a modifier so that it can logically attach to the words or phrases on either side of it. For example, the following sentence poses this problem:

They decided on Tuesday to visit the castle.

Is Tuesday the day that they made the decision, or is Tuesday the day that they visited the castle? To clear up the ambiguity, the sentence may be amended two ways:

On Tuesday, they decided to visit the castle.

They decided to visit the castle on Tuesday.

Split Infinitives

The split infinitive is viewed by some grammarians as another kind of coherence problem. A split infinitive rarely affects the clarity of a statement, but because it interrupts a part of speech, it can be a distraction. The following are examples of split infinitives and appropriate corrections:

SPLIT INFINITIVE	AMENDED
to immediately go	to go immediately
to quickly finish	to finish quickly
to admirably work	to work admirably

SENTENCE FRAGMENTS

In checking your essay for undesirable fragments—incomplete sentences written and punctuated as if they were complete—reread what you have written in reverse, from last sentence to first. This practice can help you to see statements out of context and to identify more easily those sentences which are incomplete. Examine the common types of fragments below. Although they may seem relatively easy to recognize, they can be quite troublesome to identify when in context, for they often read as extensions of the sentences which follow or precede them.

SENTENCE FRAGMENT	COMPLETE SENTENCE
nonfinite verb:	
The car being the problem.	The car was the problem.
dependent clause:	
That women may be as fallible as men.	That women may be as fallible as men is true.
If he returns.	If he returns, we shall win.
Which was just in the eyes of God.	The action was one which was just in the eyes of God.

SENTENCE FRAGMENT	COMPLETE SENTENCE
noun phrase:	
Not only his words but his actions.	Not only his words but his actions showed his concern.
prepositional phrase:	
In another life.	Happiness comes in another life.

Sometimes a fragment may be used for special emphasis, as in the following example. However, you may want to check such usage with your instructor.

> It is necessary for the newcomer to be particularly wary of walking in the park. Passing through the area without a gun or vicious dog at your side can make the journey quite dangerous. *Especially after dark.*

FUSED SENTENCES

In rereading your essay, check to see that your sentences aren't fused. Each independent clause should have punctuation that separates it from other independent clauses or sentences. Examine the following:

> The man knocked on the door he was selling gopher tonic.

Though two independent clauses appear in the statement, there is no indication of the point at which the first unit of thought ends and the next begins. To clarify the relationship between the two thoughts, the statement can be rewritten in a number of ways:

> The man knocked on the door. He was selling gopher tonic.
>
> The man knocked on the door; he was selling gopher tonic.
>
> The man knocked on the door, and he was selling gopher tonic.
>
> The man who knocked on the door was selling gopher tonic.
>
> The man who was selling gopher tonic knocked on the door.

The first two choices are satisfactory because the period and semicolon provide adequately strong pauses; the reader is signaled that a separate and significant unit of thought is to follow. The third choice is grammatically correct, though the resulting sentence seems wordy. The fourth and fifth choices economically embed one clause—now a dependent clause—in the other; they are also grammatically correct. In revising fused sentences, determine how best to emphasize the more important clause. (Note the different emphases in four and five.) But keep in mind that sometimes the two clauses may be equally important. In such cases, employ a coordinating conjunction.

THE COMMA SPLICE

Comma splice refers only to a specific type of comma error: the use of a comma alone to separate two independent clauses not joined by a coordinating conjunction. For example:

The man knocked on the door, he was selling gopher tonic.

The simplest means of correcting the comma splice is to use a semicolon or a period in place of the comma:

The man knocked on the door; he was selling gopher tonic.

The man knocked on the door. He was selling gopher tonic.

Comma splice errors occur frequently with *conjunctive adverbs* ("however," "therefore," "besides," "indeed," "in fact," "also," "moreover," "furthermore," "nevertheless," "still," "thus," "hence," "consequently," and "accordingly"). A conjunctive adverb is not the same as a coordinating conjunction, which always is positioned between the two independent clauses it links. Rather, a conjunctive adverb can take different positions within the second clause. When a conjunctive adverb appears at the beginning of an independent clause, the word must be preceded by a semicolon and followed by a comma. When a conjunctive adverb appears within the clause, it is both preceded and followed by commas. Comma splice constructions occur when a conjunctive adverb begins an independent clause but is preceded by a comma instead of a semicolon. Compare the following:

COMMA SPLICE	COMMA SPLICE ELIMINATED
I am a writer, however, none of my stories has been published.	I am a writer; however, none of my stories has been published.
	or
	I am a writer; none of my stories, however, has been published.

COMMA SPLICE	COMMA SPLICE ELIMINATED
There was no snow last weekend, therefore, we could not go skiing.	There was no snow last weekend; therefore, we could not go skiing.

or

There was no snow last
weekend; we could not,
therefore, go skiing.

REFERENCE AND AGREEMENT

Errors in reference and agreement can cause not only distraction but misunderstanding. To understand why, be aware that certain words *refer* to other words in the surrounding context. When the word to which reference is made occurs first in the sentence, it is called an *antecedent*. Problems of reference and agreement occur largely with pronouns and their antecedents, and between subjects and verbs of sentences.

Pronoun and Antecedent

A pronoun must *agree* with its antecedent in number (singular or plural) and in gender (masculine, feminine, or neuter). Pronouns must also *refer* clearly to their antecedents. Consider this sentence.

Mary told Joan that she lacked a sense of humor.

Because "she" and "her" have no antecedents to which they clearly refer, the reader may be confused as to who needs the sense of humor. Rewording with a single pronoun clears up the faulty reference:

Mary chided Joan on her lack of a sense of humor.

Or, perhaps:

Mary said, "Joan, you lack a sense of humor."

Agreement errors signify a lack of clarity in language use, as in the following:

The present school system exceeds *their* normal operating capacity.

"System," the antecedent of "their," is singular, but "their" is plural. The reader may be led to conclude that a plural referent for "their" exists in an earlier statement. Upon discovering no plural antecedent, the reader has no choice but to impose his own logic on the writer's statement and conclude that the pronoun "their" should be "its." The agreement error causes distraction if not irritation.

Problems with *remote antecedents* can arise with the pronouns "it," "that," "this," "these," and "those." Consider the following:

> The current war in Albania has caused severe problems for the American government as well as for the Canadian government. We Americans cannot tolerate this.

The referent for "this" is so remote that you cannot identify any precise antecedent. Amended, the last sentence should read "We Americans cannot tolerate this war."

Give special attention to the antecedents "everyone," "no one," "one," "a person," and "each." These referents are singular, but the common tendency is to regard them as plural.

INACCURATE	BETTER
The income level of a person has nothing to do with *their* room assignments.	The income level of a person has nothing to do with *his* room assignment.

In the inaccurate sentence, the plural pronoun "their" is used as the referent for the singular antecedent "a person."

Current Thinking on Pronoun Gender

Recent attempts to guard against sexist language—that is, language that one sex will find offensive—have drawn attention to pronoun reference. A noticeable percentage of those who write for publication currently use "he or she" and "his or her," while others find such practice unnecessarily wordy or distracting.

Some writers have attempted to invent new forms ("s/he," for example) to supply a solution to the controversy. So far, none has achieved prominence, and most have been criticized as inelegant. For purposes of this text, we resolved this sensitive issue by using the traditional "he" to refer to anyone, male or female. We do not find this solution entirely satisfactory, though we appreciate the economy of words it allows. Where possible, you may wish to avoid the problem in your own writing by rephrasing so as to eliminate the pronoun.

Subject and Verb

A sentence's subject and verb, like pronouns and their antecedents, must be in agreement. If the subject is singular, the verb must be singular; if the subject is plural, the verb must be plural.

Here is a list of certain subject-verb combinations that often cause problems.

If "and" combines two or more elements in a subject, the verb should be plural:

The Smiths and their pet dachshund *are* going to Europe.

If "or," "nor," "either . . . or," or "neither . . . nor" combines two or more elements in a subject, the verb will usually be singular:

March or April *is* a good month for scheduling a long weekend.

Neither rain nor snow *keeps* the campus police from taking their walks.

However, if one subject is singular and the other plural, the verb usually agrees with the closer of the two subjects:

Either the teacher or the students *are* going to be dissatisfied.

"Each," "every," "nothing," "no one," "everyone," and "someone" require singular verbs:

Everyone *needs* clean air to breathe.

Nothing *is* going to prevent her from graduating.

Someone *has* played a trick on us.

Collective nouns (such as "herd," "majority," "family," "couple") and nouns of quantity that are followed by prepositional phrases take singular verbs when they refer to a single unit:

The audience *was* thrilled with the performance.

The committee *plans* an elaborate investigation.

Ten gallons of gasoline *is* all the tank holds.

Three minutes of the second period *remains.*

But when a collective noun or noun of quantity refers to individuals within a group rather than the group as a unit, a plural verb is required:

A majority *were* unable to leave their houses because of the snow.

Four quarts of milk *are* in the refrigerator.

"There" takes a singular or a plural verb, depending on the form of its complement:

There *is* a hole in the wall.

There *are* holes in the wall.

A relative pronoun ("that," "which," "who") takes a singular or plural verb, depending on whether the antecedent is singular or plural:

He will sell the prize chicken that *was* raised on his farm.

He will sell the prize chickens that *were* raised on his farm.

The law, which *is* unfair, needs to be repealed.

The laws, which *are* unfair, need to be repealed.

I gave food to the beggar who *was* poorly dressed.

I gave food to the beggars who *were* poorly dressed.

"Any," "some," "none," "all," "more," and "most" take either singular or plural verbs, depending on their context:

Any of these answers *is* correct.

Were any of you able to attend the lecture?

Of the three hundred students, some *are* not going to graduate.

Some of the food *has* spoiled.

All of our hopes *were* fulfilled.

All of my money *was* lost.

Do not mistake the object of a preposition for the subject of the sentence:

One of the hamsters *was* sick.

VERB TENSE AND MOOD

Because verbs carry the action of your sentences, they need to function well together. In addition to indicating action or state of being, verbs also reveal tense—the time the action took place (*past* tense), takes place (*present* tense), or will take place (*future* tense). Verbs, with their auxiliaries, may also indicate whether the action has been completed (*perfect* tense) or is in progress (*progressive* tense).

PRESENT: I accomplish
PRESENT PROGRESSIVE: I am accomplishing
PRESENT PERFECT: I have accomplished
PAST: I accomplished
PAST PROGRESSIVE: I was accomplishing
PAST PERFECT: I had accomplished
FUTURE: I will accomplish
FUTURE PROGRESSIVE: I will be accomplishing
FUTURE PERFECT: I will have accomplished

To avoid distracting the reader, maintain a logical, consistent sequence of tenses from clause to clause and from sentence to sentence. Check particularly for shifts from past to present and from present to past. Note, for example, the tense shifts in the following paragraph:

> As the month of November *progressed,* the anticipation I *feel begins* to grow. I *am* aware that at the end of this month would come the happiest day of my life. It *was* impossible to pay attention to my school assignments, because my mind *is* always wandering. Soon I would be married.

In the first sentence, the tense shift from the past to the present is illogical and distracting. Moreover, the tense shift in the first sentence, coupled with the present tense in the second sentence, causes confusion about "this month": does the writer mean the past November, or is she referring to the present time at which she is writing the account? In the third sentence the tense shifts again and raises another question: does the writer's mind always wander, or did it wander only at that time because she was preoccupied with marriage plans?

Here is the paragraph revised:

> As the month of November *progressed,* the anticipation I *felt began* to grow. I *was* aware that at the end of that month would come the happiest day of my life. It *was* impossible to pay attention to my school assignments, because my mind *was* always wandering. Soon I would be married.

The Historical Present

Writers sometimes use the *historical present* in a narrative to create a sense of closeness between the reader and events that took place in the past. This use of the present tense usually occurs in works of literature and in literary criticism. The first of the two paragraphs that follow is a historical account of a village gravedigger; the second is a brief literary analysis. Both use the historical present:

He *works* incredibly hard and with great independence, travelling from village to village on a moped to the carrier of which *is* tied a gleaming spade and fork. He *drives* well out towards the centre of the road and the Anglo-American traffic *has* to swerve and swear to avoid him. Quite a lot of people *recognize* him, however, for he *is* a famous person, and *give* him a wide berth. They *know* they *are* seeing Time's winged chariot with a two-stroke.

Ronald Blythe,
Akenfield, Portrait of an English Village

Chaucer's Wife of Bath *shows* how a person can have many faults, yet remain cheerful and likable. The Wife *tells* how she mistreated her five husbands, and, in essence, *seems* to be asking if among the pilgrims there *is* a volunteer for the role of sixth husband. The implied request *is* mirrored by the actions of the loathsome hag in the Tale the Wife *tells.*

The Subjunctive Mood

Formal usage, and sometimes informal usage as well, requires use of the subjunctive mood when *conditions contrary to the facts* are referred to. The following sentences properly employ the subjunctive mood:

If he *were* (not *was*) coming, he would be here by now.

Were (not *was*) the point untenable, John would not stand by it.

Becky would attend the convention if more money *were* (not *was*) in the travel fund.

ADJECTIVES AND ADVERBS

Adjective Degrees

Adjectives have two degrees, comparative and superlative. Use the *comparative degree* (signaled by *-er* or *more*) only when making a comparative statement about *two* objects, persons, or concepts:

Of the two texts, John's is the *better* one.

Milton's poetry evokes *more* interest than Dryden's.

Rita is *happier* than anyone else.

Use the superlative degree (signaled by *-est* or *most*) to make a comparative statement about *more than two* objects, persons, or concepts:

Of the five texts, John's is the *best*.

Of Dryden's play, Wordsworth's sonnet, and Milton's epic, the *most* interesting work is Milton's.

Rita is the *happiest* of the three.

Adverb Degrees

Like adjectives, adverbs have two degrees. The comparative degree is marked by *more* and the superlative by *most*:

The first problem is *more* difficult than the second.

The first problem is the *most* difficult of the five.

Adjective-Adverb Confusion

Use adjectives to modify nouns and pronouns. Use adverbs to modify verbs, adjectives, and other adverbs. Do not confuse the adjective and adverb forms.

INCORRECT	CORRECT
Wayne did his job *good*. (adjective modifying verb)	Wayne did his job *well*. (adverb modifying verb)
Wayne did a *real* good job. (adjective modifying another adjective)	Wayne did a *really* good job. (adverb modifying adjective)

EXERCISES

1. Correct the problems with point of view in each of the following sentences:
   a. I enjoy visiting Niagara Falls because one feels the power of nature there.
   b. By attending the revival, I learned that you should obey the Ten Commandments.
   c. She asked would I like to follow her.
   d. When a person graduates from college, you find that jobs are still scarce.
   e. We had trouble locating a policeman; one is usually not there when you need him.
   f. He asked me would I attend the game.
2. Rewrite each of the following paragraphs to improve sentence variety:

   In crossing the railroad, I found many tracks. I tried to avoid one engine. I was knocked down by another. I was dragged a distance of a block or more. I got cuts on my face and hands, and I got coal ashes in the cuts. I didn't get any broken bones, and that was eight years ago. It took me two years to recover though.

He was a good boy until he got to card-playing and drinking. He didn't like to work after that, and he often stayed out till morning. He'd sleep late, and I couldn't wake him. The farm got run down, and the family got further in debt. We sold the farm, and we bought a house in town. He got worse than ever. He couldn't do any work. He wouldn't do anything but gamble and drink. A garbage truck ran over him one Monday morning.

3. Determine whether or not the following sentences are properly coordinated. (Is the most appropriate conjunction used? Are the coordinated statements closely related and of equal importance?) Correct any errors that you find.
   a. I voted for the man, and I still don't like him.
   b. He took the course four times, and he may have to take it a fifth.
   c. I didn't vote for him, but I've only lived in his district for a year.
   d. A good means of learning to succeed is to study three hours a night, and I haven't been able to do that.
   e. In order to save gasoline, don't drive when you can walk, but always consider the extra time that walking requires.
   f. Visit us again, and we always love to see you.
   g. I am not going to quit, nor shall I ask for a promotion.
   h. He will drive the blue sports car, or he will use his limousine.
   i. I did eat their porridge, but I didn't kill them.
4. Explain whether the subordination properly emphasizes the more important element in each of the following sentences:
   a. She had just arrived in class when word reached her that she had won the lottery.
   b. In addition to having to go to jail for ten years, he will miss the weekly poker game.
   c. After graduating from college, she became an assistant to the senator.
   d. Until he learns to get to places on time, he'll remain unemployed.
   e. According to the surgeon general, cigarette smoking is dangerous to your health.
   f. I was only mildly surprised when the doctor said my wife had delivered triplets.
   g. When the bus carrying the football team was four hours late in returning, the victory celebration was marred.
5. Correct the faulty parallelism in each of the following sentences:
   a. Corn products, wheat products, oat products, and Cheerios are my favorite breakfast foods.
   b. John likes to cook, reading historical novels, and classical music.
   c. His eyes grew brighter and brighter, his cheeks redder and redder, and his knees weaker.
   d. I remember my college years as being happy and carefree, and the sadness that came when I graduated.

    e. The boys were running, the girls laughing, and the parents were screaming.

    f. We picked tomatoes from the garden, apples from the orchard, and went home.

    g. I will either call you tonight or first thing tomorrow morning.

    h. The trees are lofty and beautiful, the sky is blue and clear, and the grass is green but feels prickly.

    i. Neither a bowl of chicken soup nor taking two aspirins made Joe feel better.

    j. He loved his wife not for her beauty, but because of her brains.

    k. They are enjoying football more.

    l. This issue is of paramount concern to the legislators, the taxpayers, and to welfare recipients.

6. Correct the errors in coherence in the following sentences:

    a. Shuddering convulsively, the pill was popped into the patient's mouth.

    b. Jumping to our positions, the contest started.

    c. When a poor immigrant boy of ten, my father took me to my first baseball game.

    d. The cannibal ate the missionary with zest.

    e. They ate the hotdogs with relish.

    f. Joe bought a Ford from the used car salesman with bucket seats.

    g. The university counselor is very understanding when crying and upset.

    h. Cruising at 3,000 feet, the people looked like ants.

    i. While drinking Scotch, the glass fell out of his hand.

    j. To play the scene correctly, words must be enunciated with precision.

    k. The couple went to the party on the bus.

7. Identify and correct the fragments in the following paragraph:

    Centerville is a hot, quiet town during the summer. Main Street consists of three stores and a gas station. The awnings over the fronts casting a welcome shade. When Mr. Argus arrives to unlock the doors to his optometrist office. Everyone knows it is eight o'clock sharp. As the sun gets higher, the air immediately over the street looks wavy and thick. Hardly any customers come. Because the population has pretty good vision.

8. Rewrite the following fragments to make them complete sentences:

    a. Especially after John's friends showed up at her house.

    b. This being that consumers are pressed for time and are therefore unable to compare prices.

    c. Without the report having been completed.

    d. The box which I left on the table.

    e. In the beginning of the month of April, in 1966.

    f. Until we met at the train station in the western part of Ohio.

    g. Where the row of ash trees meets the white fence.

    h. Which I have never been guilty of before.

    i. The problem being that he is incompetent.

    j. A travel guide to the United States.

9. Among the following sentences, identify and correct those which are fused and those which contain comma splices:

    a. The game was important for our school's reputation, it was being broadcast over national television.

    b. I was lying on the floor then I decided to get a snack.

    c. I awakened from a deep sleep, and then I made breakfast.

    d. You left the room you weren't properly dressed.

    e. I was standing in the elevator with nothing on but my thermal underwear, I really felt embarrassed.

    f. I went to school knowing that I wouldn't be able to study.

    g. He had just bought a new house, two new cars, and a boat, and then his employer fired him.

10. Correct the problems with reference and agreement in the following sentences:

    a. The times he attended was the most enjoyable.

    b. Each person should understand that their problems do have solutions.

    c. No one ever likes to turn their back on a person in need.

    d. The Johnsons and their son agrees to vote for the Republican.

    e. The problems with the men the two sisters married are quite complex; I don't even like to discuss them.

    f. Neither Ed nor Willard were in class today.

    g. Joe, along with his family, are attending the state fair.

    h. Every one of the Smiths go to church on Sunday.

    i. The army is building their own defenses.

    j. A writer like Chaucer or Shakespeare were well known by their contemporaries.

    k. Every time we fly through a cloud it rains.

    l. As Jane watched the lioness, she became quite interested in her movements.

11. Correct the problems with tense and mood in each of the following sentences:

    a. It made no difference to the prisoner whether the fence is electrified or not.

    b. If the decision was mine, I'd marry him.

    c. Whenever I went to Philadelphia, the restaurants don't serve grits.

    d. After I arrived at the university, I proceed to the dining hall.

    e. The difficulties between the two countries are insurmountable when a third country intervened.

    f. Napoleon arrives at the camp, issues his orders, and departed in haste.

    g. Henry James makes the ghost story believable when Miles ran away from the governess.

    h. By the time the train arrived, I have completed my plans.

    i. Was he here, the party would be ruined.

12. Correct the errors in use of adjectives and adverbs in the following sentences:

a. John sure knows how to drive a truck!
b. The man sat continuous atop the flagpole for three days.
c. Drowning the cat was a real bad thing to do.
d. Of the three brothers, John is the more likely to do good in school.
e. The Smiths determined to fix up the house as good as their finances permitted.
f. Tennis and basketball are enjoyable sports to watch, but I like to watch basketball the most.
g. I sometimes forget to do my math assignments very careful.
h. Mr. Scott is the less helpful of the three teachers.
i. Fred complained of feeling nauseous.
j. Dr. Clark's prescription aggravated the rash real bad.
k. Kate's head felt poor when she awoke.

Checking   14
Mechanics

It is inefficient to spend time and energy planning and writing a paper, only to type it hurriedly and rush to submit it. Time spent revising and polishing can make the difference between a successful written communication and a piece of writing that doesn't quite jell. It can also reveal errors or sources of possible confusion or distraction that you will want to fix before giving your work to someone else to read. As perhaps your last task in the revision process, you need to become your own proofreader. In this role, you read through the composition checking the nuts and bolts of punctuation that hold the language together.

It is best to stick to conventional usage in capitalizing, punctuating, and the like, for two reasons. First, you run the risk of making a poor impression on readers who know the usual practices if you do not observe them. You are writing not to alienate readers but to draw them toward your line of thinking. Second, following standard usage leaves you free to devote your energy to questions of thought and of language. At the same time, use of conventional mechanics offers you considerable control over your writing, as is shown in this discussion. For definitions of terminology used here, consult Appendix C.

THE COMMA

A comma indicates a pause between sentence parts. It is possible to "listen" for places where a comma is required, but in general you can gain greater control of your writing through conforming to accepted uses of the comma.

With Coordinating Conjunctions

▶ Place a comma before coordinating conjunctions ("and," "but," "or," "nor") to separate independent clauses in compound sentences:

> I thoroughly enjoyed our recent meeting, and I want to thank you for the useful information you gave me.

> Charles eagerly sought membership in the country club, but he was dismayed to discover its social bias.

> The Irish cannot unite behind a common view of the English, nor can the Scots agree on one view of the Irish.

The comma is optional when the independent clauses are short:

> The sky is blue and the sun is shining.

> Elvis stayed but Carol went home.

▶ Place a comma before coordinating conjunctions to separate independent clauses in a compound-complex sentence:

> The football game that we won last Saturday was attended by many alumni, but it was not our homecoming game.

> The children who were in the play stayed indoors to rehearse, and the rest of the class went outside to the playground.

With Adverb Clauses

▶ Place a comma after introductory adverb clauses:

> As soon as we heard the cannon, we realized that all was lost.

> If we attempt to debate the speaker, we will have to be sure of our facts.

> When the General Assembly returns to the Hall of Nations, the press gallery will be full.

Omit the comma when the adverb clause that follows the independent clause is essential to sentence meaning:

> Wilson stole third while Barringer waited for the ball.

> The crowd roared as the umpire signaled "Safe!"

▶ Place a comma before an adverb clause that follows an independent clause when necessary for clarity or smoothness:

I understand that many people find the President unappealing, although I think him a man of great charm.

The Republican party must unite behind its candidate, because this election is the most significant in years.

With Transitions

▶ Place a comma after transitional words or phrases:

In the first place, Roberts fails to understand the concept he is dealing with.

In fact, doesn't she deserve a scholarship?

With Introductory Phrases

▶ Place a comma after long introductory or modifying phrases:

Yearning for her lover, the countess stopped eating and drinking.

To enlist the cooperation of oil-rich nations, we will reevaluate our tariff program.

With Interjections

▶ Place a comma after a mild interjection that opens a statement:

Oh, did you see that car?

Yes, we do have what you require.

With Series

▶ Place a comma between items in a series:

Pick up the bottle, raise it to your lips, and swish the liquid over your tongue.

We devoured candy, plums, and yams.

(Some popular publications consider the comma preceding the conjunction optional; however, the preferred form is to retain the comma.)

Generally, omit commas when items in a series are joined by conjunctions:

Violence or drought or poverty or inflation or drugs—which will be the focal point of the next decade?

Sometimes it is necessary to place a comma between items in a series that is joined by conjunctions to avoid ambiguity or confusion:

> She attended William and Mary and Emory and Henry and the University of Oregon.

In this sentence, commas are needed to distinguish the "and" in the names of the institutions from the conjunction "and":

> She attended William and Mary, and Emory and Henry, and the University of Oregon.

▶ Place commas between two or more adjectives that equally and independently modify the same noun:

> The heavy, short man was eating cheese.
>
> Goldie, my beautiful, friendly retriever, died this morning.

In the sentences above, a comma is indicated only when both adjectives refer directly to the noun. When the first adjective modifies the whole idea that follows, it is not separated from the second adjective with a comma:

> The sad short story made me cry.
>
> Look at these beautiful blue jeans!

There are two tests that can help you decide whether a comma is needed between two adjectives. If the adjectives can be reversed and still make sense, or if "and" can be inserted between them, then the adjectives can be separated by a comma.

With Nonrestrictive Elements

▶ Place commas around nonrestrictive phrases and clauses:

> Byron Maguire, a noted actor, is my uncle.
>
> Mrs. Brown offered the Waldorf salad, made with fresh apples, to the entire team.

Do not place commas around restrictive clauses and phrases:

> He tripped over the box that was full of turtles.
>
> The carpenter on the ladder dropped his hammer.

With Contrasting Elements

▶ Place commas around contrasting elements:

> She comes from Minneapolis, not Chicago.
>
> Churchill, not Eisenhower, saved Europe.

With Localities

▶ Place commas around the parts of an address or geographical location:

> I grew up in Stone Harbor, Cape May County, New Jersey.
>
> The Millers' address is 143 Beach Street, Houston, Texas.
>
> Most government buildings in Washington, D.C., are open to tourists.

With Titles

▶ Place commas around a title or a degree that follows a proper name:

> Bernard Townsend, M.A., was the keynote speaker.
>
> The chairman of the board, J. Randolph Jones, Sr., called the meeting to order.
>
> Greg Dunning, M.D., and John Williams, Ph.D., are the authors of this article.

With Dates

▶ Place commas around the parts of a date:

> The building was dedicated on July 13, 1944.
>
> January 21, 1976, is the date on his letter.

If the day is given before the month, omit the comma:

> The last entry in the journal is dated 3 October 1859.

If the day is not given, the comma following the month is optional:

> I haven't seen her since June 1968.
>
> In December, 1956, my family moved to California.

With Salutations

▶ Place a comma after the salutation in an informal letter:

> Dear Hepsibah,
>
> My dear Aunt Mildred,

THE COLON

With Independent Clauses

▶ Place a colon after an independent clause to announce that clarifying material follows:

> What separates Chaucer from his contemporaries is his deep appreciation of the wide variety of English life: he welcomes the genteel with the bawdy, the spiritual with the worldly.

> The following delegates from the Tenth Congressional District voted "aye" to the controversial resolution: Barry Adams, Heather Fulton, D. Jason Landis.

With Quotations

▶ Place a colon before a formal quotation when the quotation is a complete sentence. The quoted statement following the colon begins with a capital letter:

> Perhaps John F. Kennedy said it best: "Ask not what your country can do for you; ask what you can do for your country."

> Churchill's words after the Battle of Britain are immortal: "Never have so many owed so much to so few."

With Numbers, Biblical References, and Salutations

▶ Place a colon between hour and minute, between Biblical chapter and verse, and after a formal letter greeting:

> 8:45 A.M.
>
> Luke 2:13
>
> Dear Mr. Turner:

THE SEMICOLON

With Independent Clauses

▶ Place a semicolon between independent clauses not connected by a coordinating conjunction:

> The candle was lit; there still was insufficient light for reading.

> The cat was a gourmet; he demanded shrimp, scallops, and lobster.

▶ Place a semicolon between two independent clauses linked by a conjunctive adverb. A comma follows the conjunctive adverb:

> The ever-expanding Soviet Navy may prove troublesome to the West; in fact, it is now the largest military sea force in the world.

> Bill found he could not get a clear shot to the goal; therefore, he passed to Richard.

With Series

▶ Place a semicolon between elements in a series when commas appear within an individual item in that series:

> Griselda bought three new pets: Clarence, a goldfish; Seymour, a scorpion; and Magnolia, a mouse.

THE PERIOD

With Sentence Endings

▶ Place a period at the end of all sentences except questions or exclamations:

> There is nothing so appealing as the mating song of the hornbilled egret.

> "Herman Melville's life is really a study of contrasts," claimed Professor Snort.

With Abbreviations

▶ Place a period after an abbreviation:

Dr.	Sr.
Ms.	R. E. Jones
B.A.	Ave.

Current usage allows omitting the period from certain abbreviations, particularly those of organizations and agencies:

NATO	UNESCO
FBI	NAACP

With Indirect Questions

▶ Place a period (not a question mark) after an indirect question (a declarative statement that concerns a question):

> She wanted to know if Congress would continue the education funds.

> The district attorney asked Randolph the source of his income.

THE QUESTION MARK

With Direct Questions

▶ Place a question mark after a sentence that asks a direct question:

> Are you going to the party?

> "Do you really think," he asked, "that the government will fail?"

With Implied Uncertainty

▶ Use a question mark to imply uncertainty concerning dates or facts:

> Bede, 673(?)–735

> Eric the Red, born 950(?)

THE DASH

With Interruption

▶ Place a dash before and after a parenthetical statement that clarifies a sentence:

The black mass—a corruption of the Christian service—continues in parts of Eastern Europe.

The basics of democracy—equality, choice, expression, freedom— are still thriving in our country.

With Qualification

▶ Use dashes to indicate strong hesitation or doubt:

They'll arrive at nine—I hope.

You're an honest person—aren't you?

THE HYPHEN

With Word Division

▶ Place a hyphen between syllables of a word when your margin does not leave you room to write the entire word on one line:

secre-   handker-
    tary   chief

Do not hyphenate single-syllable words even if they are long ("thought," "could," "straight"), and do not hyphenate words so that a single letter is set off ("a-bove," "weight-y"). If you are not sure how to divide a word, check the dictionary.

With Two-Word Adjectives

▶ Place a hyphen between two-word adjectives that function as a single adjective:

They sat on the moss-covered stone and ate their lunch.

The air-conditioned theater is always crowded in the summer.

With Compound Words and Numbers

▶ Place a hyphen between the elements in compound words and numbers:

My mother-in-law gave me another new tie.

Sparta was a Greek city-state.

Thirty-seven students have signed up for the new class in astrology.

With Prefixes

▶ Place a hyphen after prefixes followed by proper nouns, and after "ex" and "self":

> "You are un-American," stated Senator Pringle.

> As France entered the post-World War I period, her citizens rallied around the new government.

> He is an ex-union official.

> Snodgrass, forever suffering the pain of self-doubt, became entirely superfluous within the organization.

THE EXCLAMATION POINT

With Exclamatory Sentences

▶ Place an exclamation point after exclamatory sentences:

> Touch me and I'll scream!

With Interjections

▶ Place an exclamation point after an emphatic interjection:

> Damn! The hot rivet fell inside my shoe.

> We're having deep-fried artichokes for brunch? Great!

PARENTHESES

With Enumeration

▶ Place parentheses around numerical or alphabetical points within a sentence:

> There are three central questions we must confront if this project is to be successful: (1) the total cost, (2) the required number of man-hours, and (3) the long-range effects on the international market.

With Explanatory Elements

▶ Place parentheses around material that explains but is not essential to the meaning of a sentence. Sometimes an entire sentence, with appropriate punctuation, may be placed in parentheses:

The character of Sherlock Holmes ("Elementary, my dear Watson") was actually drawn from a man known to Sir Arthur Conan Doyle.

Because of the North Sea oil fields, Aberdeen (population 225,000) has become Scotland's first "boom town."

You may need additional information. (If so, consult the card catalog.)

BRACKETS

With Direct Quotations

▶ Place brackets around material not part of a direct quotation but added for clarification:

> "I believe," said the ambassador, "that he [the Shah of Iran] is a loyal friend of the United States."

The Latin word *sic* in brackets in a direct quotation indicates that an error appears in the original source:

> Her journal entry for April 24, 1869, reads, "We leave today for Calafornia [*sic*], a long and perilous journey."

QUOTATION MARKS

With Direct Quotations

▶ Enclose direct quotations (the exact words and punctuation of the speaker or writer) in quotation marks. When using a quotation within your own sentence, quote only the words that belong to the secondary source:

> Ibsen maintained that "all men require a pleasing illusion to make the ugliness of reality more palatable."
>
> "There are two major problems plaguing the nation," James Wilson explained. "The first is inflation; the second is unemployment."

For further discussion of the use of quoted matter, see Appendix B, pp. 231–232.

Indirect quotations (that is, restatements of the original words of someone else) do *not* take quotation marks:

Mr. Jackson said, "The divorce rate in America is a symptom of the nation's moral degeneration." (direct quotation)

Mr. Jackson said that he considers the divorce rate in America to be symptomatic of the nation's moral laxity. (indirect quotation)

▶ Quotations within quotations should be indicated by single quotation marks:

At the convention, the speaker told the members of the N.E.A., "I disagree with Professor Jamison's charge that we are 'a bunch of muddle-headed intellectuals' who 'cannot separate theory from reality.' "

With Titles

▶ Place quotation marks around titles of essays, magazine articles, chapters of books, short stories, individual poems, and television and radio programs:

MacQuirk's new essay, "A New Theory of Relativity," is not as complete as Rankin's "Understanding Relativity."

Hemingway's "Indian Camp" is my favorite short story.

The class read Robert Frost's excellent poem "Birches."

With Other Marks

▶ Place the period and the comma inside quotation marks:

I believe," said John, "that we are on the brink of disaster."

▶ Place the colon and the semicolon outside quotation marks (unless they are part of the quotation itself):

The novelist accused his audience of "ignorance which is an insult to the arts"; I noted, however, that some of his comments were also ignorant.

He claimed that "we are a lost civilization": morally and spiritually we are bankrupt.

The speaker, attacking the quality of education in the contemporary classroom, stated, "We have only three options: reorganize our schools; hire better teachers; establish appropriate funds for necessary materials."

▶ Place the question mark inside the quotation marks when the quotation itself is a question and outside the quotation marks when the quotation is included within a question:

"Do you love me?" he asked.

Did the courtship proceed "with all deliberate speed"?

THE APOSTROPHE

With Possessives

▶ "Use 's with singular nouns that do not end with s to indicate possession:

John is Bill's brother.

The book's jacket is gorgeous.

▶ To make a singular noun ending with s possessive, use the apostrophe alone or 's:

I enjoy reading Dickens' (or Dickens's) novels.

The actress' (or actress's) performance was outstanding.

▶ Place the apostrophe after the s to form the possessive of plural nouns:

The Smiths' house is for sale.

The players' shirts were stolen.

▶ Place 's after the last letter of plural nouns that do not end with s to show possession:

The children's bicycles are in the yard.

The geese's honking kept us awake.

▶ Use 's to form the possessive of indefinite pronouns:

Someone's coat is on the floor.

Is everybody's work finished?

Do not use an apostrophe with possessive pronouns:

I'm not sure whose turn it is.

The decision was both theirs and ours.

With Some Plurals

▶ Use the 's to form the plural of words being referred to as words:

Jack has five misspelled *separate*'s in his paper.

How many *yes*'s do I hear?

▶ Use 's after letters of the alphabet and numbers to form their plurals:

Richard's three F's made his father angry.

Paula's 7's are poorly formed.

With Contractions

▶ Use the apostrophe to show contractions in words and dates:

I'm meeting Jill at 2 o'clock.

He's a member of the class of '78.

ITALICS AND UNDERLINING

With Titles

▶ Underline (to indicate italic type) the titles of books, magazines, newspapers, long poems, films, plays, and works of art:

Although originally produced in 1939, *Gone with the Wind* continues to attract the moviegoing public.

We are going to read Milton's *Paradise Lost* in literature class next term.

I subscribe to *Time* and *Sports Illustrated*.

With Foreign Words and Phrases

▶ Underline (to indicate italic type) foreign words that have not become part of the English language:

The candidate, summing up his successful campaign, said, "*Veni, vidi, vici.*"

Your chocolate mousse is the *pièce de résistance*.

With Words, Letters, and Figures

▶ Underline (to indicate italic type) words, letters, and figures referred to as such:

> You spelled Mississippi with too many *s*'s.
>
> John's 7's look like 1's.
>
> The word *tranquility* means different things to different people.

CAPITALIZATION

▶ Capitalize proper nouns:

William Shakespeare	Los Angeles, California
John the Baptist	University of Michigan
Hudson River	Bell Telephone Company
Fifth Avenue	United Nations

▶ Capitalize adjectives derived from proper nouns:

Shakespearian	Greek
Californian	Platonic

▶ Capitalize specific events or periods in history, months, days of the week, and holidays:

the Civil War	Monday, April 24
the Stone Age	Christmas

▶ Capitalize titles immediately preceding a name:

President Lincoln	Reverend Witherspoon
Dean Smithers	Captain Pierce

▶ Capitalize abbreviations immediately following a name:

John L. Meadows, Jr.	J. P. O'Malley, D.D.S.
Margaret Winkler, Ph.D.	Arthur Roth, M.D.

▶ Capitalize the first word in every sentence.

▶ Capitalize all words in a title, except articles, the "to" of infinitives, conjunctions, and prepositions—unless these appear as the first or last word in a title:

An Inquiry into the Assassination of President William McKinley

"In Darkness and Confusion"

▶ When quoting a complete sentence, capitalize the first word and any other word that the author capitalized:

Citing the current campus crisis, Dean Blather wrote: "Action must be taken now if the University is to survive."

Capitalization is not necessary when incorporating a quoted phrase into your sentence:

The creature laughed at "this strange little planet."

▶ Capitalize abstract nouns when they are personifications:

the stench of Pity

the rape of Romance

EXERCISES

1. Insert commas where they are needed:
   a. Today is January 13 1980.
   b. "Oh I really do like chocolate" squealed Sarah.
   c. She was the daughter of a merchant from London and she married the son of a merchant from Brussels.
   d. Please bring in the groceries especially the sack with the ice cream in it.
   e. He prided himself on his athletic ability particularly his skill in basketball hockey and polo.
   f. Chris not Susan smoked all Marty's cigarettes.
   g. Budapest Hungary was poorly represented at the conference.
   h. Rasputin who was purported to be the queen's lover exerted great influence in czarist Russia.
   i. The thatched roofs were very very flammable.
   j. And now ladies and gentlemen here is Walter Schmurtz the anchorman for the six o'clock news team.
   k. The third assault was led by Philip Augustus king of France.
   l. Accordingly we should enlist the cooperation of the commissioner of baseball.
   m. To keep his harem safe the king hired six eunuchs.
   n. I don't in fact plan to attend the class reunion.

    o. Tamara was an angel but an angel with fangs.

    p. The bill is here from John Grove M.D.

2. Correct the punctuation and capitalization problems in the following:

    a. Bill is this Mikes' pen or is it Gretchens'.

    b. That you lisp, George is nothing to be ashamed of.

    c. Ugh, the cheese in the cellar turned rancid, I knew I shouldn't have left it there.

    d. Johnson stated The Gulf of Tonkin Resolution is essential to our Foreign Policy.

    e. The train arrived at 4 35, John my boyfriend wasnt on it, he came on the bus the next night.

    f. Is it your turn or our's to bring refreshments?

    g. Shots rang out and general Lee shouted "no surrender".

    h. Do'nt get the idea that you're here for a vacation you are'nt.

    i. He divorced punctuality, and married eccentricity.

    j. James Madison the third president of the United States courted and married: the beautiful Dolly Madison.

    k. consider the following proposition; i have two coins totaling fifty five cents one of the coins is not a nickel. What are the two coins.

    l. He caressed her lovingly. all the while munching on a candy bar.

    m. Country music defies classification to analyze it is to spoil it.

    n. While composing his symphonies Beethoven was deaf.

    o. Bankruptcy obliged the family to move from Berlin Germany, on August 17 1808, when Hortense celebrated her tenth birthday and look for a new home near Billings Montana.

    p. cheer up cried Heathcliff!

    q. Mr Moore the president of Union bank, Ms Nathanson the bankers wife, and Ella Snyder PhD the famous botanist combined their efforts in the third annual greater Gibson county talent show.

    r. There are four steps to washing your dog—1 immerse the animal 2 scour it thoroughly with soap 3 dry it off 4 comb its fur.

    s. Yes! That's my coat in the closet.

    t. His most recent novel, "Beyond the Horizon," was acclaimed by critics. (See the review by Waldo Flink in Time, December 20 1976.)

    u. It was not; however, the flood that made me late

    v. At four am Linus tumbled out of bed; went to the kitchen; then realized his clock was on eastern standard time.

    w. He wore new shoes hush puppies.

Appendices

Appendices

A Paper Undergoing Revision   **A**

The value of thorough revision is illustrated by the following three drafts of a student paper. Note that the changes made from draft one to draft two, and again from draft two to draft three, involve an ever-sharpening thesis statement, improved diction, more supporting detail, and correction of illogic and grammatical and mechanical errors. A comparison of drafts one and three reveals that essay elements are constantly being modified and amended as the writer more clearly perceives the scope and direction of his paper.

The marginal annotations in the following drafts indicate certain problems that the student identified. Even though draft three is an obvious improvement over drafts one and two, you may find additional ways that the student could have improved his paper.

OUTLINE

I.   INTRODUCTION

     A. Main point: Today's college students are exploited.

     B. Thesis statement: Today's college students are exploited by large class sizes, by impersonal teaching in an impersonal manner, and by being forced to buy books and materials that they do not need.

II.   BODY

    A.   Many college classes have 200+ students in them.

        1. Large classes make discussion impossible.

        2. Large classes make questions impossible.

        3. Large classes mean that tests will be objective.

    B.   Many teachers seem not to care about their students.

        1. Some are unprepared.

delete

        2. Some are under such pressure to publish that they have

           little time for discussions, tutorials, and office hours.

    C.   Students often have to buy books and materials that they do

       not need.

        1. Some teachers require students to buy books and materials

           that will be used only once or twice all semester.

        2. To make money, some teachers require students to buy

           books that they themselves have written.

III. CONCLUSION: Class sizes should be reduced, (teachers must be

       delete

    made to live up to their professional responsibility,) buying

    books should only be required when the book is central to the

    course.

Note that even before the first draft is written, alterations of the outline have been made.

FIRST DRAFT

paper's purpose needs to be clearer

Today's college students are exploited by large class sizes, ~~by~~ *improve* ~~impersonal~~ and being forced to buy books and materials that they do *parallelism*

not need.

From the <u>Ivy League to the Pacific Eight</u>, many college students

   restate — suggests athletics   *ref?*

attend ~~classes that have too many people~~ in them. This causes problems

too much repetition *sp* in the education they <u>recieve</u>, problems that stem from the impossibility

of class discussions in <u>these large classes</u>. The teacher, <u>because of</u>

<u>class</u> size, can only lecture. He doesn't have time to answer students

relevant?

questions, (even if they were encouraged to ask them, which they aren't.) *awkward*

The result of all this is lectures which often just <u>skim the surface</u> *trite*
parallelism of the material, bored students, and finally objective tests that only
point of view require <u>you</u> to fill in the blanks or match answers to questions. A̶lot
of these students work many hours each week so that they can afford to
logic: appeal to pity attend college. Many of their parents <u>scrimp and save</u> to help put their *trite*
offspring through college. And all they get are huge classes and tests
that demand nothing more than <u>memerization.</u> *sp*

Better transition between ¶s. The other thing that causes college students to get <u>ripped off</u> is *diction?*
professors who make their classes buy books and materials that they do
not need. In a̶lot of cases, a professor will demand that his class buy
a book and then (only) use the book once or twice during the semester.

Still too general? In other cases, a professor will have his students buy a book and then
simply tell them to read around in it. The students doesn't know what
they're suppose to read. ~~They don't know~~ *or* why they should read it. But
they do it because the professor says they should. The worst example
ref of <u>this</u> is the professor who makes his students buy a book that he has
written only so that he can make money from the sales. He has no
intention of using the book in class but he has every intention of
using the money he gets from it's sale!

Most college students are interested in learning. They deserve
More forceful conclusion? better than they often get. What needs to be done is to make class
sizes smaller and to force professors to order only books and materials
that the content of the course requires.

SECOND DRAFT

TITLE?

The ever-increasing cost of a college education has resulted in
many students questioning whether or not they are getting what they
pay for. Some students beleive that they are being exploited by *sp*
Never supported colleges that make large classes standard and by professors who force
them to buy books and <u>materials</u> that they do not need.
too broad? College classes of one-hundred to six hundred have become the *no hyphen*
standard in many of the nation's schools, with the result that students
are being deprived of the educational opportunities that should be part

Still not convincing— of learning. Because they cannot possibly answer all the students'

questions in such classes, professors often do away with discussion,

Make specific and the class becomes nothing more than a thrice-weekly lecture

directed at a sea of faces. The result is often boredom, students sit

poasively as words echo all about them, the professor has no opportunity

to engage in debate with active and interested students, and the

diction too strong? intellectual stimulus and depth that is part of discussion is lost. The

ultimate exploitation occurs during examinations. The class size often

forces the professor to give objective tests consisting of true/false

or multiple choice questions. Thus, examinations become nothing more

than regurgitation sessions, and those students who sincerely want to

investigate an area of knowledge are left with no where to go. "The

answer to number 10 is a"; "number two in column b matches number seven *parallel*

in column a." Sadly enough, it is the student most in need of small

agreement classes—the freshman and sophomores—who ~~are~~ *is* shunted into Introduction *expand these points for specific examples*

to Psychology with an enrollment of 300, and into Introduction to

Biology with 250 students.

Equally upsetting to many of today's students are thoughtless

professors who demand they buy unnecessary textbooks and materials.

With the average hard-back text costing $8 or $9 (paperbacks are a

few dollars less,) students are reluctant to buy books, that will be

Make Specific of little use to them. Yet one of my recent classes, I was told to buy

a text costing $9.95, that the class would use it from time to time.

I bought the book. The professor referred to it twice during the rest

of the semester. In other instances, a text appears on a course

syllabus, the professor tells the class to "read around in it," and

the students buy it. But they are never told what to read or why.

be specific When one of my friends complained to a professor who was guilty of

this practice, the professor simply brushed the complaint aside with

the remark that "It's a good book to have around." Serious as such

instances are, they pale next to the practice which some professors

Specific example— delete? use: forcing the class to buy a book written by that same professor.

Naturally, there is nothing wrong with this practice providing that

argument too weak, too general the book will be used in the class. However, a number of professors

demand that students buy their texts simply to make money from the

sales.

The three to five thousand dollars per year that students pay for a college education is high enough. Like everyone else, students are exploited by inflation and the cost of living. But for their money, they deserve an educational experience not found in large classes, and they do not deserve to be exploited by thoughtless and, at times, unscrupulous professors.

THIRD DRAFT

COLLEGE RIP- OFF

The rising costs of a college education have prompted many students to ask if they are getting what they pay for. At State University, tuition has gone up over $300 in the last three years; the cost of certain basic texts, an upperclassman told me, has risen by one-third in that same period of time. ~~I think I~~ Students are being exploited not only by large classes but also by being forced to purchase texts ~~and materials that~~ they do not need.   deprive

The large sizes of several of my classes ~~show that~~ students ~~are~~ ~~deprived~~ of certain learning opportunities. In my biology lecture section, for example, there are at least 250 students. Last Tuesday the professor lectured on crustations; twice I had difficulty under-standing her because she spoke so rapidly, but she never noticed my raised hand, and I was unable to get my questions cleared up. After class, six or eight other students approached her with questions. I didn't have time to wait in line since I had to get to Introduction to Psychology in ten minutes. I never did get my questions answered, and now I'm not even sure what they were. When I arrived at my psy-chology class, I took my seat among 300 other students. The ~~class was so large and the~~ lecture ~~so~~ was really boring—in part because the professor was so far away that many students couldn't even see his facial expressions. Students near me were snoring, writing letters, and reading the student newspaper. In both my biology and psychology courses, I am given only ~~objective~~ multiple-choice tests for ease of grading. On these, I regurgitate memorized facts; I am never asked to synthesize information in a discussion, and therefore I get no

instructor reaction to my general ideas. I think much of my tuition
is wasted.

A second way in which students are exploited is through being made
to buy unnecessary books. My psychology text cost me $11.95 (plus tax).
I have never had a specific assignment from it, and the objective tests
in the course are only over the material the professor has lectured on.
I must admit, though, that the professor told ~~me~~ to /read around in it."
the class
I'm not sure what to read or why. When my friend Jim asked the professor
why the class had to buy the book/the professor replied, "It's a good
book to have around." ~~Another example of exploitation is the~~ ~~An even~~
An even
~~worse~~ Another example of unnecessary ~~expense~~ text expense is that of ˄
students
an
having to buy˄expensive text/ and then ~~use~~ be˄assigned only one-tenth of
ing
it for class; my friend Ann bought a $16 book for her Music Appreciation
course last year and was assigned only two of the twenty chapters.

The $3,000 to $5,000 ~~that~~ per year that students pay for a college
education is high enough. For that kind of money a person˄an educational
deserves
experience not found in large classes, and no one should have to ~~endure~~
~~buying high~~ go to the additional expense of buying a needless or almost
needless book.

The essay is now ready to be recopied for submission.

The Research   B
Paper

The research paper is similar to any composition insofar as it involves prewriting, developing supporting material, and revising. It is, however, the nature of the research paper that makes it seem complex, for as the name implies, "research" means dealing with sources of information outside of your experience. For this reason, it is helpful to think of a research paper as a partnership between you and the information that you will locate, shape, arrange, and present.

The following pages illustrate the components of the research process: selecting a topic, researching material, and documenting that material. The appendix concludes with a sample research paper.

ARRIVING AT A TOPIC

Writing a research paper does not begin with a visit to the library; it begins with you. To go to the library without first having a clear idea of what you will write about will result in much time wasted.

Selecting a topic for a research paper requires going through the prewriting process as described in chapters two and three. You must confront at least some of the strategy questions (particularly the question of what you are attempting to do to or for your audience), and you must impose limitations on a broad subject area. Assume, for example, that you have been assigned a 2,000-word research paper by your biology instructor on the broad subject of "digestive systems." Your major objective is to explain, but you realize that to write on such a broad subject would result in a paper so general that it would have no value. A few moments of directed thinking, however, will enable you to narrow your focus as you move from subject to topic.

SUBJECT	NARROWING FOCUS	TOPIC
digestive systems	in man——in animals——in plants——in insects——**in insects**——digestive systems in insects——in nonflying insects——in ants——in the fire ant——in the South African fire ant——components of digestive systems in the South African fire ant ——pincers——thorax——enzymes——mandibles——the function of the mandibles in the South African fire ant	**the function of the mandibles in the South African fire ant**

As the above example reveals, arriving at a topic for a research paper requires an ever-narrowing focus (similar to that described in chapter three). Naturally, the more you know about any subject area, the easier it will be to narrow your focus. But even if you have been assigned a subject you know very little about (a rare occurrence in college), a few minutes of thought will enable you to place some commonsense limitation on the subject, thereby making your task easier when you do visit the library. Remember, researching material on the Siamese fighting fish is considerably less complicated than researching material on tropical fish.

The assigned length of any research project will also help determine the limitations of your topic. A 10,000-word paper would obviously enable you to cover a broader area and provide more supporting detail than would a 2,000-word paper. If, for example, you begin thinking about the broad subject of "war," you may narrow your focus to "Napoleonic Wars," further narrow it to "Napoleon's strategy at the Battle of Waterloo," and finally arrive at "Napoleon's pincer tactic against the Russians at the Battle of Waterloo." The subject "war" is far too broad for even a hundred books, and the topic "Napoleonic Wars" might be treated in ten volumes. But "Napoleon's strategy at the Battle of Waterloo" could be explored in a 10,000-word paper, and "Napoleon's pincer tactic against the Russians at the Battle of Waterloo" could be treated in a 2,000-word paper. Remember, as with any essay, a successful research paper depends on finding a topic that can be treated thoroughly within specific limits. Do not assume that a short research paper should have less depth than a long one. Remember your obligation to your audience.

RESEARCHING MATERIAL

You should visit a library only after you know the limitations that have been imposed by the assignment, after you have confronted the appropriate strategy questions, and after you have narrowed your focus as much as possible. (You may, of course, continue the narrowing process as your research acquaints you more fully with components of your topic.)

This section is designed to familiarize you with the following: (1) the arrangement of materials in the library, (2) the major resources that will aid your research, and (3) the basic research process.

Library Classification Systems

Materials in libraries are arranged either by the Dewey decimal system or by the Library of Congress system. Some libraries use both. Learning the basics of each system will aid you in locating material.

The following lists the major subject divisions and corresponding classification numbers for the Dewey decimal system:

000	General Works
100	Philosophy
200	Religion
300	Social Sciences
400	Philology (Language)
500	Pure Science
600	Applied Science (Technology)
700	The Arts
800	Literature
900	History and Geography

The following lists the major subject divisions and corresponding classification letters for the Library of Congress system:

A	General Works
B	Philosophy, Psychology, Religion
C	History
D	Topography (except America)
E–F	American History and Topography
G	Geography, Anthropology, Sports
H	Social Sciences
J	Political Science
K	Law
L	Education
M	Music

N	Fine Arts
P	Language and Literature
Q	Science
R	Medicine
S	Agriculture, Forestry, Animal Husbandry
T	Technology
U	Military Science
V	Naval Science
Z	Bibliography and Library Science

Resources for Research

The library contains three broad resources for research: (1) general reference materials, (2) periodical indexes, and (3) the card catalog. Knowing how to use each of these resources will allow you to save considerable research time.

General Reference Materials

Libraries contain general reference works—encyclopedias, special dictionaries, yearbooks, bibliographies—that provide background material on a variety of subjects. These materials are appropriate sources to consult when *beginning* your research. However, because their information is simply a compendium of research done by others, they should never form the substance of your paper.

There is one basic text to be aware of when launching a research project in an area in which you are not expert: Constance M. Winchell's *Guide to Reference Books*, 8th ed. (Chicago: American Library. Association, 1967). It is an index of bibliographies and reference books on the following:

A. General Reference Works

1. Bibliography
2. Librarianship and Library Resources
3. Societies
4. Encyclopedias
5. Language Dictionaries
6. Periodicals
7. Newspapers
8. Government Publications
9. Dissertations
10. Biography
11. Genealogy

B. Humanities

1. Philosophy
2. Religion

    3. Linguistics and Philology

    4. Literature

    5. Languages

    6. Fine Arts

    7. Applied Arts

    8. Theater Arts

    9. Music

C. Social Sciences

    1. General Works

    2. Education

    3. Sociology

    4. Anthropology and Ethnology

    5. Mythology

    6. Folklore and Popular Customs

    7. Statistics

    8. Economics

    9. Political Science

    10. Law

    11. Geography

D. History and Area Studies

    1. General History

    2. The Americas

    3. Europe

    4. Africa

    5. Asia

    6. Australia and New Zealand

    7. Oceanica

    8. Arctic and Antarctic

E. Pure and Applied Sciences

    1. General Works

    2. Astronomy

    3. Biological Sciences

    4. Chemistry

    5. Earth Sciences

    6. Mathematics

    7. Physics

    8. Psychology and Psychiatry

    9. Engineering

    10. Medical Sciences

    11. Agricultural Sciences

Here is a brief list of some of the best-known general reference works for certain fields (your library will probably contain many others):

HUMANITIES

> *Social Science and Humanities Index*
> Bateson, F. W., ed., *Cambridge Bibliography of English Literature*
> Modern Language Association of America, *MLA International Bibliography*
> R. E. Spiller et al., eds., *Literary History of the United States*

SOCIAL SCIENCES

> *Social Science and Humanities Index*
> *International Bibliography of Social and Cultural Anthropology*
> *International Bibliography of Sociology*
> *International Bibliography of Economics*
> Harmon, Robert B., *Political Science: A Bibliographical Guide to the Literature*
> *Education Index*
> *Business Periodicals Index*

SCIENCES

> *Harvard List of Books on Psychology*
> U. S. National Agricultural Library, *Bibliography of Agriculture*
> U. S. Geological Survey, *Bibliography of North American Geology*
> Whitford, Robert H., *Physics Literature: A Reference Manual*
> *Guide to Mathematics and Physics*
> *Index Medicus*
> *Index Chemicus*
> *Engineering Index*

Periodical Indexes

Any magazine, journal, or newspaper published on a regular basis constitutes periodical literature. Your library will have a list or a file of the periodicals it contains.

Because of the large number of periodicals on the market and because many of them are aimed at specialized segments of the populace, *periodical indexes* are published to aid research. There are many such indexes, each of which lists articles published in periodicals concerning a particular subject or professional area. For example, for research on engineering, start with the *Engineering Index;* for research on economics, consult the *Index of Economic Journals;* for research on music, examine the *Music Index.* Your library will have a list of available indexes.

The *Reader's Guide to Periodical Literature* deserves special mention. This index surveys many general magazines and journals, from *House and Garden* to *Time* to the *Education Digest.* Published bimonthly, the

Reader's Guide contains information that is always current, and, like most periodical indexes, it is easy to use because it includes at its beginning a list of the periodicals that it surveys and a list of the abbreviations that it uses. Articles are indexed in the *Reader's Guide* by both subject and author.

The following annotations are designed to familiarize you with the abbreviations common to the *Reader's Guide.* The first is a subject entry:

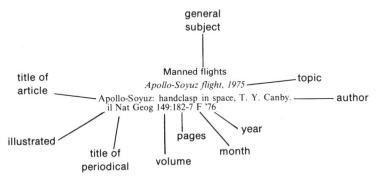

This is an author entry:

> SKOW, John
> Call of the champion. il por Outdoor Life 157:
> 54-7+ F '76

Like any index, the *Reader's Guide* contains cross-references which guide you to additional information under separate headings. Here is a sample cross-reference entry:

> SKILLED labor
> *See also*
> Trade unions—Skilled labor

The Card Catalog

The card catalog is a file of all the books, pamphlets, and films that the library possesses. It consists of a three-part system of index cards arranged alphabetically under (1) the subject(s) of the book, (2) the title of the book, and (3) the author's name (last name first). The basic three-part makeup of the card catalog allows you to find relevant books without knowing specific authors or titles. If, for example, you want to locate a book on tropical fish but you cannot remember the author or title, you can still find the book by thinking of subjects that the book is likely to embrace: ichthyology, fish, tropical fish. One of your subject headings will likely correspond to a heading in the card catalog. Because it requires less information, the subject catalog is perhaps more useful than the author or title catalogs.

When you locate a specific reference in the card catalog, you will see that it contains considerable information:

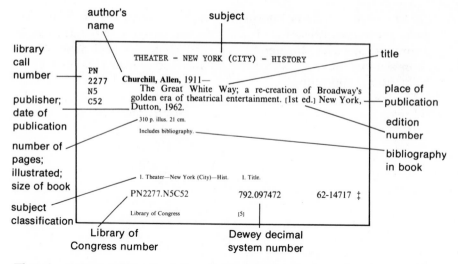

The above is a *subject card,* but there are two other cards in the card catalog for the same book: the *title card* and the *author card.* The title card is identical to the subject card except that the subject is omitted and the book's title appears on the first line:

```
         The Great White Way
PN
2277   Churchill, Allen, 1911—
N5          The Great White Way; a re-creation of Broadway's
C52    golden era of theatrical entertainment. [1st ed.] New York,
       Dutton, 1962.
            310 p. illus. 21 cm.
            Includes bibliography.



            I. Theater—New York (City)—Hist.    I. Title.
       PN2277.N5C52              792.097472          62-14717  ‡
       Library of Congress             [5]
```

The author card is identical to the subject and title cards with the exception of the subject and title lines, which are omitted:

```
PN
2277   Churchill, Allen, 1911—
N5          The Great White Way; a re-creation of Broadway's
C52    golden era of theatrical entertainment. [1st ed.] New York,
       Dutton, 1962.
            310 p. illus. 21 cm.
            Includes bibliography.



            I. Theater—New York (City)—Hist.    I. Title
       PN2277.N5C52              792.097472          62-14717  ‡
       Library of Congress             [5]
```

In addition to the author, title, and subject cards, the library's card catalog contains *cross-reference* cards. If, for example, you are checking through the catalog for books on "transmitters," you will find "see also" cards at the end of this section. These cards list other headings that pertain to "transmitters": "see citizen band radio" or "see mobile radio."

The Research Process

After you have narrowed your focus and after you know the location of research materials, you are ready to begin your active research. There are three steps in this process: (1) examine research materials, (2) compile a tentative bibliography, and (3) take notes.

Examining Research Materials

Effective research, like effective writing, requires method, and the best method for research is one of ever-increasing focus as you move from the general to the specific.

Your first stop in the library should be at the general reference collection. The encyclopedias, special dictionaries, and bibliographies (which you have become aware of through the appropriate guides and indexes) will supply you with valuable background information which may enable you to limit your topic further. In addition, the general reference collection may provide you with clues for further research. You may notice, for example, that a particular book, article, or author is mentioned prominently in a number of these references, a signal that you should investigate this specific reference further.

The background information and clues furnished by the general reference collection should lead you to the appropriate periodical indexes. Do not at this point attempt to locate specific periodicals; simply make a note of articles that, from what you gather in the indexes, might later prove useful. Do not be reluctant to use periodicals, for they have a number of advantages. First, because articles in periodicals are shorter than most books, the information they contain is often more accessible—it's easier, after all, to thumb through a 20-page article than a 400-page book. Second, many periodicals (particularly scholarly journals) cater to specialized groups and professions; thus, they are easily classifiable. Finally, periodicals are current, and this is particularly valuable when you are dealing with a timely topic or issue.

The background information and clues provided by the general reference collection also should lead you to titles, authors, and subjects in the card catalog that may aid your research. Again, do not attempt to locate specific books at this point; simply make a note of works that may be of interest. Also, bear in mind that many books contain bibliographies of additional works on the same topic, and you may want to pay particular attention to these. (The card catalog will tell you if a book contains a bibliography.)

Compiling the Tentative Bibliography

A tentative bibliography is simply a list of articles and books that may be of use to you when gathering information for the research paper. You should compile your tentative bibliography as you examine the library's indexes and card catalog. The indexes and card catalog contain all the information you will need for the tentative bibliography.

Here are some guidelines for compiling a tentative bibliography:

1. Be selective. Look for the most timely and comprehensive works as indicated by titles, number of pages, bibliographies, illustrations, and the like.

2. Be practical. There's no sense in listing forty-five books on the same topic. Again, be guided by those works that seem the most promising.

3. Be critical. For example, a book entitled *The Whole Truth about the War in Vietnam* that contains only 175 pages may offer sketchy and simplistic information.

4. Be accurate. Make sure that each entry in the tentative bibliography contains all the information necessary for your final bibliography (see pp. 227–230).

Use 3″ × 5″ index cards to list each of the works in your tentative bibliography, and use only one card for each reference. Using separate cards will enable you to organize your material better. The cards that make up the tentative bibliography will later be keyed to correspond with *note cards* (see p. 221).

Each tentative bibliographic card should contain the following information:

1. the reference call number for a book

2. a bibliographic reference number that you assign to each work in your tentative bibliography for later reference to corresponding note cards

3. author's name, last name first (if no name is given—as, for example, with a government pamphlet—begin with the title of the work)

4. title of book (underlined) or title of article (in quotation marks) and title of the periodical (underlined) that contains the article

5. publication data: for a book, place of publication, publishing company, date of publication, edition of book if given; for an article, the volume number, date, and page numbers containing the article

You may also want to add a note at the bottom of the card if the reference is illustrated, contains a bibliography, or has any other information useful for your topic.

The following is a sample tentative bibliography card for an article in a magazine:

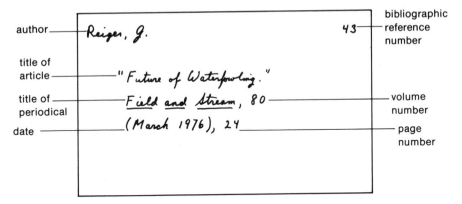

Here is a sample tentative bibliography card for a book:

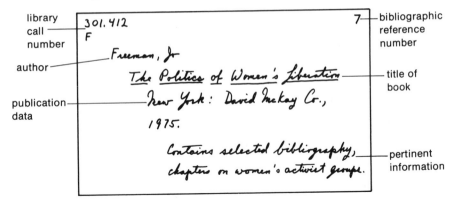

Here is a sample tentative bibliography card for an essay in a book:

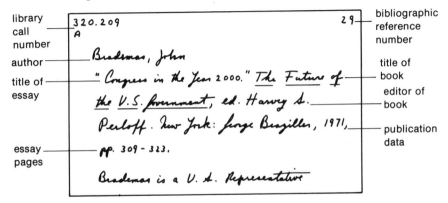

Taking Notes

Only after you have completed the tentative bibliography are you ready to begin taking notes. To select works that are particularly suited to your topic requires reading or scanning with close attention. You will probably find that some of the sources in your tentative bibliography are not relevant to your topic. Discard them. Careful scanning is the first rule of good note taking.

Compile notes in a manner that will aid you in organizing your information. Most experienced researchers use index cards for note taking because cards enable them, prior to writing the research paper, to shuffle and reshuffle their information until they have found the best way to organize it. The preferred size for note cards is 4" × 6" (which distinguishes them from the 3" × 5" bibliography cards and also provides more room for writing). Each note card should contain one note (again, for ease in later organizing), and each should have the following information:

1. a subject heading that identifies the basic content of the card
2. the author of the book or article
3. the exact title of the book or article
4. the exact page numbers in the book or periodical that the information is taken from

It is a good idea to include also a number that corresponds to the bibliographic reference number in your tentative bibliography. Note card 17, for example, would indicate that the information has been taken from bibliographic source 17 (see p. 218). This procedure helps ensure that you will be able to locate the source of your information even if you have omitted material from a note card.

The content of the note card should be the product of careful reading. Note cards should contain summaries, facts, figures, paraphrases, and direct quotations. Be neat and orderly with your notes. For ease in later reshuffling, avoid writing on both sides of a note card, and use two or three cards for a single note that runs to some length.

Three sample note cards appear on p. 221.

DOCUMENTING MATERIAL

To *document* a research paper is to give credit to sources. You document in two ways: (1) through *footnotes* and (2) through a *final bibliography*.

The following note card summarizes points in an essay:

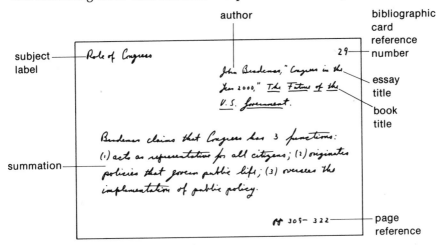

The following note cites specific figures from a book:

The following note contains a direct quotation from a periodical:

Failure to document your sources may result in *plagiarism,* a sophisticated term that means, quite simply, cheating. Plagiarism, whether intentional or not, occurs when you fail to credit information, ideas, or words that are not your own. Penalties for plagiarism are usually severe. At the college level, plagiarism may lead to expulsion or, at the very least, to a failing course grade.

Footnoting

A footnote usually signals *indebtedness.* It tells the reader that the information which precedes it has been taken from a primary or secondary source.

Use a footnote under the following conditions:

1. when you present a direct quotation
2. when you paraphrase or summarize material that is not your own
3. when you present facts that are not common knowledge
4. when you copy a chart, table, or diagram or construct one based on someone else's research

A number is assigned to each footnote; it follows immediately after the quoted or paraphrased matter, usually at the end of a sentence, and is typed slightly above the line. The footnote number should come *after* the punctuation (except in the case of a semicolon, colon, or dash). Footnotes should be numbered consecutively throughout the paper.

The footnotes themselves may be placed either at the bottom of the pages on which they occur or at the end of the research paper listed on a separate sheet. (Check with your instructor for the preferred form.) If footnotes are placed at the end of the paper, the reference information they contain should be double-spaced. If footnotes are given at the bottom of the pages, they should be set up as follows:

1. The information in the first footnote on each page should be separated from your text by a triple space.
2. The information in each note should be single-spaced.
3. The first line of each note should be indented five spaces.
4. Each footnote should be separated from others on the same page by a double space.
5. Each footnote should end with a period.
6. Be sure that the footnote correctly corresponds with the number assigned to it in the text.

The reference information that corresponds to each footnote number should contain all the facts necessary for your reader to locate the source. For a book, include the following information:

1. author's name (first name first)
2. title of book (underlined)
3. edition number (if other than a first edition)
4. place of publication
5. publisher
6. date of publication
7. page(s) of citation

Note the annotations in the following sample footnote for a book:

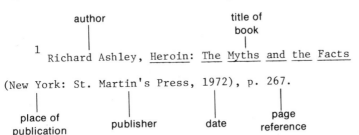

For an article in a periodical, include the following information:

1. author's name (first name first)
2. title of article (in quotation marks)
3. title of magazine, journal, or newspaper which contains the article (underlined)
4. volume number (if available)
5. date of publication
6. page(s) of citation

Note the annotations in the following sample footnote for a periodical:

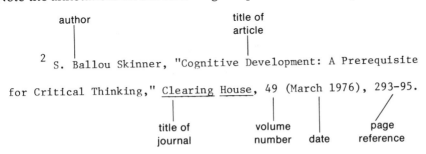

In documentation, use abbreviations with care. Here are some of the more common abbreviations. If you are in doubt, check with your instructor.

anon.	anonymous
ed.	editor or edition
eds.	editors or editions
et al.	Latin for "and others"
ibid.	Latin for "in the same place"
p.	page
pp.	pages
trans.	translator
vol.	volume
vols.	volumes

You may also use footnotes to explain material that would be intrusive if presented in the main body of your text. Such *explanatory* footnotes do not usually suggest indebtedness; their function is solely to present a message from writer to reader.

First References

The *first time* that a reference occurs in your paper it should follow the conventions demonstrated in the following sample footnotes:

BOOKS

▶ One author:

¹ Charles Marden Fitch, *The Complete Book of Houseplants* (New York: Hawthorn Books, 1972), p. 73.

▶ Two authors:

² Thomas Boslooper and Marcia Hayes, *The Femininity Game* (New York: Stein and Day, 1973), p. 136.

▶ More than three authors:

³ Horatio P. MacSwine et al., *Life on the Farm: A Serious Inquiry* (Corncob Corner, Ind.: Chicken Press, 1977), pp. 13–15.

▶ An edited book:

⁴ Rebecca West, ed., *Selected Poems of Carl Sandburg* (New York: Harcourt, Brace and Company, 1926), p. 3.

▶ An edition other than the first:

⁵ Nathan Hurd, *Sweet Songs of Sunshine*, 4th ed. (Philadelphia: Tawdry Press, 1937), p. 13.

▶ An essay published in a book:

> ⁶ Lester R. Brown, "The Nation-State, the Multinational Corpora-
> tion, and the Changing World Order," in *The Future of the U.S.
> Government*, ed. Harvey S. Perloff (New York: George Braziller,
> 1971), p. 114.

(Include the names of both the author of the essay and the editor of
the book.)

▶ A multivolume work:

> ⁷ Gunther L. Ambrose, *Sexist Language in Guinea Pig Disease Man-
> uals* (New York: People's Press, 1977), I, 345.

(Because a volume number is given, the abbreviation for "page" is
unnecessary.)

▶ A translation:

> ⁸ Pierre Teilhard de Chardin, *The Future of Man*, trans. Norman
> Denny (New York: Harper and Row, 1964), p. 39.

(Acknowledge the translator of a work cited that originally was published in a foreign language.)

ARTICLES

▶ From a popular magazine:

> ⁹ William Warriner, "RN for RF Interference," *Hi Fi*, March 1976,
> p. 57.

(A comma is unnecessary between month and year if no day is given.)

▶ From a scholarly journal:

> ¹⁰ Vivian Lindbeck, "Needed: A New Status for the Single
> Woman," *Catholic World*, 202 (December 1965), 151.

(When a volume number is given, drop the abbreviation for "page" or
"pages" and enclose the date in parentheses.)

▶ From a general reference source:

> ¹¹ J. Carson McGuire and G. Thomas Rowland, "Jean Piaget: Theo-
> ries," *The Encyclopedia of Education*, 1971, VII, 143–44.

(Because this is a general reference source, no place of publication or publisher is necessary. Note also that because this reference contains a volume number, the "pages" abbreviation is not necessary.)

▶ From a newspaper:

[12] Kathleen Connoly, "Experts Fear Financial Collapse," *San Francisco Examiner*, February 17, 1931, p. 9.

(Reprint the name of a newspaper exactly as it appears in its banner but note omission of the article "the" from the title. Some newspapers indicate place of origin in their names—*Chicago Daily News*. When dealing with a little-known newspaper, it is a good idea to indicate in brackets its place of origin—*Hawkins* [West Va.] *Herald*.)

MISCELLANEOUS

▶ An anonymous pamphlet:

[13] *Parental Involvement in Title I ESEA* (Washington, D.C.: U.S. Government Printing Office, 1972), pp. 2–5.

(If no author is given, begin the citation with the title.)

Later References

Subsequent references to works previously cited in full require only author and page:

[14] Trimble, p. 37.

If your paper cites more than one work by the same author, include the title so as to eliminate confusion:

[15] Fitch, *The Complete Book of Houseplants*, p. 19.

If two or more authors have the same last name, include the first name and initial:

[16] Lester R. Brown, p. 175.

You may use "ibid." (from the Latin *ibidem*, "in the same place") when the citation is the same in all respects, including page number, as the one that *immediately precedes* it:

[17] Fitch, p. 73.

[18] Ibid.

If the page number is different from the preceding reference, include the page number following "ibid."

¹⁹ Fitch, p. 17.

²⁰ Ibid., p. 79.

The Final Bibliography

Each source cited in a footnote must appear in the final bibliography, a list of the sources used in compiling the research paper. The final bibliography appears at the end of the paper on a separate sheet or sheets entitled "Bibliography" or "List of Works Cited."

Follow these rules for preparing the bibliography for your paper:

1. Alphabetize all references by author (last name first); when dealing with an anonymous work, alphabetize by title (excluding the article —"a" or "the"—that appears as the first word in the title).
2. Do not indent the first line of each reference; indent the second and subsequent lines five spaces.
3. Do not number references.
4. Type reference information double-spaced within each entry; double-space between entries.

For a book, include the following information:

1. author's name (last name first)
2. title (underlined)
3. place of publication
4. publisher
5. date of publication

Note the annotations in the following sample bibliographic entry for a book:

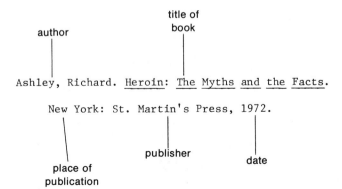

For an article in a periodical, include the following information:

1. author's name (last name first)
2. title of article (in quotation marks)
3. title of periodical or book (underlined)
4. volume number (if given)
5. date of publication
6. pages on which article appears

Note the annotations in the following sample bibliographic entry for an article:

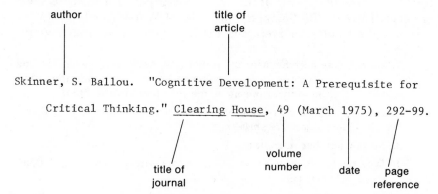

Skinner, S. Ballou.   "Cognitive Development: A Prerequisite for

Critical Thinking." Clearing House, 49 (March 1975), 292–99.

There are certain conventions involved in compiling the final bibliography for research work. The following sample bibliographic entries detail and explain these conventions. Note that most of these are bibliographic entries for the footnotes on pp. 224–226.

BOOKS

▶ One author:

Fitch, Charles Marden. *The Complete Book of Houseplants.* New York: Hawthorn Books, 1969.

▶ Two or more books by the same author:

Delderfield, R. F. *Diana.* New York: Pocket Books, 1972.

——. *Farewell the Tranquil Mind.* New York: Pocket Books, 1973.

(The long dash substitutes for repeating the author's name.)

▶ Two authors:

Boslooper, Thomas, and Marcia Hayes. *The Femininity Game.* New York: Stein and Day, 1973.

(When listing a book by two or three authors, note that only the first author's name is inverted.)

▶ More than three authors:

> MacSwine, Horatio P., et al. *Life on the Farm: A Serious Inquiry.* Corncob Corner, Ind.: Chicken Press, 1977.

▶ An edited edition:

> West, Rebecca, ed. *Selected Poems of Carl Sandburg.* New York: Harcourt, Brace and Company, 1926.

▶ An edition other than the first:

> Hurd, Nathan. *Sweet Songs of Sunshine.* 4th ed. Philadelphia: Tawdry Press, 1937.

▶ An essay published in a book:

> Brown, Lester R. "The Nation-State, the Multinational Corporation, and the Changing World Order." In *The Future of the U.S. Government.* Ed. Harvey S. Perloff. New York: George Braziller, 1971, pp. 93–117.

(Include the names of both the author of the essay and the editor of the book.)

▶ A multivolume work:

> Ambrose, Gunther L. *Sexist Language in Guinea Pig Disease Manuals.* 2 vols. New York: People's Press, 1977.

(Indicate when you consult all volumes of a multivolume work.)

> Bowser, William T. *Basic Photography.* Vol. 1. New York: Delray Publications, 1973.

(The above volume citation indicates that only one volume of a multivolume work has been consulted.)

▶ A translation:

> de Chardin, Pierre Teilhard. *The Future of Man.* Trans. Norman Denny. New York: Harper and Row, 1964.

(Acknowledge the translator of a work cited that originally was published in a foreign language.)

ARTICLES

▶ From a popular magazine:

> Warriner, William. "RN for RF Interference." *Hi Fi*, March 1976, pp. 55–58.

(Use "pp.," the abbreviation for pages, when no volume number is given.)

▶ From a scholarly journal:

> Lindbeck, Vivian. "Needed: A New Status for the Single Woman." *Catholic World*, 202 (December 1965), 147–53.

(Use parentheses to separate volume from date in a journal. Note also that the pages appear without the "pp." abbreviation.)

▶ From a general reference source:

> McGuire, J. Carson, and G. Thomas Rowland. "Jean Piaget: Theories." *The Encyclopedia of Education*, 1971, VII, 143–50.

(Because this is a general reference source, no place of publication or publisher is required.)

▶ From a newspaper:

> Connoly, Kathleen. "Experts Fear Financial Collapse." *San Francisco Examiner*, February 17, 1931, pp. 9–10.

MISCELLANEOUS

▶ An anonymous pamphlet:

> *Parental Involvement in Title I ESEA*. Washington, D.C.: U.S. Government Printing Office, 1972.

(If no author is given, begin the reference with the title and alphabetize the entry according to the first word in the title.)

A NOTE ON USING QUOTATIONS

Some inexperienced researchers devote too much time and space to copying direct quotations, with the result that their final research papers are often little more than a series of quotations strung together. A research paper that leaps from quotation to quotation indicates that the researcher has done little more than *copy* material. Therefore, refrain from quoting except (1) when the source of the quotation lends great authority to a particular point or (2) when the quotation is so aptly or emphatically stated that too much would be lost in a paraphrase.

The following conventions will assist you with quoting:

1. Keep quotations as short as possible. Avoid, for example, a 200-word quotation in a 1,500-word paper. It would be better to summarize such a quotation.

2. Incorporate quotations of five lines or less (as they appear on *your* paper) directly into the body of your text and indicate them with quotation marks.

3. Center and set off from your text quotations of more than five lines (as they appear on *your* paper). Do not use quotation marks with set-off quotations and indent the quotation five spaces from both sides of your text. Type it single-spaced.

4. Insert [*sic*] into a quotation to indicate that you are exactly reproducing that quotation; [*sic*] points up that the error or outdated usage appears in the original.

   "The Order of Battle is given to evry [*sic*] commander of a Regiment or Squadron."

5. Use brackets to clarify references within a quotation. For example:

   "The use of this new weapon will end civilization as we know it."

   "The use of this new weapon [the titanium bomb] will end civilization as we know it."

6. Indicate words omitted from the middle of a quoted sentence with three spaced dots (ellipsis points). For example:

   "When 24 percent of our children fail to graduate from high school, the schools must be at fault."

   "When 24 percent . . . fail to graduate . . . the schools must be at fault."

7. Indicate words omitted at the end of a quoted sentence with four ellipsis points (one to show the end of the sentence). For example:

   D. K. Elkins states, "The use of this new weapon will end civilization. . . ."

8. When omitting words from a direct quotation, make sure that the omissions do not alter the original meaning of the quotation. For example:

   The noted Broadway critic said of the play, "Miss Smith is marvelous but the play is a disaster."

   The noted Broadway critic said of the play, "Miss Smith is marvelous. . . ."

9. Establish the context of a direct quotation before presenting it. For example:

> In his defense of ancient science, the noted archaeologist Philander Sweetwater claims that "the Egyptian process of mummification was capable of preserving a human body for thousands of years."

A SAMPLE RESEARCH PAPER

The following sample research paper illustrates the principles of the research process discussed in this appendix. Note in particular the limited topic, variety of secondary material, and form of both footnotes and bibliography. In addition, note that the writer establishes context prior to quoting and paraphrasing.

FROM DUCKING STOOL TO JOB DISCRIMINATION

Contemporary society tends to glorify medieval woman, and mention of her likely evokes visions of a luxuriously robed Queen Guinevere presiding next to Arthur at a feast, or of Saint Joan of Arc in shining armor valiantly leading a ribbon-bedecked cavalry. But most women in the period were, of course, neither saints nor queens, and the status of the woman in medieval times offers certain parallels to the status of the woman today. A general historical overview of early and late medieval woman's status may help today's woman see just how far she has come--and how far she has to go. In the medieval era, women were paradoxically treated sometimes as ideals and at other times as mere beasts or property. The treatment of women in the twentieth century is perhaps also paradoxical, though the extremes are currently less severe.

Although the status of woman in the Middle Ages was "perpetually oscillating between a pit and pedestal,"[1] man did allow more dignity to the woman in the early part of the Middle Ages (500-1100) than he did during the later part (1100-1500). As Dorothy Whitelock points out, a woman did have the right to hold and sell land, to defend herself in court, to testify to the innocence of others, to make religious dona- tions, and to free slaves.[2] "She was, in short, very much more inde- pendent than were women after the Norman conquest [1066]."[3]

[1]Marjorie Rowling, Life in Medieval Times (New York: G. P. Putnam's Sons, 1968), p. 72.

[2]Dorothy Whitelock, The Beginnings of English Society (Baltimore: Penguin Books, 1952), p. 94.

[3]Ibid.

2

Even with the above rights, woman's status in the early Middle Ages remained inferior to man's. A woman was subject to being married off for purposes of political alliance if a close male relative, such as a father or a brother, so desired.[4] In the ninth century, the powerful emperor Charlemagne had five wives.[5] Polygamy heightens the status of the male by subordinating the rights of several women to a single male ego. It seems that a woman, during this period, could not call her body her own.

How far have women progressed since these views were established? As recently as the nineteenth century, polygamy was still practiced in the United States by members of the Mormon faith. Today, polygamy is still a common practice in many countries of the Middle East, including Saudi Arabia and Kuwait. But women today are indeed allowed to hold property in this country, and they are allowed to vote--though that right came only recently, in the early part of this century. And a woman today may defend herself in court. Yet continuing challenges to the United States Supreme Court ruling on abortion remain as a vestige of medieval society's view that a woman has no rights insofar as her own body is concerned.

Let us now see what perspective we may gain from examining woman's status in the latter part of the Middle Ages.

After the Norman Conquest, woman's lot did indeed change. The differences between the pit and the pedestal became more obvious.

[4]Christopher Brooke, The Structure of Medieval Society (New York: McGraw-Hill, 1973), pp. 70-74.

[5]Peter Munz, Life in the Age of Charlemagne (New York: G. P. Putnam's Sons, 1969), pp. 44-45.

3

The twelfth century brought the rise of the concept of Courtly Love, a belief in the woman as an ideal.[6] As Morris Bishop states:

> The female sex gained status. Previously women
> had been merely unpaid domestic laborers or
> symbols of sin. Now they attained dignity and
> commanded respect. The concept of chivalry and
> the code of courtly love elevated women, or at
> least upper-class women. They had leisure to
> learn to read and to enjoy the long poetic romances
> that were written for them. Women's conversation
> was prized, their friendship sought. . . . Social
> life, as we understand the term, really began in the
> thirteenth century.[7]

If, as Bishop suggests, it was only the upper-class woman who was elevated, a woman of such status also had to live with the paradox of great inequality to men at the same time. One case in point is that of the wife of the knight of La Tour-Landry, who suffered having the knight kick her in the face and break her nose because she had scolded him in public.[8] Other examples of abuse are provided by Christopher Brooke's account of how upper-class women were married off in "a kind of dynastic game" to consolidate land holdings and political alliances.[9] Perhaps, however, it is most interesting to note that at all class levels the woman's chief occupation was to run the household, be it castle or hovel.[10]

Women in the middle classes also had status less than equal to that of men. In many parts of Europe a woman had no legal rights to

[6]For a discussion of the actual ritual of Courtly Love, see W. T. H. Jackson, "The De Amore of Andreas Capellanus and the Practice of Love at Court," Romanic Review, 49 (1958), 243-51.

[7]Morris Bishop, The Middle Ages (New York: American Heritage Press, 1970), p. 37. See also Rowling, p. 81.

[8]Bishop, p. 73.

[9]Brooke, pp. 70ff.

[10]Bishop, p. 121

4

speak of; she was not allowed to testify in court or even to make a
will.[11] It was not, however, the lack of legal standing that made
conditions so deplorable for a woman but rather the power that a male
relative--particularly her husband--held over her physically. Apparently
a husband could subject his wife to nearly any kind of physical torture
as long as he stopped short of murder.

> [One] fourteenth-century writer, instructing his maiden
> daughters, warns them of the fate of a certain disobedient
> wife. Her husband consulted a surgeon and made a deal for
> the mending of two broken legs. He then went home and broke
> both his wife's legs with a pestle, remarking that in the
> future she wouldn't go far to break his commandment again.[12]

Middle-class wives, as well as upper- and lower-class wives, were
subject to a thirteenth-century law of Gascony, which stated that
"all inhabitants of Villefranche have the right to beat their wives,
provided they do not kill them thereby."[13]

Women of the lower class, however, were much worse off than those
of the middle and upper classes. "Village women," reports Marjorie
Rowling, "who dared to rail against their husbands were doused in
the ducking stool in the village pond." She adds, "Court rolls show
that villages were repeatedly threatened or fined for failing to
provide these punitive instruments."[14] The peasant woman very likely
remained unaware of the codes of chivalry and Courtly Love and had to
continue her daily drudgery in the fields.[15] These women had other
injustices to suffer, injustices inflicted upon lower-class men as

[11]Ibid., p. 219.

[12]Ibid., p. 271.

[13]Rowling, p. 72.

[14]Ibid., p. 73.

[15]Bishop, p. 37.

5

well. "Said a noble poet: 'Why should the villein [serfs] eat beef,
or any dainty food? Nettles, reeds, briars, peashells are good enough
for them.'"[16] And another social historian adds, "The woman serf
[was] regarded as little more than a beast."[17]

Today it would be safe to generalize that society prizes women's
conversation and seeks their friendship. Some men still will open
a door for a lady; traces of chivalric treatment remain. An upper-
class woman today need not fear being kicked in the face if she were
to scold her husband in public—her husband, should he break her nose,
would face the possibility of arrest. But perhaps the "dynastic game"
of marriage for political alliance and consolidation of land holdings
is still in effect today: Why did Jacqueline Kennedy marry Aristotle
Onassis? Is it likely that Princess Grace of Monaco will allow her
daughter to marry a person who is not already quite wealthy? And
who will be the lucky woman that England's Prince Charles will choose?
There are surely many exceptions to wealthy persons marrying other
wealthy persons, but such marriages are still common enough among the
upper classes that it is tempting to argue that de facto marriages
of political and economic convenience are still strongly encouraged
if not, as in the Middle Ages, openly forced. Today there are no
ducking stools in the village ponds of America; "peasant" women in
this country usually enjoy somewhat better fare than "nettles,
reeds, briars, and peashells." But managing the household is still
the main occupation of the majority of contemporary women, even of

[16]Ibid., p. 243.

[17]Rowling, p. 74.

6

those who hold jobs outside the home.[18] Job discrimination, in

other words, has taken the place of the village ducking stool. In

a recent series of interviews, a sociologist found that "almost twice

as many housewives as employed wives said they were dissatisfied

with their lives . . . and believed that their husbands' work was

more interesting than theirs."[19] Guinevere ended up in a convent

after King Arthur's realm was destroyed by civil war; Joan of Arc

ended up at the stake. Today women face job discrimination instead

of the convent or the stake and the kitchen sink instead of the

ducking stool.

---

[18]Myra Marx Ferree, "The Confused American Housewife," Psychology
Today, 10 (September 1976), 76.

[19]Ibid.

7

LIST OF WORKS CITED

Bishop, Morris. The Middle Ages. New York: American

    Heritage Press, 1970.

Brooke, Christopher. The Structure of Medieval Society.

    New York: McGraw-Hill, 1973.

Ferree, Myra Marx. "The Confused American Housewife."

    Psychology Today, 10 (September 1976), 76-80.

Jackson, W. T. H. "The De Amore of Andreas Capellanus and

    the Practice of Love at Court." Romanic Review, 49

    (1958), 243-51.

Munz, Peter. Life in the Age of Charlemagne. New York:

    G. P. Putnam's Sons, 1969.

Rowling, Marjorie. Life in Medieval Times. New York:

    G. P. Putnam's Sons, 1968.

Whitelock, Dorothy. The Beginnings of English Society.

    Baltimore: Penguin Books, 1952.

Grammar Terms   C

The definitions provided in this section are intended to aid you in understanding the conventions of grammar discussed earlier. Certain terms that were not used in the chapters are included here, since your instructor may refer to them. This appendix consists of definitions, *not rules,* so you may wish to consult the index to locate examples of usage.

Some of the terms are necessarily defined by use of other terms; some are explained through examples. If you need explanation of a term used to define another term, consult the index.

NOUNS

A *noun* is conventionally defined as the name of a person, place, or thing. However, a working definition is that a noun is any word which can fit into the following blank: the ——.

Types of Nouns

Proper noun: a word that names a specific person, place, or thing.

> *John* is from *Canada.*

Common noun: a word that names a general category or class of persons, places, or things.

> Put your *coat* in the *closet.*

Collective noun: a word that names a group or collection (and usually takes a singular verb or pronoun).

The *committee* plans to present its report at the next meeting.

Concrete noun: a word that names something that can be perceived by the senses.

George smelled *smoke*, but he didn't see a *fire*.

Abstract noun: a word that names something that is intangible and cannot be perceived by the senses.

Mr. Carr took great *pride* in his son's *intelligence*.

Functions of Nouns

Subject: a noun about which a sentence or clause makes a statement. (The subject usually appears near the beginning of a sentence or clause.)

John is hiding in the closet.

Possessive: a noun that serves as a modifier of another noun and indicates ownership.

The guest broke *Greg's* bottle.

Object of a preposition: a noun that is linked to another sentence element by a preposition.

I am going to *California* for the *summer*.

Direct object: a noun that receives the action of the verb.

Abigail threw the *book*.

Indirect object: a noun that indirectly receives the action of the verb and states to whom or for whom something is done. (When the indirect object follows the direct object, the prepositions *to, for,* or *of* are used. When the indirect object precedes the direct object, the preposition is understood.)

Joan hit the ball to the *fielder*.
Joan hit *him* the ball.

Ethel bought a new tie for her *friend.*
Ethel bought her *friend* a new tie.

Pat asked a tough question of the *theologian.*
Pat asked the *theologian* a tough question.

Predicate noun (also called **predicate nominative** or **subject comple-ment**): a noun that appears in the *predicate* and is equivalent to the subject. (The main verb in a sentence containing a predicate noun is *be, seem,* or the equivalent—see *copulatives,* p. 247.)

John is the *captain.*

PRONOUNS

A *pronoun* is a word that stands in the place of a noun or noun element (a phrase or clause functioning as a noun). Pronouns therefore function in sentences in the same ways that nouns do.

Simple personal pronoun: a direct substitute for a noun.

Subject:

I	we
you	you
he, she, it	they

He likes ice cream.

They decided to cancel the meeting.

Object:

me	us
you	you
him, her, it	them

Tom called *her* for the assignment. (direct object)

The judges awarded *him* first prize. (indirect object)

Sally can't go to the movies with *us.* (object of preposition)

Possessive:

my, mine	our, ours
your, yours	your, yours
his; her, hers; its	their, theirs

Is this book *yours?*

Their new apartment has five rooms.

Reflexive personal pronoun: a pronoun that indicates that the subject of the clause acts upon itself (*myself, yourself, himself, herself, itself, ourselves, yourselves, themselves*).

He blamed *himself* for the accident.

Did you hurt *yourselves?*

Intensive personal pronoun: a pronoun used to intensify or emphasize its antecedent. Intensive personal pronouns have the same forms as reflexive personal pronouns.

I built the table *myself.*

The students *themselves* graded the exam papers.

Impersonal pronoun: the pronoun *it,* with no antecedent (nothing preceding to which *it* refers). An impersonal pronoun may stand in place of a clause or phrase that follows the main verb, operating as the subject of the sentence.

It was wrong for her to laugh.
(*Compare:* For her to laugh was wrong.)

It was appropriate that he got a raise.
(*Compare:* That he got a raise was appropriate.)

An impersonal pronoun may also refer to an understood concept.

It is hot in Mexico.
(*Compare:* The air feels hot in Mexico.)

Demonstrative pronoun: a pronoun that calls attention to or points out the thing being referred to (*this, these, that, those*).

This is the book I told you about.

Those aren't my glasses.

Relative pronoun: a connective that joins a *dependent clause* to an *independent clause,* normally having the immediately preceding noun or noun substitute as its antecedent (*who, whoever, whose, whom, whomever, that, what, whatever, which, whichever*).

The queen honored the man *who* axed Aethelflat.

John loved the girl *whom* his mother picked.

They live in a town *that* has no sidewalks.

The trees, *which* are yellow, are full of spiders.

Note that, in formal English, *who, whose,* and *whom* refer only to persons, and *that* and *which* refer to nonhuman concepts.

Interrogative pronoun: a pronoun that introduces a question; it has the same form as a relative pronoun, except for the *-ever* words.

> *Who* is knocking at my door?

> *Which* is the most difficult test?

Indefinite pronoun: a pronoun that does not refer to a particular person or thing *(none, both, one, each, all, any, few, some, much, more, many, several, something, someone, somebody, anything, anyone, anybody, everything, everyone, everybody).*

> *Someone* left an umbrella in my car.

> Helen did *much* of the work herself.

ADJECTIVES

An *adjective* is a word that modifies (describes or limits) a noun or pronoun. A working definition is that an adjective is any word which you can fit into this blank: the —— (noun).

Descriptive adjective: names a quality or condition of the noun or pronoun it modifies.

> The *small* boy wore a *red* jacket.

Limiting adjective: points out or identifies the noun or pronoun it modifies or indicates number or quantity.

> *My* house is the *third* one from the corner.

Indefinite, possessive, relative, demonstrative, and *interrogative pronouns* sometimes serve as limiting adjectives.

> *Few* students attended the lecture.

> *My* house has no electricity.

> I located the man *whose* wallet was found.

> She wore *that* hat to the opera.

> *What* reason did you give?

Adjectives that are also pronouns agree in *number* (singular or plural) with the noun or pronoun they modify.

> *These* hats are made in China.
>
> *This* dog is Warren's.

Though adjectives usually precede the word modified, they may also appear following, or in the *post position*.

> Patsy likes her meat *rare*.
>
> The dog, *large, black,* and *menacing,* appeared suddenly.

Degrees of Comparison

Positive: a modification that simply suggests how the thing modified is different or distinct from other things like it.

> The *black* dog is named Porthos.

Comparative: a modification designated by *-er* or *more* and used to differentiate two items.

> Of the two paintings, Rob prefers the *larger*.
>
> Esther is *more* confident than Leona is.

Superlative: a modification designated by *-est* or *most* and used to differentiate one item from among more than two items.

> Of the five chairs, Bryan's is the *most* comfortable.
>
> Jimmy is the *strongest* boy in the school.

VERBS

A *verb* is a word that states an action or asserts a condition. It may or may not have a direct object (transitive/intransitive); it may state an equivalence between subject and predicate (copulative); and it may indicate if the subject acts or receives action (active/passive).

Transitive verb: indicates an action and requires a direct object to complete its meaning.

> Travis *threw* a ball into the pond.

Intransitive verb: indicates an action but is complete without a direct object.

> The sun *appeared.*

Some verbs may be transitive or intransitive, depending on the context. For example, in the following sentences, the verb "paint" is transitive in the first sentence and intransitive in the second.

> Jo Ann *paints* guinea pig hutches.
>
> Sharon *paints* beautifully.

Copulative or linking verb: states equivalence between subject and predicate or states a condition of the subject by connecting it to the predicate. A copulative verb is always intransitive.

> Carol *became* a beauty queen.
>
> Jerry *is* the chairperson.
>
> Karen *seems* angry with her roommate.

Active voice: subject performs the action indicated by the verb.

> The dog *smelled* a beaver.

Passive voice: subject receives the action indicated by the verb.

> The beaver *was eaten* by a fox.

Auxiliary Verbs

An *auxiliary* or *helping verb* combines with a main verb (1) to indicate tense, (2) to form the passive voice, (3) to make negative statements, (4) to add emphasis, or (5) to ask questions.

> Martha *was* provided help with her homework.
> (auxiliary indicates past tense, passive voice)
>
> A porkchop *is* tied around Alice's neck.
> (auxiliary indicates present tense, passive voice)
>
> Tyler *did* not enjoy visiting his friend.
> (auxiliary used with negative)
>
> You *do* eat bananas often!
> (auxiliary indicates emphasis)
>
> *Do* you eat bananas often?·
> (auxiliary indicates question)

Modal: an auxiliary that indicates condition, such as ability, obligation, permission, possibility, or habit is termed a *modal*. Some auxiliaries that function as modals are *can, must, may, should, would.*

Principal Parts

The *principal parts* of a verb—the present infinitive, the past tense, and the past participle—supply the basic forms for the different tenses of the verb.

Regular verbs: form the past tense and the past participle by adding *-d* or *-ed* to the present infinitive. Most verbs in the English language are regular.

PRESENT INFINITIVE	PAST	PAST PARTICIPLE
laugh	laughed	laughed
walk	walked	walked
hope	hoped	hoped

Irregular verbs: form the past tense and the past participles in some way other than adding *-d* or *-ed* to the present infinitive. The following is a brief list of examples of the three principal parts of some verbs that are irregular and often misused.

PRESENT INFINITIVE	PAST	PAST PARTICIPLE
do	did	done
get	got	got (or gotten)
go	went	gone
eat	ate	eaten
lay	laid	laid
lie	lay	lain

For both regular and irregular verbs, the past participle is used with an auxiliary *(have, had)* to form additional past tenses of the verb *(have laughed, had eaten).*

Mood

Mood is a verb property that indicates whether the speaker is expressing a command; a fact or question; or a wish, supposition, or uncertainty.

Imperative: makes a request or gives a command.

Attach the gas line to the fuel pump.

Indicative: states a fact or asks a question.

> We *fed* cornflakes to the owl.
>
> *Was* he ready on time?

Subjunctive: expresses a wish, supposition, or uncertainty.

> I wish that I *were* rich.
>
> Suppose that you *were* he.
>
> If it *were* to snow on Saturday, we could go skiing.

Verbals

A *verbal* is a form that is derived from a verb but operates as another part of speech. It may appear as a *participle*, a *gerund*, or an *infinitive*.

PARTICIPLE

A *participle* is a verbal that operates as an adjective. It may appear in present, past, or perfect form.

Present participle: a verbal ending in *-ing*.

> Roger's business is a *going* concern.
>
> Lend a *helping* hand.
>
> There is a goldfish in your *swimming* pool.

Past participle: a verbal in the form of the third *principal part* of the verb.

> The *lost* dog was hungry.
>
> Hector drove a *stolen* car.
>
> Judy handed in her *written* work.

Perfect participle: a verbal in the form of auxiliary + *-ing* + past participle (active) or in the form of auxiliary + *-ing* + *been* + past participle (passive).

> *Having gone,* Suzie missed the ice-cream truck.
>
> The blind man crossed the street, his dog *having led* him there before.
>
> Their liquor *having been drunk,* Paula and Linda left the party.

GERUND

A *gerund* is a verbal that operates as a noun. It may appear in present or perfect form.

Present gerund: a verbal in the form of the first *principal part* + *-ing.*

> *Swimming* is my favorite pastime.

> The coach prefers *losing* to *winning.*

Perfect gerund: a verbal in the form of auxiliary + *-ing* + third *principal part* (active) or in the form of auxiliary + *-ing* + *been* + third *principal part* (passive).

> The couple argued over *being divorced.*

> The senator was glad at *having been saved* from scandal.

INFINITIVE

An *infinitive* is the present-tense form of a verb preceded by *to* (sometimes, however, *to* is understood rather than openly stated). As a verbal, an infinitive may operate as a *noun, adjective,* or *adverb.*

Noun infinitive:

> *To sing* and *(to) dance* was all the happy frog desired.

Adjective infinitive:

> Few persons find time *to read.*

Adverb infinitive:

> John went *to complain.*

A *split infinitive* occurs when a word or phrase (usually a single adverb) intrudes between the *to* and the main verb. (The split infinitive is usually considered unacceptable usage in formal English.)

> We need *to* carefully *study* the problem.

Verb Phrases

Participial phrase: consists of a participle, its modifiers, and an object. It operates as an *adjective.*

Anticipating a barrage of mortar fire, the troops ducked for cover.

Mr. Jones saw the thief *hiding from the police.*

A *nominative absolute* is a special kind of participial phrase that grammarians have traditionally claimed is grammatically unrelated to the rest of the sentence; the nominative absolute does in fact operate adverbially, serving the function of answering a *why* or *when* question.

His partner having wrenched his knee, the tennis player called off the game.

Gerund phrase: consists of a gerund and, sometimes, its modifiers and an object. It operates as a *noun.*

Being respectful is important.

Bill enjoys *watching "Bowling for Dollars"* with the vice-president.

Infinitive phrase: consists of an infinitive and, sometimes, its modifiers and an object. It operates as a *noun* or as an *adverb.*

To dine with Allison is a true pleasure.

Archie tried *to wax his moustache.*

ADVERBS

An *adverb* is a word that modifies (describes or limits) a *verb, adjective,* or another *adverb.* Adverbs have relative freedom of position in the English sentence but usually appear near the word modified. An adverb may be defined as a word that answers one of the following questions: Where? When? How? Why? How long? How often? How much? (However, some adjectives also respond to the last three questions.) Many adverbs are marked by *-ly.*

John ran *upstairs.*
(adverb answers the *where* question)

Judith ate fish *yesterday.*
(adverb answers the *when* question)

The cannibal ate the missionary *zestfully.*
(adverb answers the *how* question)

Vengefully, Roland struck the target.
(adverb answers the *why* or *how* question)

It seems that we must wait *forever*.
(adverb answers the *how long* question)

We sell books *frequently*.
(adverb answers the *how often* question)

Amy had *scarcely* slept.
(adverb answers the *how much* question)

Note the difference between *there* as an adverb of place (in answer to the *where* question) and *there* as an *expletive* (an expletive is a filler in the word order, itself empty of meaning; it stands in the place of another word or phrase as does the impersonal *it*).

Set the book *there*.
(*There* is an adverb.)

There is a communication problem.
(*There* is an expletive. *Compare:* A communication problem exists.)

Degrees of Comparison

Positive: a simple modification of the verb.

We must wait *forever*.

Comparative: a modification designated by *more* and used to distinguish between two items.

Jeff learns *more quickly* than Mary does.

Superlative: a modification designated by *most* and used to distinguish one item from among more than two items.

Of the three, Jeff learns the *most quickly*.

Conjunctive Adverbs

See p. 253.

INTERJECTIONS

An *interjection*, a word or phrase conveying emotion, is grammatically independent of any sentence that may accompany it.

Hurrah! Our team won!

Oh, I don't care.

Excellent! What a fine movie!

CONJUNCTIONS

A *conjunction* is a word that connects words, phrases, or clauses.

Coordinating conjunction: a connecting word *(and, but, or, nor)* conveying the idea of equal importance for the items connected.

> Mr. Halligan vacuumed the floor *and* washed the windows.

> The livingroom was clean *but* not the kitchen.

Correlative conjunction: a coordinating conjunction that is used in paired form *(either . . . or, neither . . . nor, not only . . . but also, both . . . and).*

> Bob will *either* attend summer school *or* go to the shore.

> Sue looked *not only* tired *but also* angry.

> *Neither* job *nor* family could keep her from the golf course.

Subordinating conjunction: see *relative pronoun*, p. 244.

Conjunctive adverb: an adverb that acts as a conjunction, joining two independent clauses *(however, therefore, besides, indeed, in fact, also, moreover, furthermore, nevertheless, still, accordingly, consequently).*

> The train was late; *consequently,* I missed my appointment.

> John is an excellent tennis player; *in fact,* he has won many tournaments.

> The doctor is busy today; *however,* he can see you tomorrow.

PREPOSITIONS

A *preposition* is a word that operates to connect or embed a phrase within a clause; prepositions signal meanings of time, space, direction, agency, or some other relation that the connected or embedded phrase has to a verb, noun, adjective, or adverb in the clause. A *prepositional phrase* consists of a preposition, its object, and any modifiers of the object; the phrase may operate as an *adjective* or as an *adverb*.

Milton worked *in the dark.*
(prepositional phrase used adverbially)

His problem is a matter *of chronic self-abuse.*
(prepositional phrase used adjectivally)

CLAUSES

A *clause* consists of a *subject* and a *predicate*. Both the subject and the predicate may be spoken of as *simple, complete,* or *compound*. The *subject* is the noun or noun substitute (pronoun, phrase, or clause that operates as a noun) about which the clause makes a statement. It usually appears as the first noun element in the clause. The *predicate* is the verb and any modifiers and objects that apply to the verb or to one of its objects.

Simple subject: the noun or noun substitute about which the clause makes a statement.

The *man* in the car drives too fast in school zones.

Complete subject: the simple subject plus the words that modify it.

The man in the car drives too fast in school zones.

Compound subject: two or more subjects joined by coordinating conjunctions.

The *man* and his *wife* drive too fast in school zones.

Simple predicate: the main verb of the clause.

The man in the car *drives* too fast in school zones.

Complete predicate: the simple predicate plus its complements, modifiers, and objects.

The man in the car *drives too fast in school zones.*

Compound predicate: two or more predicates joined by coordinating conjunctions.

> The man in the car *drives* too fast in school zones and *stops* without warning on freeways.

Types of Clauses

Dependent (subordinate) clause: serves the function of a *noun, adjective,* or *adverb* in relation to an *independent clause;* it may not stand alone as a sentence.

> Ben likes *whatever he reads.*
> (noun clause)
>
> Dot is in love with the man *who delivers pizza.*
> (adjective clause)
>
> *When Linda is ready,* we can leave.
> (adverb clause)
>
> I'm in agreement with *what Bruce said.*
> (noun clause)

Restrictive clause: an adjective clause that limits the noun or noun substitute that it modifies. A restrictive clause is not set off by commas; it is essential to the meaning of the noun or noun substitute and cannot be omitted.

> Children *who wear galoshes* catch few colds.

Nonrestrictive clause: an adjective clause that provides additional information about a noun or noun substitute while placing no restrictions or limits on what it modifies; that is, the information provided by the nonrestrictive clause is not crucial to identifying the noun or noun substitute modified.

> Lettuce, *which contains Vitamin C,* should be fed to your guinea pig regularly.

Independent clause: a clause capable of standing alone as a sentence.

> *Jenkins hit the ball.*
>
> *Jenkins hit the ball and ran to first base.*
>
> *Jenkins hit the ball, and he ran to first base.*
>
> If you want great poetry, *read Rod McKuen.*

Although Connors is a clever boxer, *Smith can defeat him handily*.

The colonel and the general do eat marshmallows in their chili; however, they never put garlic powder in their orange juice.

SENTENCES

A *sentence* consists of at least a single independent clause. According to the number and kind of clauses they contain, sentences may be classified as *simple, compound, complex,* or *compound/complex.*

Simple sentence: consists of a single independent clause.

The girl never cheats on tests.

Compound sentence: consists of at least two independent clauses.

The girl never cheats on tests, and she always writes well-organized essays.

Complex sentence: consists of an independent clause and one or more dependent clauses.

When Jane finishes with the hair dryer, I get to use it.

Compound/complex sentence: consists of one or more dependent clauses and two or more independent clauses.

When Agnes handed in her test, she stapled it carefully, but she forgot to fold it properly.

Index

Symbols for Revision

The following symbols are commonly used in revision. Each symbol is keyed to the pages in the text where the problem is discussed. Space is provided after each symbol should your instructor wish to use an alternate symbol.

ab	faulty abbreviation	189-190, 197
adj	wrong form of adjective	177-178, 245-246
adv	wrong form of adverb	178, 251-252
adj/adv	adjective-adverb confusion	178
agr	faulty agreement	172-175
amb	ambiguous	48, 137-138
apos	apostrophe needed or misused	195-196
awk	awkward expression	159-166
[ ]	brackets needed or misused	193, 231
cap	capital letter needed	197-198
coh	lacks coherence	68-78, 166-169
:/	colon needed or misused	188
;	comma needed or misused	183-188
cs	comma splice (or comma fault)	171-172
coord	faulty coordination	161-162, 253
dm	dangling modifier	167-168
dash	dash needed or misused	190-191
def	define term	138
dev	inadequate development	69-78
d	inappropriate diction	137-145
div	faulty word division	191
el	ellipses needed or misused	231
emph	weak emphasis	159-166
!/	exclamation point needed or misused	192
frag	sentence fragment	169-170
fs	fused sentence	170-171
hy	hyphen needed or misused	191-192
ital	italicize (underline)	196-197
lc	lower case (no capital letter)	197-198
log	faulty logic	149-155